The Complete
GUITAR**TECHNIQUE**
SPEEDSTRATEGIES
Collection

A Three-In-One Compilation of Sweep Picking, Speed Picking & Legato Methods For Guitar

CHRIS**BROOKS**

FUNDAMENTAL**CHANGES**

The Complete Guitar Technique Speed Strategies Collection

A Three-In-One Compilation of Sweep Picking, Speed Picking & Legato Methods For Guitar

ISBN: 978-1-78933-231-5

Published by **www.fundamental-changes.com**

Copyright © 2020 Fundamental Changes Ltd

By Christopher A. Brooks

Edited by Tim Pettingale & Joseph Alexander

www.fundamental-changes.com

Over 13,000 fans on Facebook: **FundamentalChangesInGuitar**

Instagram: **FundamentalChanges**

Instagram: **chrisbrooksguitarist**

For over 350 Free Guitar Lessons with Videos Check Out

www.fundamental-changes.com

Cover Image Copyright: Author photo used by permission & Shutterstock, Carlos Castilla

Thanks to Charvel Guitars and Bareknuckle Pickups

Compilation Foreword

Welcome to my first collection release for Fundamental Changes – a suite comprising three books with enough material to keep even the most ardent practice maniac busy for a long time. The titles chosen for this compilation will take you from *player* to *slayer* as you master the right- and left-hand techniques essential to shred guitar mastery.

Neoclassical Speed Strategies for Guitar focuses on speed picking in the tradition of Yngwie Malmsteen, where picking technique is approached using biomechanics, strategy, and progressive advancement to create blazing single- and multi-string licks, sequences, and etudes. While the examples draw from minor, harmonic minor, and diminished sounds, you will be able to put the system to work in just about any style you choose.

Sweep Picking Speed Strategies for Guitar continues the theme of creating systems and using deliberate and economic motion mechanics to blaze through just about any arpeggio line smoothly. With eighty arpeggio shapes that work over a dozen chord types, you will maximise your ability to cover large amounts of fretboard real estate using fast and logical moves.

For the fretting hand, *Legato Guitar Technique Mastery* will help you to dazzle with smooth lines, comprehensive neck coverage and various mechanical combinations. As you perfect your fretting technique, build stamina and use sequences, number systems, hybrid picking, swybrid picking and chromatic passing tones, you'll develop a sense of dexterity and control that will prove beneficial in many areas of playing.

Some readers will benefit the most from studying this volume cover to cover. Others might maintain their interest by bouncing around a little. My one piece of advice is to *always be escalating*. Don't sit on one exercise for too long, waiting for permission to move ahead. While there can be a danger in moving too fast when you're not quite ready, waiting for the perfect moment to see what's next might be just as limiting.

A great way to advance is to review what you've done, spend a decent amount of time on the next task, then take a peek at what comes next. By keeping track of the past, present and future, you'll feel a sense of progression, even when you have to take a step back now and then to review or tidy things up a bit.

Happy Shredding,

Chris Brooks

Get the Audio

The audio files for this book are available to download for free from **www.fundamental-changes.com.** The link is in the top right-hand corner. Simply select this book title from the drop-down menu and follow the instructions to get the audio.

We recommend that you download the files directly to your computer, not to your tablet, and extract them there before adding them to your media library. You can then put them on your tablet, iPod or burn them to CD. On the download page there is a help PDF and we also provide technical support via the contact form.

For over 350 Free Guitar Lessons with Videos Check out:

www.fundamental-changes.com

Twitter: **@guitar_joseph**

Over 12,000 fans on Facebook: **FundamentalChangesInGuitar**

Instagram: **FundamentalChanges**

Contents

Book 1: Neo-Classical Speed Strategies For Guitar

Introduction   2

Part One: A System of Strengths   4

Chapter One: Biomechanics   5

    Active Principle One: Forearm Rotation and Auxiliary Mechanics   18

    Active Principle Two: Single String Alternate Picking   22

    Active Principle Three: Multi-string Even Numbers Strategy   26

    Active Principle Four: Ascending Odd Numbers Strategy   27

    Active Principle Five: Descending Odd Numbers Strategy   29

Chapter Two: Tonalities and Signature Sounds   33

Part Two: Technical Development   43

Chapter Three: Single-string and Even Numbers Alternate Picking   44

Chapter Four: Ascending Economy Picking Drills   54

Chapter Five: Descending Pick-gato Drills   58

Chapter Six: Loop and Sequence Drills   62

Part Three: Advanced Studies   71

Chapter Eight: Studies in E Minor   72

Chapter Nine: Studies in A Minor   78

Chapter Ten: Studies in B Minor   87

Conclusion   92

Glossary of Terms   93

Book 2: Sweep Picking Speed Strategies For Guitar

Introduction   97

Chapter One: Rudiments of Flow   98

Chapter Two: Ascending Strategy   106

Chapter Three: Ascending Etudes   114

Chapter Four: Descending Strategy   119

Chapter Five: Descending Etudes   124

Chapter Six: Bidirectional Strategies   128

Chapter Seven: Bidirectional Etudes   139

Chapter Eight: Fretboard Coverage – Triads   146

Chapter Nine: Fretboard Coverage – Sevenths   169

Chapter Ten: Seventh Arpeggio Etudes   189

Conclusion   198

Book 3: Legato Guitar Technique Mastery

Introduction	201
Get the Audio and Video	202
Setting Up Your Tone	203
Chapter One: Biomechanics	204
Fretting Arm Positioning	204
Finger Orientation and Sound Control	206
Picking Hand Function and Control	207
String Changes and Articulation Options	208
Chapter Two: Technique Builders	213
Chapter Three: Making (and Breaking) Scale Patterns	226
Chapter Four: Liquid Lines and Scorching Sequences	235
Chapter Five: Number Systems and Omissions	252
Chapter Six: Chromatic Passing Tones	264
Chapter Seven: Legarpeggios	272
Chapter Eight: Styling and Ornamentation	280
Chapter Nine: Monster Licks	290
More From Chris Brooks	298

NEOCLASSICAL
SPEEDSTRATEGIES
FORGUITAR

Master Speed Picking for Shred Guitar & Play Fast – The Yng Way!

CHRISBROOKS

FUNDAMENTALCHANGES

Introduction

The incredible and fiery guitar style of Swedish neoclassical shred pioneer Yngwie Malmsteen (born June 30, 1963) turned the guitar world on its head in the early 1980s with a smorgasbord of extended single-string lines, positional and shifting scale patterns, blistering sequences, pedal-point licks and arpeggios. Malmsteen's playing delivered a bombastic baroque/metal hybrid that the styles of Ritchie Blackmore, Uli Jon Roth and Randy Rhoads had hinted at before him but, arguably, the amalgam had never delivered with this kind of unapologetic fury.

When the nimble-fingered Swede relocated to the U.S.A. in the midst of the Los Angeles hair-metal scene, new standards were set almost overnight regarding hard rock styling, technical vocabulary and picking fluidity in the post-Van Halen era. Guitar enthusiasts clamoured to understand what they were hearing and, for a time, assumed that the power behind Malmsteen's high-speed skillset was the result of strict alternate picking in the tradition of Al Di Meola or John McLaughlin. Early method books and transcriptions sometimes compounded the growing mythology, with incorrect fingerings and vague but well-intentioned advice about *starting slow and building it up* to achieve success, but to teenage me in the late 80s and early 90s, there was a nagging feeling that something was amiss.

Malmsteen's use of single string sequences and ostinatos did, of course, display a fantastic and accurate command of alternate picking, but for multi-string picking sequences, it certainly sounded as though there were other forces at work. Learning many of the lines by ear and using primitive methods of slowing music down, it became increasingly evident to me that licks which sounded like they finished on down strokes in Yngwie's playing, ended on upstrokes in mine. The aggression of his ascending sequences, contrasted by the liquid-smooth flow of descending lines, and the seamless integration of sweep-picked arpeggios just didn't fit the alternate picking blueprint somehow. What was it?

Over the years, observations and breakthroughs were made as I progressed from slowing down records, moving to frame-by-frame VHS with a handful of 1990s Japanese instructional tapes, to digital video and the YouTube age. This exploration revealed a fascinating and seemly intuitive system to deliver *all* Yngwie's licks. Where at first it may have seemed like a matter of *one technique for this, another for that*, time revealed Malmsteen connects a tapestry of musical ideas with a set of principles that provide a method of delivery that is so original, consistent, and masterful that it rarely contradicts itself. It offers what I believe is a valid third option in the alternate vs economy picking debate.

The various chapters of this book take the guesswork out of the Malmsteen picking system by breaking it into the three parts that I consider essential for mastery: understanding, development, and application. Part One is all about grasping the why and how of The Yng Way. Part Two is about developing the chops to execute the system through drills and practice routines. Part Three is a virtual lick pack, with practical uses of all the concepts explained, plus a few expansions upon them.

It's been 27 years since I started dissecting this style, and formulating the right method for study has been more akin to a slow-cooker than a hot pan. I've drawn several parallels between learning this system and the study of sports science. I've even consulted some expert therapists to get the terminology right, so please take your time understanding the terms used. Thanks to those whom I called upon for linguistic help!

To my delight, Troy Grady's *Cracking the Code* video series reinforced a lot of what I'd theorised and applied in own my years of playing Yngwie material. Grady has also spearheaded some very useful phraseology on picking mechanics, some of which I've integrated here to establish a level of conformity. Hats off to Troy for great discoveries and trailblazing what I see as new standards in guitar pedagogy.

I'm thrilled that it's once again *cool* to talk about Yngwie's technique, and I'm confident that this book offers an authentic, verifiable and usable method to master the speed systems of a true great of rock guitar!

How To Use This Book

This book has been designed to give you the understanding, developmental tools and real-world experience to perform not only the music contained within it but to help you determine the best and most authentic ways to decipher and execute your favourite Yngwie Malmsteen licks and solos in your study of his vast catalogue of neoclassical rock guitar. Furthermore, I hope that you can take the concepts explained here and use them in your improvisation, regardless of the genres you play.

When practising anything fast, it's imperative that you remain relaxed, take plenty of breaks, and listen to your body when it's time to quit for the day. Remember that unnecessary tension is the enemy of speed. Keep good posture, warm up sufficiently, and avoid using any *No pain, no gain* mentality. The best gains are the ones you can make by playing clean, fluid and precise. Think of it more as *Jujutsu* (from the Japanese *Ju* meaning *pliable* and *Jutsu* meaning *technique*) than weight lifting.

Use Part One to empower your understanding, Part Two to hone your technique and structure a practice regime, and Part Three to apply your new picking powers to practical musical examples. Borrow the licks I've presented, transpose them into other keys and tonalities, and remember that an idea is only as useful as the ways you can apply it.

My philosophy is that speed is a result of efficiency working at maximum potential. Read that sentence again. *Speed is a result of efficiency working at maximum potential.* I'm referring to neural efficiency as much as physical. By increasing your facility through good habits, consistent repetitions and focused execution, you are building and reinforcing the motor skills that make fast passages seem a lot more natural in the long run.

The number of times a skill is correctly executed improves the chances of it being performed correctly again. Always be working on keeping your ratio of clean to sloppy well in favour of clean playing.

Take your time and enjoy the process!

Chris Brooks

Part One: A System of Strengths

There's a piece of advice that I pass on to all who study with me: *Work on your weaknesses, but systemise your strengths*. Seeing both as essential but very different steps is something I believe ties into The Yng Way system discussed in this book.

Working on weaknesses is vital because as players it is crucial not to abandon our musical ideas because of an inability to execute them. We are motivated to break through the barriers because the thought of being able to play the music we like serves as a constant motivation.

Systemising your strengths is a concept that goes even further. Now that you're proficient at an element, how can you exploit that skill or musical device and multiply it into a thousand licks? Often the most powerful concepts you can work on in the practice room are the ones that solve the most problems or adapt to the most applications within your style.

I believe that The Yng Way is a system of strengths as it pertains not only to Malmsteen's style, but also in the way it may provide solutions to *your* challenges. Take the opportunity to make these strategies your own. I've adapted many things within my playing to this system to bypass elements I didn't like about other systems and enjoyed the sonic results as well!

As you work through the various principles, such as picking mechanics, ascending, descending, and "even-notes" strategy, keep in mind that these all form part of a brilliant conceptual tapestry. The challenges you find in various study lines may seem isolated at first, but as you increase your scope, you will see how the parts come together, and how getting better at each element is, in fact, getting better at the system as a complete manifesto for execution.

Chapter One: Biomechanics

I divide the mechanical precepts of The Yng Way into *rested principles* and *active principles*. Rested principles are about setting up your body for the best starting position to execute the material, and active principles are the motions and playing strategies used to create fast and fluent picking lines in the Malmsteen style. These principles aren't restrictions, but a checklist of barrier-breakers for anyone who has struggled with Yngwie's material or is attempting it for the first time.

In the rested principles, we have:

1. *Pick grip*

2. *Pick edge offset*

3. *Picking orientation (including pick slant)*

4. *Picking hand anchoring*

In the active principles, we have motion mechanics and picking strategies. These include:

1. *Rotational picking motion and auxiliary mechanics*

2. *Single-string strategy*

3. *Multi-string even numbers strategy*

4. *Ascending odd numbers strategy*

5. *Descending odd numbers strategy*

Rested Principle One: Pick Grip

Yngwie's pick grip falls into a category that I've dubbed the *D-Grip* because the thumb rests on the side of the index finger and spells out an uppercase letter D. This is by far the most common pick grip, so there's a good chance you're already doing it. Figures 1a and 1b illustrate this grip with and without a pick.

Neither the index finger or the thumb protrudes from each other by more than a few millimetres. The pick is an extension of the point where the fingers come together. Yngwie uses a 1.5mm Delrin 500 pick by Jim Dunlop. I recommend using a pick that doesn't bend, as too much pliancy can drastically increase the time it takes for each pick stroke to leave the string.

The pick is not held by any of the other fingers because that can hurt the flexibility, pick orientation and anchoring that are important for this approach. Thumb tension should be neutral with neither an extreme convex nor concave thumb shape as either can cause fatigue from too much tension. Start with the minimum grip necessary and see if you need to adjust it from there.

Figure 1a:

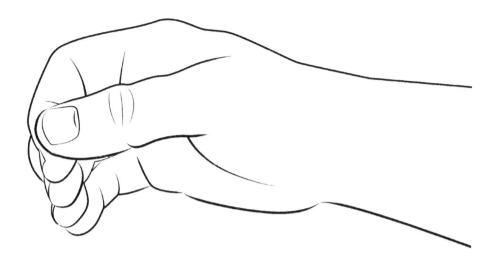

Figure 1b:

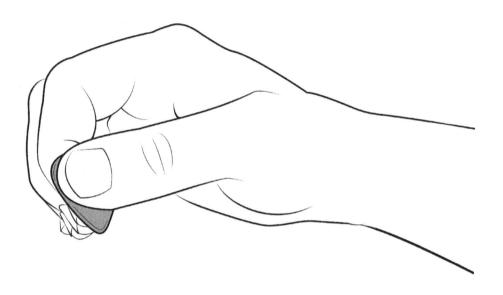

Rested Principle Two: Pick edge Offset

Pick edge Offset is a means of reducing friction by using the edge of the pick to attack the strings rather than the flat surface area. Edge offset is different to *picking orientation* because it happens in a different axis.

When a pick hits the string with no edge offset, it creates the maximum contact and friction between pick and string. It is *on-axis*, as shown in Figure 1c. Doing this can be practical for volume but less efficient for speed.

Figure 1c:

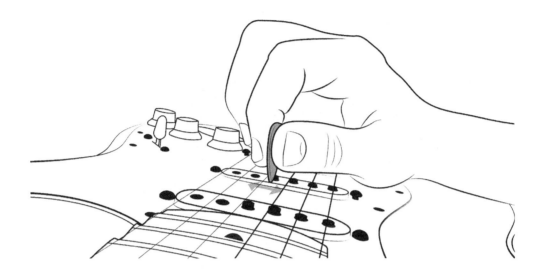

To reduce friction by rotating *off-axis* to the string, keep the pick pointed at the guitar body, then turn it either *clockwise* or *anti-clockwise* until finding your preferred sweet spot. Too much offset will have less volume and definition. For right-handed players, turning the pick clockwise from neutral point means the *outer edge* of the pick will hit the string first on a downstroke, and twisting anti-clockwise from the neutral position means the *inside edge* of the pick will hit the string first. Left-handed players need to do the reverse.

Yngwie leads with the outer edge of the pick on downstrokes, i.e., clockwise offset, while George Benson is an example of a player who uses an anti-clockwise offset, so the inner pick edge leads. Most people's outer or inner edge offset is created by wrist position and fine-tuning from the thumb.

Figure 1d: Clockwise pick edge offset:

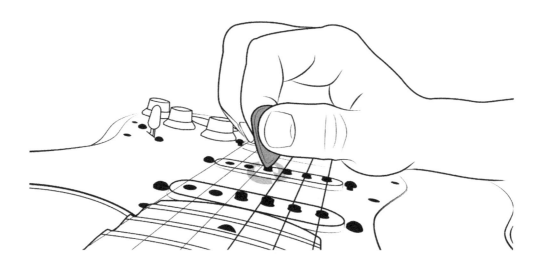

Figure 1e: Anticlockwise pick edge offset:

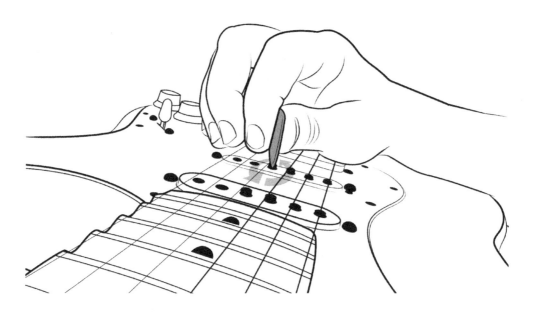

To get a feel for the difference between on-axis and off-axis pick positioning, take a tremolo picking drill like Example 1a, maintaining on-axis surface area contact with the string at first. Take note of how it feels as you work up to your clean top speed. Depending on the shape and material of your pick, this may even prove difficult if the pick tends to hook onto the string with each pick stroke.

Example 1a:

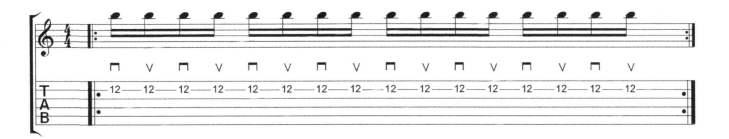

To adopt Yngwie's approach, a clockwise offset of just 20 to 30 degrees should be enough to minimise friction and maintain note clarity. Repeat the speed test in Example 1a and compare the results. If the pick edge offset hasn't been your default approach, give it some time to become natural through habit, repetition, and combination with the other principles in this book, then make an informed decision on how much offset to apply.

Rested Principle Three: **Downward Picking Orientation (DPO)**

Yngwie's picking pathways do not occur in parallel to the guitar body, so the study of picking orientation is critical in its effect on your starting position, and on the string-changing strategies in the active principles. In this section, it's essential to acquire an overview of picking orientation and *pick slant* so you can relate that knowledge to subsequent chapters. If these concepts are new to you, they may, in fact, have far-reaching application in your picking style.

The problem with parallel picking motion

When a pick goes up and down on either side of one string in parallel motion to the guitar body, it remains at a constant distance from the guitar as you push it back and forth through the string. Both strings adjacent to the one being played form a kind of boundary for the range of picking motion. In isolation, these conditions don't create any immediate problems, particular with pick edge offset to cut through.

The problem with parallel picking motion is, however, that when *changing* strings, there's a good chance the pick will be stranded on the *wrong side of the fence,* i.e., inaccessible to the string you wish to travel to next.

To see this in action, play two notes slowly on the B string, down and up, with a completely parallel picking motion. At the end of the upstroke, the pick now resides between the B string and the G string, which creates a problem affecting either direction you go from here. If the aim were to play two notes on the G string next, down and up, the pick is now on the wrong side of the G string, forcing an awkward upward semi-circle leap over the G string to get into position (Figure 1f).

If the aim were instead to play two notes on the high E string, the B string itself is now in the way, requiring a downward semi-circle leap (Figure 1g).

Figure 1f:

Figure 1g:

An example like the following could, therefore, become a mess at high speed as the picking pathway switches between parallel lines and semi-circle arcs.

Example 1b:

Replacing circles with lines

Using a pick slant is another way to solve problems using angles. In Principle Two, the issue of friction and therefore latency in one axis was resolved by pick edge offset. In this principle, the objective is to aid string changing in another axis by re-orienting the pick relative to the guitar and following oblique lines of motion. To start, let's reposition the pick.

Treating the string as a *horizontal axis* and the tip of the pick as the *zero point*, moving the back end of the pick down the vertical axis results in a *downward pick slant*. Doing the reverse, i.e., leaning the pick *up* the vertical axis, results in an *upward pick slant*.

Figure 1h:

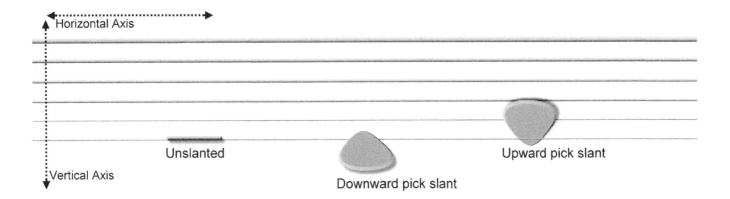

Picking consequently moves in two slanted pathways depending on the pick slant applied. In a downward slant (Figure 1i), downstrokes push through the string towards the guitar and upstrokes pull away. In an upward slant (Figure 1j), the opposite occurs.

Figure 1i:

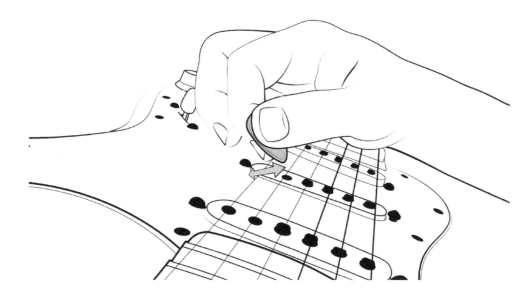

Figure 1j:

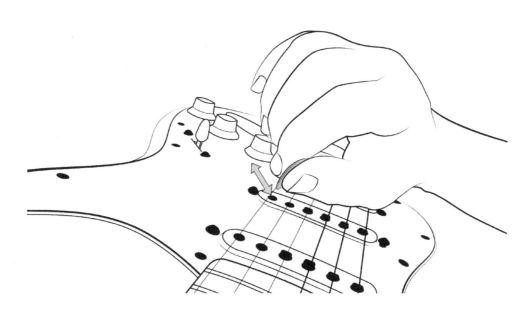

By removing the equidistant nature of the picking pathway in line with the guitar body, the pick will have an unobstructed range of movement unhindered by the obstacles described in the earlier parallel motion problem.

Re-examining Example 1b with this knowledge reveals that the string-changing problem in that situation can be overcome with a downward pick slant. The upstrokes now pull away from the guitar, and the downstrokes push through the string towards the guitar.

Figure 1k illustrates an upstroke on the B string followed by a downstroke on the G string while Figure 1l depicts a change to the E string instead, as per the last two beats of Example 1b.

Figure 1k:

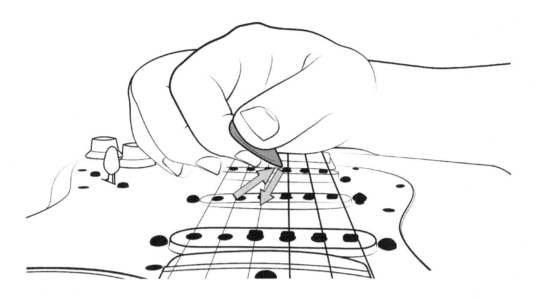

Figure 1l:

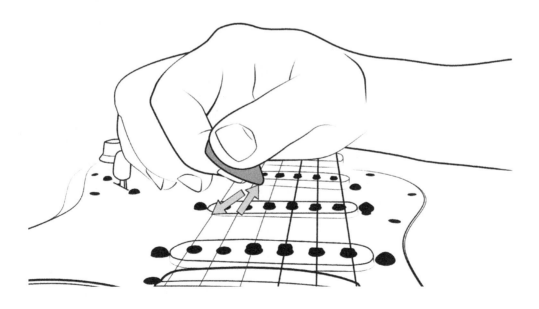

In Example 1c, the slanted pathways will enable hassle-free string changing throughout.

Example 1c:

If the last two examples had the reverse picking strokes, up and down on each string, a downward slant would create the same problem as the semi-circle leap. The solution in that scenario is to play with an upward pick slant instead. Choosing the correct slant for each application is important.

Alternating Pick Slant (*Not* part of the Yng Way)

In situations where you find yourself leaving strings on both up and down strokes throughout a lick because of odd numbers of strokes per string, the ability to alternate between pick slants is a highly useful tool to avoid entrapment. Such an approach is a trait inherent to many of the best alternate pickers, which can be considered an alternating or *two-way pick slant*. The aim is to leave each string with the pick slant that avoids the pick getting trapped on the wrong side of each new string in a phrase or scale run.

oExample 1d indicates where downward (\ p.s) and upward (/ p.s.) pick slants can alternate to create a clear picking pathway. As you can see, a change in pick slant occurs one note before a string change takes place.

Example 1d:

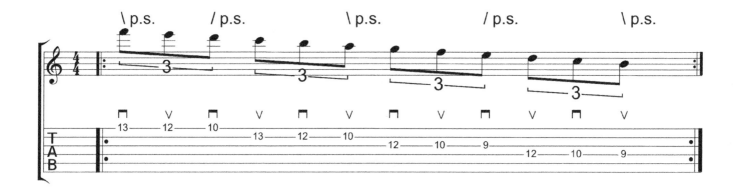

How do you create a pick slant with the picking hand?

In both cases, the rested pick slant is generated by rotation of the forearm muscles, resulting in the picking hand turning either outward or inward. You can achieve a downward slant by using an outward rotation (supination) of the forearm from the neutral position, and an upward slant by using an inward rotation (pronation) of the forearm from the neutral position.

Figure 1m:

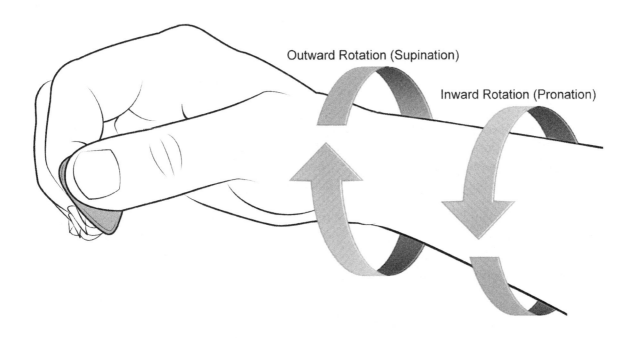

One way to identify a downward or an upward pick slant in your own or someone else's playing is to take note of the fingers, relative to the guitar. With the fingers curled up and fingertips in line as many players do, a player using a downward pick slant will rotate their thumb furthest from the guitar body, and a player using an upward pick slant will rotate their fourth finger furthest from the guitar body with the thumb being the closest.

Differentiating between pick slant and picking orientation

Many players have naturally developed a biased resting position in an upward or downward pick slant pose, meaning the forearm is in *rested supination* or *rested pronation* even before a single pick stroke has occurred. This preferred starting point is what I describe as picking orientation, where the dominant pick slant becomes the new neutral position from which up strokes and down strokes occur. Such is the case in Malmsteen's default picking pose, which exhibits a *downward picking orientation* (DPO).

Picking orientation and pick slant can overlap but need not be mutually exclusive. Many players might prefer one form of orientation, yet still be capable of alternating pick slant when their natural picking orientation doesn't provide the right picking pathway for string changing. For example, both Vinnie Moore and Andy James have visible upward picking orientation (UPO), yet are masters of alternate picking with fluctuating pick slant wherever it is required. James even seems to prefer starting many picking patterns on upstrokes to support his UPO, but still, exhibits a fierce picking style uninhibited by changing pick slant on the fly. By comparison, Paul Gilbert has a visible DPO but demonstrates a use of alternating pick slant in scale sequences where downward pick slant alone might create a trap.

Players who maintain a single picking orientation and pick slant throughout often engineer their string-changing strategies based on that preference. In the genre of *Gypsy Jazz,* for instance, this *Supination Bias* is almost a rule rather than an exception. Yngwie too falls into this asymmetrical category with a picking style that results in unconventional string-changing strategies, scale layout, and melodic choices made depending on whether lines are ascending or descending, as discussed further in the active principles section.

Rested Principle Four: Anchoring

Picking hand anchoring is a precept that results in both functional and aural effects worthy of mention. One of three contact points with the guitar (the others bring at the forearm contour and the pickguard), Yngwie's planted picking hand is a multifunctional stealth tool for stability, string control and muting.

Placed close enough to the edge of the bridge saddles to let notes ring out or mute them, the picking hand gains stability and consistency from an anchored position, can control unwanted noise from unused strings and dictates how open or closed picking passages sound with degrees of *palm muting*. Yngwie is capable of a range of fast, efficient movements with this hand that range from the simplicity of deadening unused strings to the precision of applying varying degrees of muting to strings in play for increased percussive effect, and occasional lifting and muting for riffs and heavier passages.

Developing a range of right-hand effects is a matter of finding a comfortable and functional resting position, then experimenting with various degrees of muting and string control. Movements to try from the anchored position include subtle wrist flexion and extension to mute and unmute, and combinations of wrist deviation and forearm supination to roll palm muting across different groups of strings as required.

Yngwie's fourth finger is often near or around the volume knob on a Stratocaster(TM), especially when playing the treble strings, so feel free to use it as a landmark. The other fingers often meet the pickguard but not in a planted finger approach like that of Michael Angelo Batio.

To get into the approximate position, place the side of the picking hand on the strings as shown in Figure 1n.

Figure 1n:

As you curl up the fingers somewhat, rotate the forearm inwards and turn the pick towards the strings. More of the inside of the hand will naturally become a part of the anchored position. When combining the anchor with pick edge offset and DPO, you should see a resting pose like that of Figure 1o.

Figure 1o:

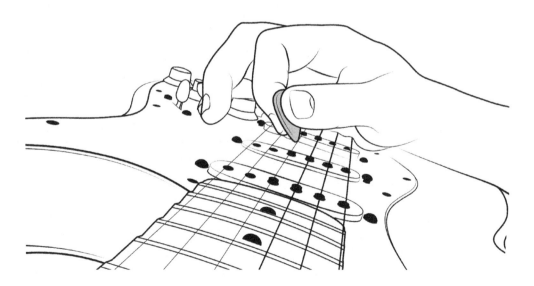

At all times, keep your picking hand relaxed without too much downward pressure since you do not wish to play out of tune by placing undue stress on the bridge. Great anchoring is a result of your hand placement rather than weight.

Note that in the case of single-string Eruption-style tremolo picking, Yngwie floats his picking hand away from the bridge and applies wrist flexion, resulting in a protruding wrist joint more akin to the position used in the Gypsy Jazz picking style.

Active Principle One: Forearm Rotation and Auxiliary Mechanics

Our upper limbs are capable of quite a few movements that can enable and influence the motion mechanics of guitar playing. Some actions can be attributed to one part of the hands or arms, and others to a compound of motions. The degree to which these movements are executed can vary widely from player to player. For one player, one motion might be a core strategy, and for another player, the same motion might be bypassed entirely.

The point of discussion in this principle is how to replicate a trademark mechanical device in Malmsteen's speed system. The dominant mechanic in Yngwie's speed-picking approach is *Forearm rotation*, which is comprised of two components: *active supination* (turning the palm outward) and *active pronation* (turning the palm inward).

That's not to say that other mechanics won't work for speed-picking in general. I could list numerous exceptional players who use different singular or compound motions to create high-velocity picking lines from mechanics like the following:

- *Elbow motion: flexion (bending) and extension (straightening)*

- *Wrist horizontal: radial (sideways inward motion) and ulnar (sideways outward motion)*

- *Wrist vertical: extension (upward motion) and flexion (downward motion)*

- *Thumb and index finger motion: flexion and extension (closing and opening of the interphalangeal and proximal interphalangeal joints respectively)*

We are all likely to use at least a few of these movements in our guitar playing but for The Yng Way, let's focus on rotational motion.

As described earlier, forearm rotation is the combination of two motions, known to physical therapists as active supination and active pronation. Both are widespread mechanics among speed-pickers, but in Yngwie's case, keep in mind that the forearm is already *passively* supinated in its rested position as described in Principle Three. It means there is further supination outward from the starting position on upstrokes, and pronation back inward to the supinated point of origin on down strokes.

The rotation rarely, if ever, pronates to the point where the pick would be in an upward pick slant, so it is a matter of using different degrees of supination from the angle that DPO has already established. Figure 1p illustrates a downstroke having pronated through G string (left) and an upstroke supinating away from the G string (right), ready for the next downstroke.

Figure 1p – Pronation (downstroke), Supination (upstroke):

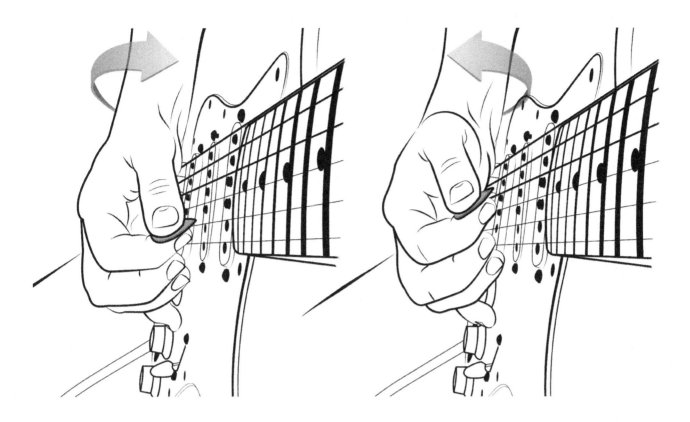

To experiment with supination and pronation in your technique, start on one string with a single note so that you can direct attention to your picking hand. Example 1e provides an example that alternates between 1/8th notes and 1/16th notes. It's important to keep your technique consistent throughout both.

Example 1e:

If your rotation and downward picking orientation are in place, you should be able to perform the string changes in Example 1f without getting the pick stuck on the wrong side of any string. With the larger distance from the E string to the G string, it's natural to use a little more supinated rotation to cover the range. Just be sure that you are not switching techniques or using any upward pick slant in this example.

Example 1f:

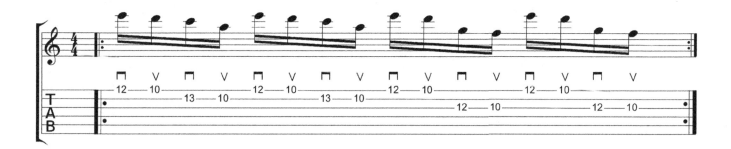

Troubleshooting with Rest Strokes

If you find yourself second-guessing the picking pathways you are creating, another way to line up your pick strokes and double-check your angles is to practice with a *Rest Stroke*. Rest strokes are more commonly associated with sweep picking and in the ascending strategies of this book, but can also be employed for troubleshooting your picking pathways.

A rest stroke develops when the pick leaves a string and simultaneously but silently arrives at the next string in anticipation of the following note. The rest stroke won't make any noise because it is just the point at which the pick has come to a stop.

Going back to Example 1e with the rest stroke in mind, down-pick the first note of the B string with DPO and let the pick come to a standstill at the high E string, which will act as a *guide rail* to make sure you are not scooping the pick up and down with the wrist. Next, play the second note of the B string with an upstroke, keeping the same slanted pathway. You should be able to pick upward as far as you like without hitting the G string. Continue to use the rest stroke for the entire drill to make downward pick orientation habitual.

You can then try the same approach by revising Example 1f, resting the pick on the E string after downstrokes on the B string, and resting on the B string after downstrokes on the G string.

You might find yourself exaggerating the motions at first, which is an entirely acceptable method of becoming acquainted with the technique. In Yngwie's playing, the rotation is almost covert in its speed and range of motion, particularly when combined with picking hand anchoring. This stealth level of refinement will come in due time as you become increasingly fluent and economical.

Anchored versus unanchored rotation

Rotational motion is made possible in both the anchored and unanchored positions by the two bones that run from the wrist joint to the elbow joint. The *radius*, located laterally in the forearm on the same side of the thumb, and the *ulna*, located medially on the opposite side, are responsible for rotating the wrist joint in pronation and supination.

The unanchored rotational motion should be reasonably apparent to the eye as the back of the hand turns side to side in equal amounts between the pronation and supination interchanges. In the anchored position, things will look a little different. The radius can still fulfil its purpose of rotation, but with half of the hand now planted on the guitar, the thumb and index finger will appear to push towards and pull away from the somewhat stationary fingers of the anchor.

It's important not to attribute what you see in Yngwie's anchored picking to an independent *thumb and index finger* motion, which would originate through the flexion and extension of the finger joints only. Focusing attention about four to five inches up from the wrist joint of Yngwie's picking arm reveals that forearm rotation is still occurring, but with less visual clues given by the stationary fingers of the picking hand.

Auxiliary effects of anchored rotation

Auxiliary mechanics is the label I've given to motions that work together with, or result from the primary mechanic of forearm rotation. These are more likely to be resultant movements in your playing rather than aspects that require a significant portion of your thinking process.

The thumb and index finger motion that *does* occur in Yngwie's playing is perhaps best thought of as *fine-tuning*. Where some movement is altered in the process of anchored picking, the thumb and index finger both add some extra range of motion that I suspect is highly intuitive rather than conceptualised. This fine-tuning process also occurs in pick edge offset, flattening out for big notes where more volume or aggressive attack is required, and reverting to slicing mode for sweeps and fluid lines. To that end, even small traces of wrist flexion and extension can have been observed for certain phrases where a lot of attack on slower passages is required. Interestingly, Malmsteen's Blues playing features a lot more instances of these auxiliary mechanics than faster consistent passages.

If you've chosen to adopt the forearm rotation mechanic that dominates Yngwie's speed-picking, use the development drills in this book to hone that technique first and foremost, and observe any auxiliary mechanics that occur in your playing, evaluating their usefulness and either keeping or correcting them as required. As vain as it may sound, practice done in front of a mirror can be beneficial in self-evaluation!

Watch the Video!

To get a bird's eye view of rotational motion and downward picking orientation at various speeds, take a look at the video example included in our download for this book, which is from my video course The Yng Way. Details are in the "Get the Audio" section on Page 7.

Active Principle Two: Single-String Alternate Picking

In the 1960s and '70s, one way that a rock guitarist could add some flash and excitement to their solos was to take short phrases and repeat them several times, no doubt a nod to the blues that influenced so many rock players of the day. Often these phrases were done in box patterns like the Pentatonic scale, so it was common to hear three-note and four-note repetitions like that of Example 1g in the solos of influential rock players like Eric Clapton and Jimmy Page.

Example 1g

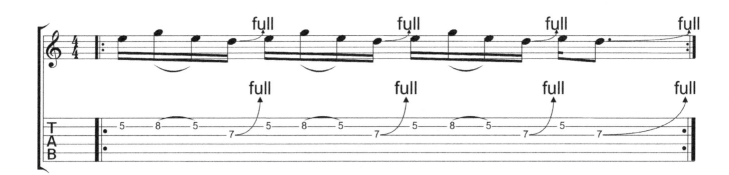

When Edward Van Halen emerged in the late '70s, things certainly opened up on a technical level as a new wave of guitar hysteria began, but Van Halen's solos still contained a lot of repetition-based licks formed around two-handed tapping (Example 1h) and tremolo picking (Example 1i).

Example 1h:

Example 1i:

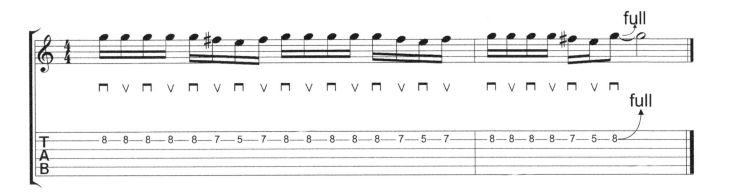

Inspired as much by Italian violinist Niccolo Paganini's (1782-1840) *24 Caprices* as Deep Purple's *Fireball*, a young Malmsteen set out to circumvent the rock clichés of the day by developing a more linear approach to speed licks and tonal sequencing which would become just one of the tricks in his magic bag. This method involves first knowing the major and minor scales up and down single strings. Example 1j contains an A minor scale in one octave on the high E string.

Example 1j:

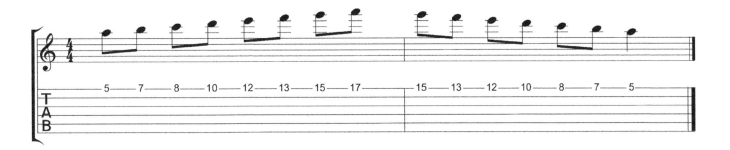

Yngwie applies a variety of sequences and position shifts to one-string scales to emulate his Italian hero, as well as recall the inverted (upper) pedal-point melodies of another significant influence, Johann Sebastian Bach (1685-1750). Malmsteen's single-string repertoire typically uses motifs consisting of three diatonic notes in each position before shifting upward or downward, executed with alternate picking.

A tonal sequence is when a motif is repeated in a higher or lower pitch, where the subsequent repetitions are diatonic transpositions of the original idea, like Example 1k which is comprised of four notes descending from each degree of the A minor scale.

Example 1k:

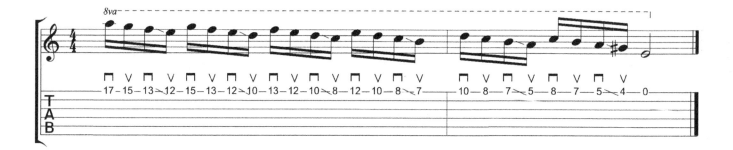

Inverted pedal-point is a device in which the highest note of the phrase is repeated between notes of a moving line. This Bach-style example in A minor is a trademark lick in the Malmsteen catalogue.

Example 1l:

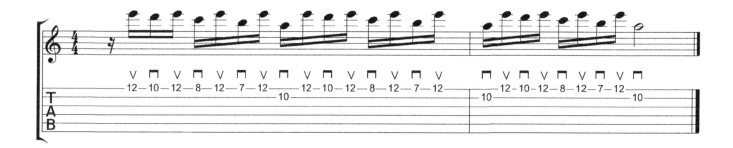

Yngwie combines elements of pedal-point and sequence along a string as shown in Example 1m, which emulates something the right hand of a harpsichordist might play in a Bach Concerto.

Example 1m:

Based on the frequent use of three notes per position, I use a numbering system to explain the melodic order of the sequences according to the lowest note, middle note and highest of the three. So, a sequence like Example 1n is described as 3-1-2-3 and means the highest note of the position is played, followed by the lowest, the middle, and back to the highest. This form is widespread in Yngwie's work.

Example 1n:

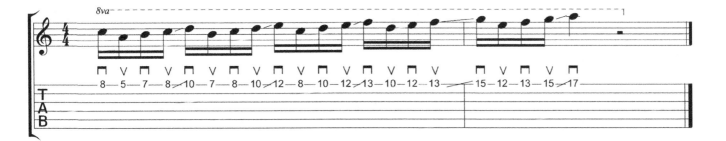

When trying these examples, remember to use the rotational motion and downward picking orientation to push towards the string and pull away from it. For shifting patterns, make sure each unit moves in perfect synchronisation with your downstrokes and the beats of your metronome.

Active Principle Three: Multi-string Even Numbers Strategy

Even numbers are a downwardly-oriented, alternate picker's dream! DPO sets up any multi-string, even-numbered picking sequence to start each string on a downstroke, exit on an upstroke, and have a clean path for changing strings in any direction without changes to pick slant. Regardless of musical style, licks based on multiples of two notes per string will give you this string-changing freedom throughout, as shown in the fusion-style A Dorian lick in Example 1o and the E Phrygian Dominant tonality of Example 1p.

Example 1o:

Example 1p:

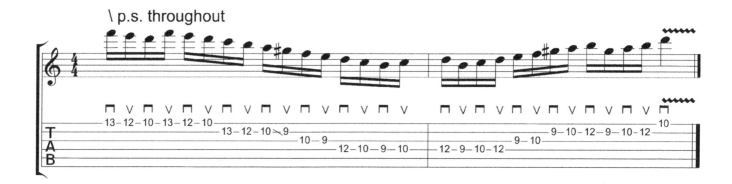

The string-changing simplicity and consistency of these patterns mean that whether each string has two, four, six or twenty notes, the picking pathway between strings need not be more complicated than a pentatonic box pattern, for example. Yngwie uses this to good effect in several of his trademark scale runs. If you remove the downward picking orientation from this category of picking licks, string changing once again becomes cumbersome. To avoid such problems, start *Evens* sequences on a downstroke and maintain DPO throughout.

Even patterns that lead with upstrokes do not naturally occur in Yngwie's playing, but if encountered in other styles and playing situations, it's important that you flip the picking orientation so that upstroke-leading is preceded by an upward pick slant. Example 1q demonstrates this with an upward pick slant on beat 2 setting up the up-driven portions of the lick before returning to a downward pick slant during the 2nd beat of bar two.

Example 1q:

Active Principle Four: Ascending Odd Numbers Strategy

At this point, you should be comfortable with alternate-picking single-string licks, and multi-string even-numbered sequences while maintaining a downward picking orientation throughout. Active principles four and five cover how Yngwie deals with odd numbers of notes, which play a big part in how the rest of the material in this book is played.

Alternate picking for odd numbers of notes per string is not a feature of The Yng Way, but it's vital to have an overview of how alternate picking is affected by odd numbers to appreciate the benefits and consistency of Yngwie's solution.

Strict alternate picking for odd numbers creates two picking pathways known as *Outside Picking* and *Inside Picking*. These terms refer to the pick travelling around the strings or directly between them. In Example 1r, the picking pathway from the G string to the B string is an outside picking stroke, and the path from the B string to the E string is an inside picking stroke. Here, the ascending *outside strokes* are best approached with an upward pick slant, and ascending *inside strokes* are best approached with a downward pick slant.

Example 1r:

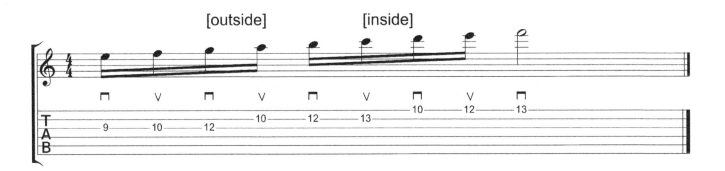

One of the pitfalls of alternate picking is that adding or removing notes from a phrase can alter where the inside and outside picking pathways occur. Example 1s starts with three new notes on the D string and follows with the notes of the previous example. As a result, a complete reversal of the prior segment of the phrase occurs, with pick strokes, pick slant, and picking pathways flipped to their opposites.

Example 1s:

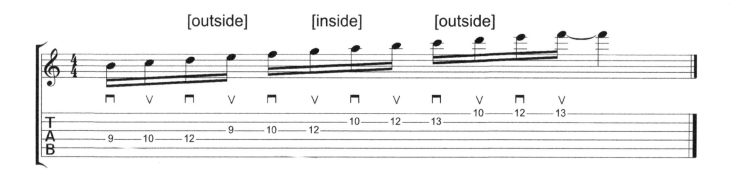

Yngwie's system, however, is built on facilitating an uninterrupted and consistent approach to each ascending string change instead of the symmetrical and oft-changing requirements of alternate picking. It preserves his preference for starting strings on downstrokes as described in the "Evens" approach.

When ascending with odd numbers, Yngwie will use a sweep or economy motion with DPO to turn the last downstroke of one string into the first downstroke of the next string. It's applying the scientific principle of *Inertia,* i.e., the tendency for an object to remain in its present state of motion until otherwise affected. Such a propensity is particularly the case with the improved velocity of outer pick edge offset, as the pick glides smoothly from one string to the next. Put simply, in Yngwie's system, the easiest way to overcome a string change is to push right through it! This directional process of changing strings with sweep-picking is known as *Economy Picking*, but Yngwie is strictly a one-way economy picker, ascending only.

Applying this approach to lines like Examples 1q and 1r demonstrates that with The Yng Way, extending a phrase need not reverse its mechanics. In Example 1t, the notes of the two previous examples are reprised but retooled with the Yngwie picking system, which remains in downward picking orientation and handles each string change the same as the next. In other words, two licks – one approach.

Example 1t:

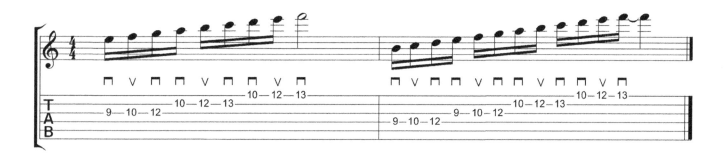

Bass players have tapped into the strengths of this Newtonian approach to string changing since the advent of upright bass fingerstyle, but in the opposite direction from higher strings to lower strings. Using a *drag method* whenever an opportunity to descend strings with the same finger presented itself, bassists continued this practice through the birth of electric bass in rock, blues, funk and jazz styles.

Back in the plectrum-using world, the asymmetrical ascending string-changing strategy has been a staple of the Gypsy Jazz genre possibly since its inception, as generational teaching methods saw it evolve into somewhat of an unspoken mechanical standard, albeit without the pick edge offset or picking hand anchoring seen in Yngwie's system.

It's imperative when developing your economy picking mechanics that you sweep as one flowing motion between strings rather than use two separate pick strokes. Develop your rest stroke technique so that exit downstrokes from the lower strings land on the following higher string without the need for a double movement. The first note of each higher string will, therefore, be created by the pick *leaving* the string rather than landing on it, as it will already be in-position from the sweep.

Watch the Video

You can see a video example of the ascending strategy at full speed and in slow motion by grabbing the download files for this book. See "Get the Audio" on Page 9 for details.

Active Principle Five: Descending Odd Numbers Strategy

Yngwie's second solution to odd numbers of notes per string is a strategy I describe with the portmanteau *Pick-gato*, combining the terms *picking* and *legato*. Legato means *tied together,* i.e., *smooth* in musical terms. For guitarists, however, it is often described as a playing technique due to the use of hammering on and pulling off notes with the fretting hand to contrast the usually stronger attack of picking.

A two-way economy picker like Frank Gambale descends by inverting his ascending approach with economy-picked string changes and an *upward* pick slant. Yngwie, being Yngwie, defiantly maintains his DPO throughout descending lines and tackles the asymmetry of his style another way.

Just like in the even numbers strategy, Yngwie uses the strengths of alternate picking to start strings with downstrokes and leave on upstrokes without forcing changes to pick orientation and picking pathway. A fretting hand pull-off is then used to execute the final odd note of any applicable string. Therefore, three notes are played *down, up, pull-off*. Five notes are played *down, up, down, up, pull-off* and so on. Example 1u is a quintessential Yngwie-style phrase with the descending Pick-gato strategy

Example 1u:

An economy picker would use a different approach to the same notes, using an upward pick slant through and using upward sweeps as shown in Example 1v.

Example 1v:

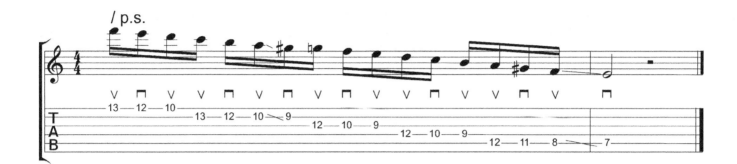

The strategy used in the former example is a cornerstone of Yngwie's fluid descending lines. The Pick-gato approach avoids inside picking, is optimised for DPO, and creates a synergy between combined even and odd numbers within a sequence, since the first pick stroke on each string is still a downstroke, and the last remains an upstroke. The strategic placement of pull-offs handles what would otherwise be a break in the even numbers strategy.

The Lone Note Exception

There is one quasi-exception to the downstroke starting-note template. I use the prefix quasi- because, despite its apparent deviation from the rules, this anomaly has a consistency to its usage.

When a single pick stroke on one string occurs before any number of notes on a lower string, the single picked note is played with an upstroke before the lower string begins on a downstroke. Handling a *lone note* in this way preserves consistency in the system amongst the remainder of the lick by treating it as an *exit note,* as though it were the last of several notes played on the higher string. The pick *leaves* the higher string on an upstroke, starts the lower string on a downstroke, and still avoids inside picking and alternating pick slant.

Example 1w is typical of the way Yngwie begins a legato phrase on one string before picking on lower strings. Even though there would be plenty of time to get to get the pick from the E string to the B string if both began on downstrokes, using the lone note upstroke removes an avoidable semi-circle leap to the B string.

Example 1w:

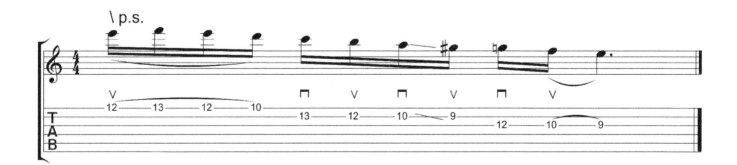

Example 1x demonstrates a direct path from the E string to the B string using the lone note exception. To reinforce how this fits into the usual descending approach rather than contradicts it, Example 1y adds an extra note to either side of the lick, keeping the picking of the original portion the same.

Example 1x:

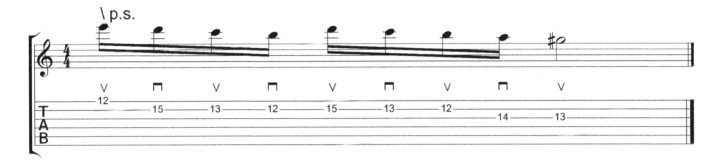

Example 1y:

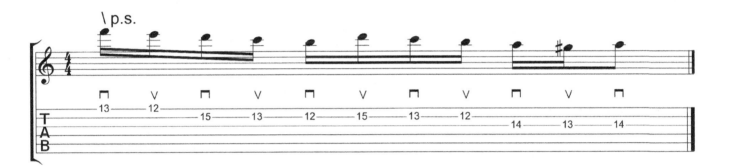

The lone note strategy will play a big part in the loop and sequence drills coming up in Chapter Six.

Biomechanics Summary

It has always been my personal view as a musician that anything is replicable if you know how, and that is precisely the motivation behind the detailed breakdown in this chapter. Where one player may appear to display a natural disposition to a concept, another may need to think harder, practise smarter, and spend more time troubleshooting than the first player. Don't be disheartened if you are the latter. Your efforts will pay dividends if you follow the method and remain self-aware.

Demystification is an essential process in our journeys as musicians, so try not to be overwhelmed with the volume of information but, instead, take logical step by logical step. Information and application build the bridge between where you are and where you'd like to be, so make sure each foundation is stable before you lay the next.

Despite the time it might take to naturally put the Malmsteen picking concepts into practice if they are new to you, the principles themselves contain some highly rewarding payoffs and time-savers. On the surface, it would appear that working on different concepts for ascending and descending directions is to work on two unrelated skills. As you'll hopefully have surmised from the principles in this book, true alternate and economy picking also require the player to master a two-pronged approach, mostly in learning equal opposites regarding pick slant, outside picking and inside picking.

The Yng Way system conserves time and energy in the following ways:

* *Allowing continuous downward picking orientation*

* *Standardising the start of each string with a downstroke*

* *Removing the alternation of outside and inside picking*

* *Systemising any exceptions to the norm with slurs and the lone note strategy*

Once you've transformed your knowledge into habits, an intuition about how the system applies to the examples in this book and the Yngwie Malmsteen catalogue at large should develop, thus enabling you to perform the material with success, confidence, and authenticity.

Chapter Two: Tonalities and Signature Sounds

This chapter is your guide to the all-important sounds of the neoclassical rock vocabulary. While Yngwie is adept in improvisation using a variety of *modes*, his signature sounds are most commonly created using variants of the minor scale and its evil cousin, the *Phrygian dominant* mode of *harmonic minor*, as well as a synthetic scale that I refer to later as the *hybrid minor* scale.

Natural Minor Scale or Aeolian Mode

Construction: I, II, bIII, IV, V, bVI, bVII.

Harmony: I min, II dim, bIII Maj, IV min, V min, bVI Maj, bVII Maj

The *natural minor* is a diatonic scale that contains semitone steps between degrees II and bIII, and between degrees V and bVI. Since each natural minor scale shares a *key signature* with a corresponding *major scale*, it is sometimes referred to as a *relative* minor. For example, the A minor scale (containing the notes A, B, C, D, E, F, G) is relative to C major (containing C, D, E, F, G, A, B).

This tonality is one of several derivatives of the major scale, called *modes*, which is why it is known to many improvisers in modern music theory as the *Aeolian mode*, the sixth of seven *modes* of the major scale. The natural minor scale is of importance in western music because we most commonly describe music as being in a major key or its relative minor key, depending on where the resolution is emphasised.

To study other modes and their application, check out *Guitar Scales in Context* by Joseph Alexander and published by *Fundamental Changes*.

On a guitar fretboard, the relative minor root note is found three frets below the major scale root note or nine frets above, adding up to the twelve chromatic notes in each octave. The study examples in this book utilise positional and shifting scale patterns, so familiarise yourself with the shapes that follow. These illustrate the A natural minor scale starting on the sixth string, the fifth string, and across the entire fretboard respectively.

A Natural Minor from 6th string root

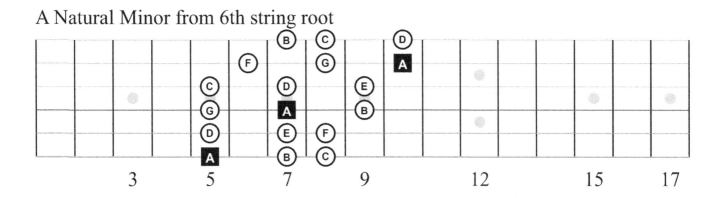

A Natural Minor from 5th string root

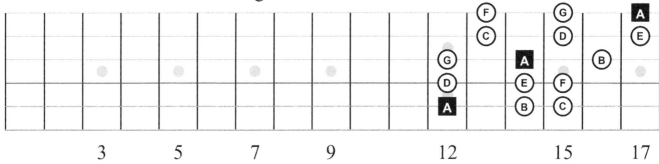

A Natural Minor across the fretboard

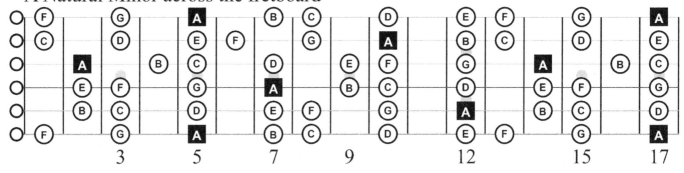

Natural Minor Scale Harmony

By stacking 3rds to build harmony, the natural minor scale produces seven triads which you can use in chord progressions underneath improvisation. Treating each scale degree as the root note of a cluster and adding a diatonic 3rd interval above it, and another diatonic 3rd interval above that results in a chord-scale. In the key of A minor, that produces the following:

A minor (containing the notes A, C, E)

B diminished (containing the notes B, D, F)

C Major (containing the notes C, E, G)

D minor (containing the notes D, F, A)

E minor (containing the notes E, G, B)

F Major (containing the notes F, A, C)

G Major (containing the notes G, B, D)

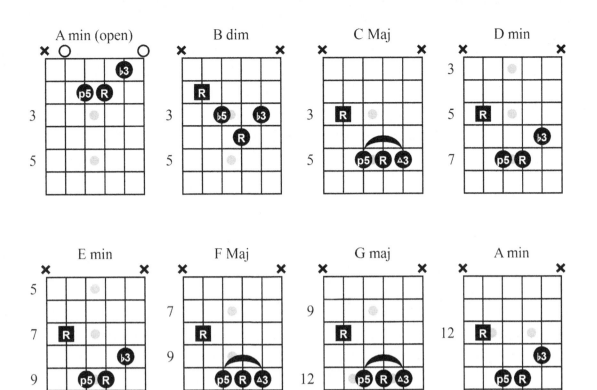

Harmonic Minor Scale

Description: Natural minor with a raised 7th

Construction: I, II, bIII, IV, V, bVI, VII.

Harmony: I min, II dim, ♭III Aug, IV min, V Maj, ♭VI Maj, VII dim.

The harmonic minor scale not only features prominently in the works of The Great Composers that influenced a young Yngwie Malmsteen's approach to composition but also in a lot of Malmsteen's improvisation, where it has become a distinct calling card of his fire-breathing solos. Even more so, harmonic minor's evil twin, the Phrygian dominant mode, is a staple you can just about bet money on appearing in any Malmsteen track.

The harmonic minor scale contains the first six scale degrees of the natural minor but concludes with a major 7th (VII) instead of a minor 7th (bVII). There is a harmonic purpose behind this alteration, which is to create a much stronger resolution from the V Maj chord (which features a major 3rd rather than a minor 3rd) to the I chord. This is called a *perfect cadence*. To hear the impact of this change, play an E minor chord followed by an A minor chord, then compare it to the pleasing resolution created by an E Major chord moving to an A minor chord. The G# note in the E Major chord becomes a leading tone to the A note.

Other engaging sounds in the harmonic minor scale include the exotic effect created by the minor 3rd leap between scale degrees bVI and VII and the fact that the scale also contains the tritones, or diminished 5th intervals, of both degrees.

A Harmonic Minor from 6th string root

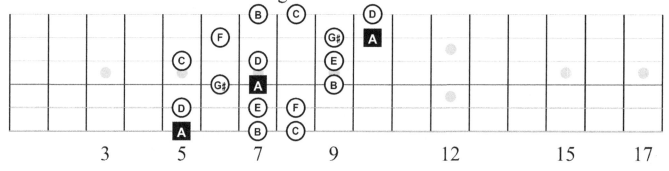

A Harmonic Minor from 5th string root

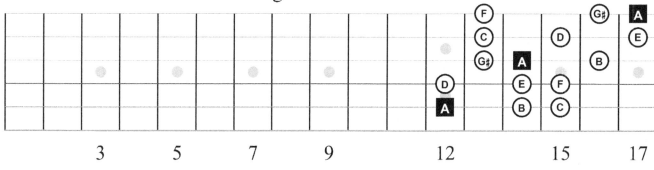

A Harmonic Minor across the fretboard

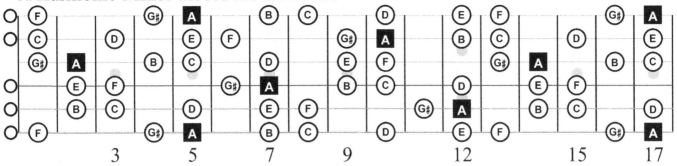

Chord V is not the only element of harmony affected by a change from natural minor to harmonic minor. Chord III Maj will become III Aug, and chord VII Maj will become VII dim (a semitone higher than its original root), giving us the following sequence of triads in the example key of A minor:

A minor (containing the notes A, C, E)

B diminished (containing the notes B, D, F)

C Augmented (containing the notes C, E, G#)

D minor (containing the notes D, F, A)

E Major (containing the notes E, G#, B)

F Major (containing the notes F, A, C)

G# diminished (containing the notes G#, B, D)

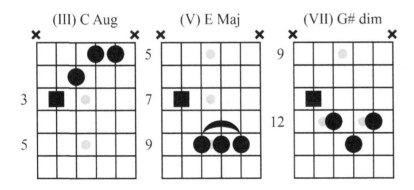

Because the natural minor and harmonic minor scales produce the same I min (and indeed the II dim, IV min and VI Maj triads), it's common for Yngwie to switch between both scales in improvisation over one-chord vamps without hitting any harmonic clams. Don't be alarmed if you see scale runs that include a bVII in one octave and a VII in the next.

Yngwie often composes and improvises around the I min and V Maj chords, the latter of which sets up perhaps the most critical Malmsteen sound, Phrygian dominant.

Phrygian Dominant Mode

Description: The fifth mode of the harmonic minor scale.

Construction: I, bII, III, IV, V, bVI, bVII.

Harmony: I Maj, bII Maj, III dim, IV min, V dim, bVI Aug, bVII minor

With its emphasis on the V chord of harmonic minor (which now becomes the I chord in context), the Phrygian dominant mode affords Yngwie the vehicle to create dark and exotic riffs and solos in an instantly recognisable way that utilises the harmonic minor scale's fifth mode. Rather than merely using the mode as a transitional device to resolve to the minor tonic chord, Yngwie composes sections and solos at length using Phrygian dominant in a modal fashion, exploring its tonality without feeling the need for a perfect cadence resolution each time.

As a mode of A harmonic minor, the E Phrygian dominant mode contains the notes E (I), F (bII), G# (III), A (IV), B (V), C (bVI) and D (bVII). Notice that each of the notes in the modal tonic triad has a semitone interval above it within the scale. Trills between these chord tones and their upward neighbour notes can be an excellent way to spell out the tonality of the mode.

E Phrygian Dominant mode across the fretboard

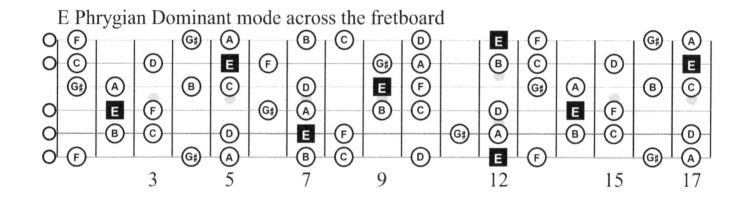

The cornerstone of good modal improvisation is thinking within the tonality at hand, so while the notes of a harmonic minor scale and the derivative Phrygian dominant are the same, it's important to think in context. Consider each note's relationship to the chord beneath, and create ideas that sound good over each chord. To that end, Yngwie favours patterns like Examples 2a and 2b within Phrygian dominant for their emphasis on its tonic triad tones, traversing the fretboard with combinations of three notes and four notes per string.

Example 2a:

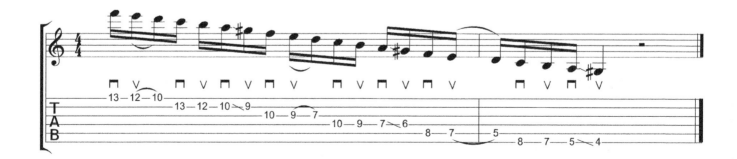

Example 2b:

Diminished 7th Arpeggios

Along with the darker sound of Phrygian dominant, *Diminished 7th arpeggios* are also a Malmsteen neoclassical signature sound. A diminished 7th arpeggio is made up of four notes that are each a minor 3rd away from each other. Phrygian dominant produces four of these which are, in fact, the same notes but inversions of each other. These are located on the bII, III, V and bVII degrees of the mode, manifesting in E Phrygian dominant as:

F Diminished 7 (containing the notes F, G#, B, D)

G# Diminished 7 (containing the notes G#, B, D, F)

B Diminished 7 (containing the notes B, D, F, G#)

D Diminished 7 (containing the notes D, F, G#, B)

The chord spelling of a diminished 7th arpeggio is I, bIII, bV, bbVII and to be enharmonically correct the note spellings above *should* be different. However, since the four arpeggios above are also inversions of each other, another way to look at them in the context of Phrygian dominant is as part of a V7b9 chord without its root. In the example key, E7b9 contains the notes E, G#, B, D and F. The root note of any underlying harmony will produce the E note, and all four diminished 7th arpeggios can be superimposed in solos to enhance the tonality and imply the complete chord.

Diminished 7th chord tones across the fretboard

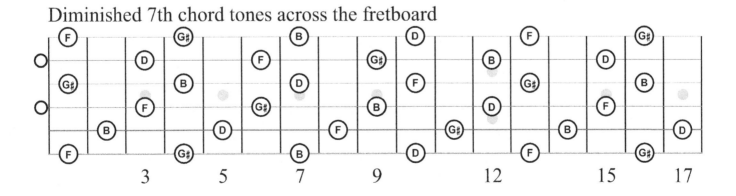

Yngwie often uses sweep picking and position shifting to connect diminished 7th arpeggios up and down the fretboard in minor 3rd steps, like the three-string form below.

Example 2c:

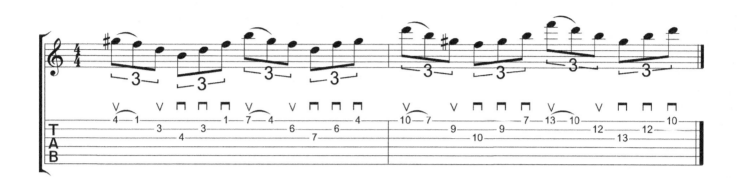

For scale lines like those focused upon in this book, diminished 7th arpeggios can also be used to create the frame of scalar picking patterns. Example 2d outlines a diminished 7th arpeggio with two notes per string, with Example 2e adding a middle note to each string to expand the arpeggio into a Phrygian Dominant line. Try these over an E or E7 chord.

Example 2d:

Example 2e:

Hybrid Minor Scale

Description: A synthetic minor scale with eight degrees.

Construction: I, II, bIII, IV, V, bVI, bVII, VII.

Harmony: Use over natural minor or harmonic minor harmony, but be careful!

Hybrid minor is my label for a synthetic scale that occurs in some of Yngwie's best-known scale runs. Whether it evolved as a matter of fretboard convenience, or as a passing tone device, the hybrid minor blurs the lines between natural and harmonic minor scales as both the bVII and VII intervals are present, creating the eight-note scale shown.

A Hybrid Minor from 5th string root

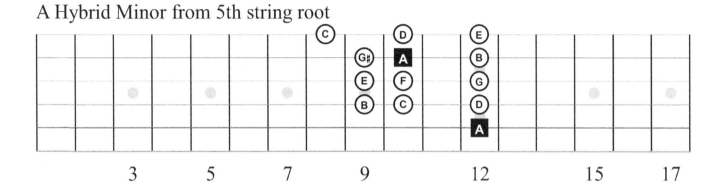

Yngwie uses the hybrid minor effect between the G string and B string, ending the third string on the bVII degree, and beginning the second string on the VII degree. This common occurrence strengthens the case for the pattern evolving as a matter of technical convenience in keeping with three notes on both strings.

In the key of A minor, the hybrid scale will include the notes A, B, C, D, E, F, G and G#. Be careful when using this scale not to hang on to any note that will create dissonance with the chord underneath. For example, when playing an A hybrid minor pattern over an E or E7 chord, use the G note strictly as a passing tone only as it will otherwise cause a direct clash with the G# note in the chord.

Yngwie frequently uses the hybrid minor pattern not only in ascending and descending runs but also in scales sequences like descending fours. It's easy to create a very unusual but recognisable sound when sequencing around the consecutive semitones of the bVII, VII and the root note above them.

Example 2f:

Each of the scales and tonalities mentioned in this chapter can be practised over the relevant tonic chord or by using *drone notes* on the low E or A strings. I recommend free-time improvisation as well as working with the metronome and backing tracks to attune your ears and fingers to the patterns and their relationship to the underlying harmony.

Part Two: Technical Development

Having studied Part One of this book, you should be familiar with the various elements of motion in Yngwie's picking style using terms grounded in science, as well as the musical terminology that will be used to describe the sounds used in the successive chapters. You should now be able to identify the different motion mechanics at play in Yngwie's style and know the sounds and fingerings of the natural, harmonic and hybrid minor scales, the Phrygian dominant mode, and diminished 7th arpeggios.

Part Two puts the mechanical precepts into practice with a series of development drills. I have categorised them into four areas of focus for progressive mastery of the entire system.

- *Single-string and Even Numbers Alternate picking*

- *Ascending Economy Picking*

- *Descending Pick-gato (alternate picking plus legato)*

- *Loops and Sequences*

For the best results, your practice routines should consist of a cross between single and multiple subjects per session. Develop one area in your *focus sessions* and cover numerous areas in *mixed sessions*. A sample development program may look something like this:

Week 1:

- Day 1: Get an overview of the entire system by taking a peek at each chapter in this part

- Days 2-6: Thirty minutes per day working through the first subject at various speeds

- Day 7: Twenty minutes of revision plus ten minutes on the beginning drills of the following chapter

Week 2-4:

- Day 1: Ten-minute review of previous material and twenty minutes working on the new chapter

- Days 2-6: Thirty minutes of focused workouts on the new chapter at various speeds with a metronome

- Day 7: Twenty minutes of revision plus ten minutes on the first few drills of the following chapter

Week 5:

- All days: work up to your clean top speed of the last few drills of each chapter with a metronome

- Take note of any issues and revise the appropriate exercises to overcome them

Week 6 and on:

- Tackle the advanced studies in Part Three, using Part Two as your warm-up material as required

Chapter Three: Single-String and Even Numbers Alternate Picking

Developing robust single-string technique is a crucial part of mastering speed picking. Not only is it a stylistic element of Yngwie's lead playing, but focusing on single string work allows you to excel at several critical technical facets before string changing becomes a factor. Even-numbered multi-string drills will also be introduced in this chapter to demonstrate how you can expand many of the single-string ideas.

The examples in this section are designed to give you the control, synchronisation, speed and timing that will put you in good stead for future chapters. I've created each drill with the aim of building your skillset progressively. When you can execute each one cleanly, accurately and with a degree of confidence, move on to the next.

Regarding Yngwie's fingering preferences, there are two fixed and two alternating fingerings in regular use. When three notes are spaced out starting with a semitone and a wider interval like a whole tone or minor third (Figure 2a), or two consecutive whole tones (Figure 2b), fingers one, two and four are used.

Figure 2a

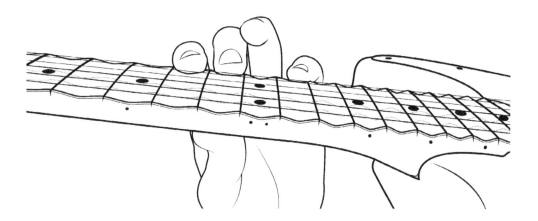

Figure 2b:

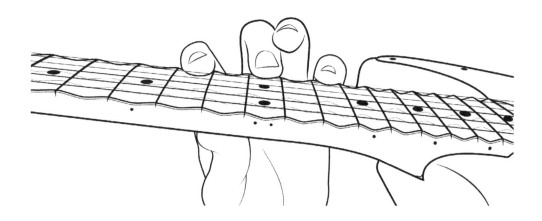

Yngwie handles note-spreads that end with a semitone in two different ways. When using a note spacing like a whole tone to a semitone in isolation, Yngwie favours fingers one, two and three (Figure 2c). For other lines and sequences where it's the logical thing to do so, he instead uses the fourth finger for the higher note and the third finger for the middle note (Figure 2d). Feel free to use either or both at your discretion, so long as you apply your choices with consistency to avoid confusion.

Figure 2c:

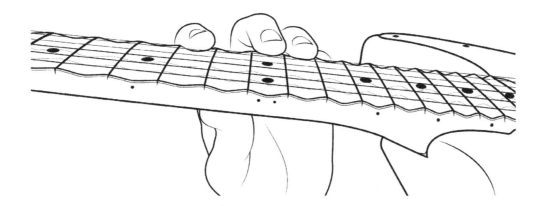

Figure 2d:

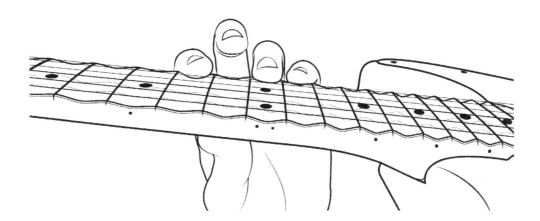

Using the picking hand principles previously covered, work on all drills in the order presented. Work on them *without* a metronome at first because this is about motor skill development. Introduce the metronome to track your progress and ensure you are playing in time once the mechanics are stable. I also suggest tapping your foot on the 1/4 note beats using the foot opposite to your picking hand. Diagonally-opposite limbs often work well together to reinforce internal rhythm, as they do in walking or running.

After a few repeats, move each exercise to the other strings of the guitar one by one, paying adequate attention to any strings that feel harder to play than others. Focus on the weak points until each string feels similar in comfort.

Beginning with Example 3a, use the high E string as a rest stroke guide rail for your picking motion along the B string. As you move the drill to each string, do the same with the higher adjacent string. On the high E string there obviously won't be a higher string to rest on, so be sure that your angles are consistent with what you did on the other strings. Focus only on your picking hand at this stage, as you incorporate pick edge offset, downward picking orientation, and anchored forearm rotation.

Example 3a:

After you've completed the first drill at various speeds and on all strings, add variety in pitch and extra fingers. Remember that you have two choices for fingering with this spacing.

Example 3b:

Examples 3c and 3d are designed to familiarise you with the natural minor scale along one string starting by moving a simple motif up and down diatonically. The 1/4 notes on beats 2 and 4 allow you to shift positions with plenty of time. Stay with the guide rail concept at this point.

Example 3c:

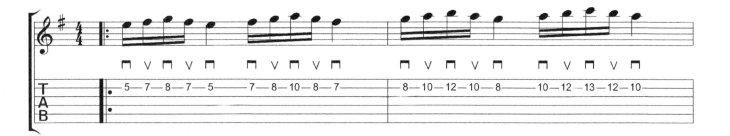

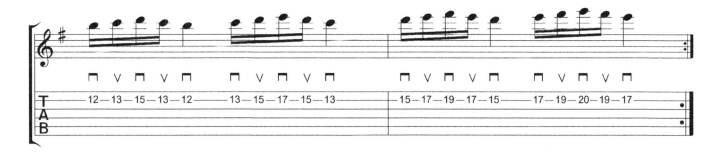

Example 3d:

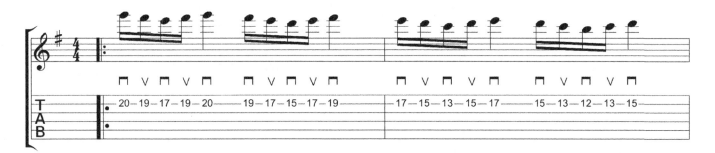

To ease into playing a steady flow of 1/16th notes along one string with position shifts, the chromatic crawling pattern of Example 3e, (which I call *The Centipede),* will build your picking hand endurance. The index finger leads each ascending group of four notes, and the fourth finger leads the descent. Aim for at least four clean repeats on each string before attempting a higher tempo, and keep track of the tempo where it falls apart to monitor your progress.

Example 3e:

The Bumblebee-style endurance drill of Example 3f involves all six strings, wider position shifts between chromatic groups, and the fourth finger leading consistently. It is crucial that DPO is used to facilitate each descending string change. Make sure that your exit upstroke on the higher string sets up the entry downstroke of the next string without the need for any second movement.

Example 3f

Ascending and descending fours are the staples of an excellent diatonic sequence repertoire, and in the next two examples, three notes from each position are extended with a shift to an additional note in the next position. Ensure that each shift synchronises with the pick stroke to avoid the fourth note of each group sounding twice. A good way to lock in your timing is to accent the downstroke that begins each unit of the sequence.

In the ascending fours of Example 3g, the index finger should synchronise with each beat of the bar. In the descending fours of Example 3h, the finger that hits each beat will depend upon your fingering preference for the *whole tone – semitone* spacing.

Example 3g:

Example 3h:

A sequence I describe as 3-1-2-3 is closely related to ascending fours, but the presence of an extra note at the beginning pushes the ascending fours portion back by one 1/16th note and reverses the picking strokes. Each position shift in Example 3i occurs at the start of each new beat and on a downstroke.

Example 3i:

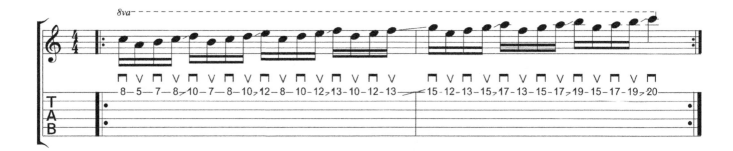

Likewise, the 1-3-2-1 descending counterpart of the previous example is a relation of the descending fours lick, consisting of position shifts at the beginning of each new beat.

Example 3j:

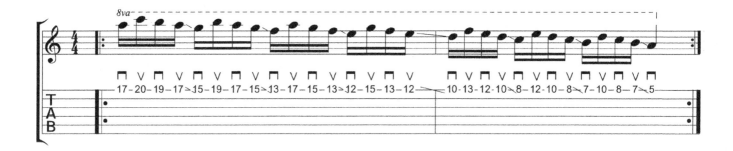

Keep in mind that sequences like 3-1-2-3 and 1-3-2-1 can be used with wider jumps along strings also, as Example 3k in A harmonic minor demonstrates.

Example 3k:

One of Yngwie's most familiar single-string licks is something I call the *Sixes Ostinato*. It appears on single and multiple strings in Yngwie's solos. In this iteration, the highest note alternates between the 13th fret C note and the 15th fret D note. Pay close attention to the suggested fingering to avoid getting knotted up. The ostinato works as a 1/16th note (Example 3l) or sextuplet (Example 3m) phrase.

Example 3l

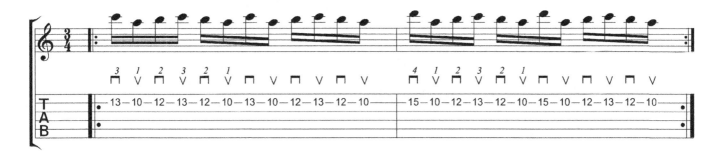

Example 3m

Example 1n is a multi-string expansion of the sixes ostinato which uses the two-string diminished 7th arpeggio form to outline an E Phrygian dominant tonality.

Example 3n:

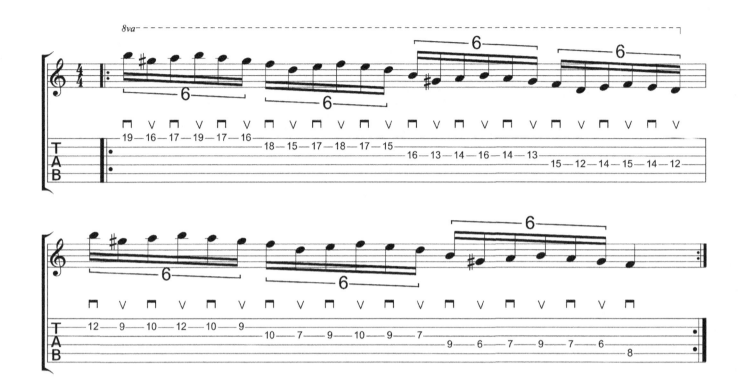

The final drill of your practice routine for this chapter is a pedal-point etude in the style of J.S. Bach, and a chance to apply your picking chops, fretboard knowledge and position shifting into one exercise. Transpose it to different keys, octaves and strings to challenge yourself. The notated key is A minor with some modulation.

Example 3o

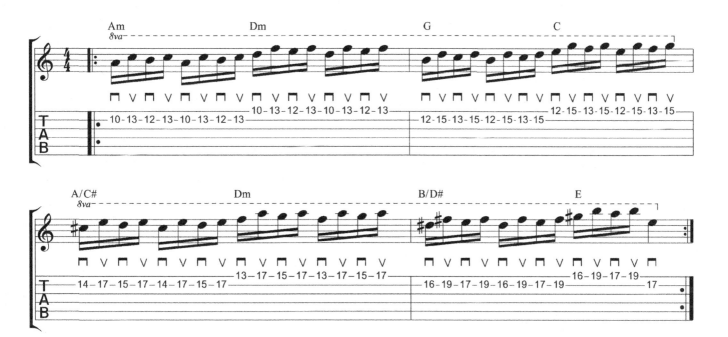

Chapter Four: Ascending Economy Picking Drills

The ascending economy picking drills in this chapter will help you develop and refine the first of two elements in Yngwie's asymmetrical string-changing system for odd numbers. Using sweep picking to finish a lower string and begin a higher string with the same pick stroke is the go-to approach anytime odd numbers of notes per string are involved.

Let's start by looking at how a string change works from the sixth string to the fifth. In Example 4a, a single downstroke sounds both the C and D notes. The sweep should be executed with rest strokes, firstly from the E string to the A string and then from the A string to the D string.

Example 4a:

This string-changing mechanic is the same used in two-string triads. In Example 4b, use an outside pick stroke with DPO to exit the A string and return to the low E string.

Example 4b:

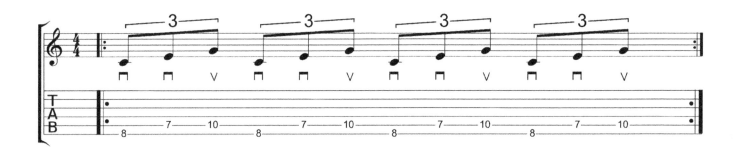

Applying the string change to a scalar situation starts in Example 4c by adding notes on either side. Make sure that the economy-picked downstrokes are neither faster nor slower than the alternate-picked notes.

Example 4c:

In Example 4d, the two alternating phrases each end on upstrokes. Downward picking orientation reinforces the outside picking pathway back to the low E string each time, which will be a valuable tool in the loops and sequences in Chapter Six.

Example 4d:

Example 4e sees a two-string drill develop into a three-octave, six-string pattern by creating diatonic pairs out of strings six and five, five and four, four and three and so on. Each unit of the lick takes up two beats and starts with the fretting hand index finger. Use this example to make sure that you are equally adept at string changing on each string pair.

Example 4e:

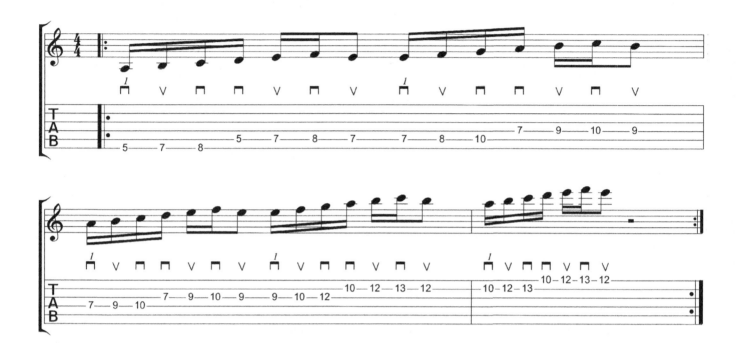

Now that you can move smaller units around the fretboard, it's time to apply the ascending strategy to scale playing. Any odd-numbered form like three-note-per-string scales (referred to herein as *three NPS*) will work perfectly with this approach. In the A natural minor run of Example 4f, pay close attention to the timing as you accelerate the tempo to your top speed. Yngwie will often rush phrases for effect, but its beneficial to your development to stay with the beat at first, applying stylistic acceleration later by choice rather than by accident.

Example 4f:

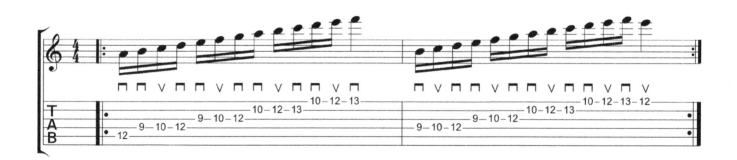

Since the integration of ideas is such a significant aspect of fluid playing in Yngwie's style, take your time mastering the final development drill in this chapter. Example 4g ascends with the same picking pattern as the first bar of Example 4f but uses an altered fingering described earlier as the *hybrid minor* scale. With this ascent taking you up the 4th beat of bar one, the drill then switches to descending fours down the high E string using the A harmonic minor scale.

You can break this drill into the two elements contained within it for memorising but, since fluidity is the goal, it's best to practise both bars from beginning to end as soon as you're able.

Example 4g:

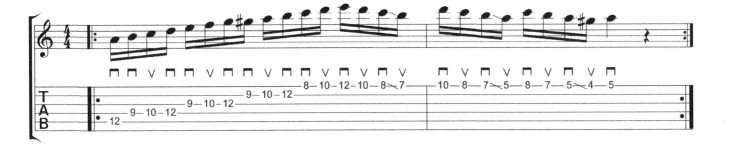

Chapter Five: Descending Pick-gato Drills

The descending drills in this chapter form a practice routine that will help the combination of alternate picking and strategised pull-offs feel like an extension of the even numbers strategy, rather than a contradiction to it.

Before commencing the Pick-gato drills, start with Example 5a, which is designed to wake up your fretting hand using hammer-ons and pull-offs. Repeat this exercise on all the other strings when practising, picking the first note of each bar only. Try to avoid any fluctuation in tempo when your fretting hand no longer has the picking hand to lock into for timing.

Example 5a:

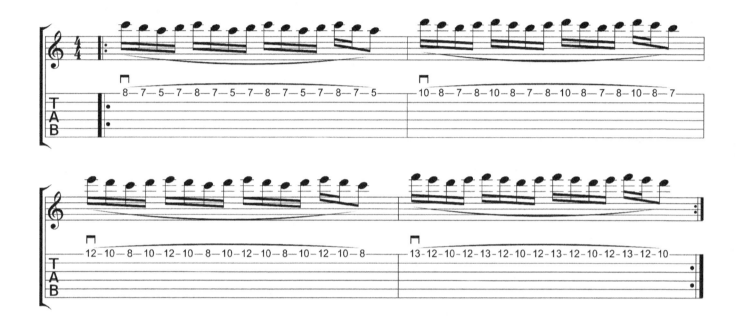

After warming up your fretting hand slurs, bring picking back into play with Example 5b. Incorporating a pull-off into the first triplet of each bar is all it takes to maintain an even number of pick strokes on both strings. After the upstroke preceding each pull-off, your pick should find its way to the next string with ease. If not, double-check your downward pick slant. When you have memorised the pattern, try it on other string pairs like the third and fourth strings, and the fifth and sixth strings.

Example 5b:

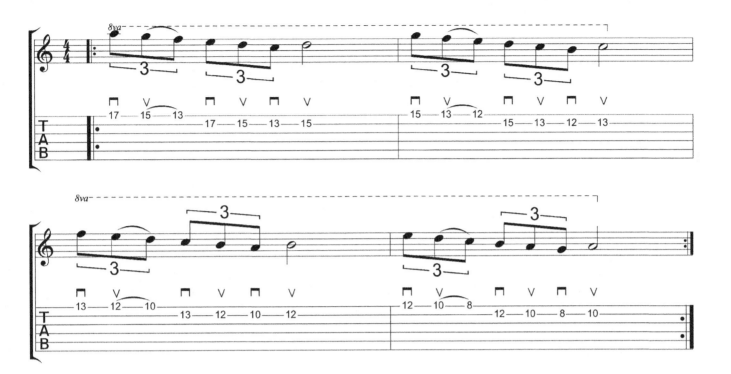

Example 5c once again uses a single pull-off to keep the system together, this time in a two-octave E Phrygian dominant lick. Yngwie stylistically starts smooth and finishes more aggressively with licks such as this, increasing pick attack towards the end of each phrase.

Example 5c:

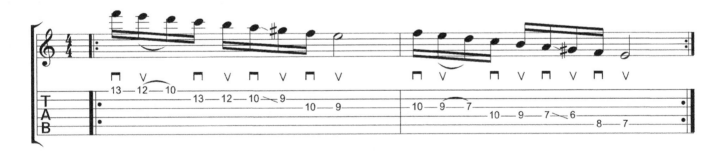

A straightforward scale like the A harmonic minor pattern in Example 5d enables the repetition of the *down, up, pull*-off picking form across multiple strings. Take care to maintain good timing, and try this picking form with all the three NPS scales that you know.

Example 5d:

In improvisation, it's important to be able to switch between odd and even numbers with ease, something that the next two examples are designed to target. Using the previous A harmonic minor shape, Examples 5e and 5f mix odds and evens by doubling the triplets on selected strings. In Example 5e, the *down, up, pull-off* form on the first, third and fifth strings is interspersed with the pure alternate picking on the second and fourth strings. Example 5f does the opposite.

Example 5e:

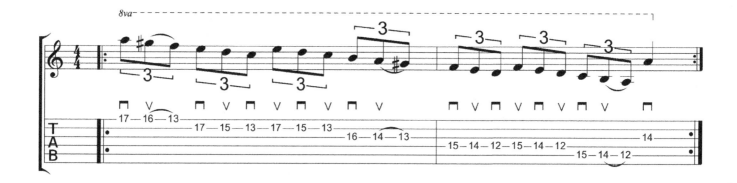

Example 5f:

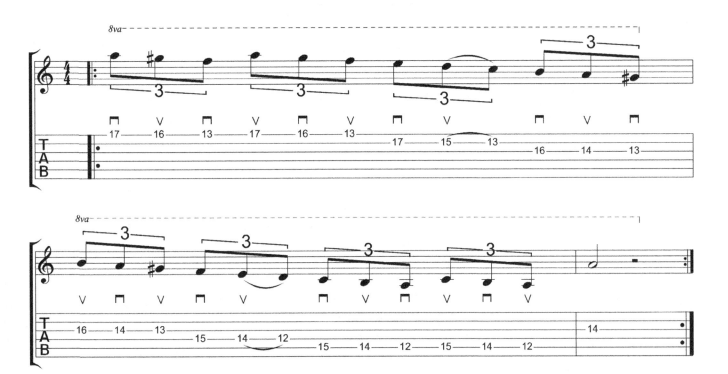

The last goal to accomplish in this chapter is to be able to play through phrases in which the placement of legato notes and string changes are irregular, i.e., not occurring in the same parts of the beat each time. Observe and work with Example 5g very slowly at first, noting where each beat falls as you play through its varying numbers of notes per string. With several slow repeats, you should be able to get a sense of where the pick strokes and pull-offs occur without reading through every time. As you increase the tempo, be vigilant in maintaining the 1/16th note rhythm, taking care to make sure that any three-note portions don't turn into triplets.

Example 5g:

Chapter Six: Loop and Sequence Drills

The purpose of this chapter is to consolidate the information and techniques you have acquired in previous chapters into a series of cyclical and sequenced exercises for practice. Building on the foundations you have created through practising chapters three, four and five, these examples will focus on bolstering your ability to seamlessly combine techniques in a musical way consistent with the Malmsteen style.

Looping is the term I give to playing short phrases that ascend and descend to create tension and interest before venturing into another idea. Yngwie does this frequently especially on the high E and B strings, but you should experiment with the loops here in multiple octaves and scale patterns.

Example 6a combines the ascending and even number strategies with odd numbers on the B string and even numbers on the high E string. Each ascending string change occurs with a sweep and each descending string change occurs after an upstroke with an outside picking path back to the B string. Melodically, this loop starts with four ascending notes and continues with two beats of descending fours, repeating in total after three beats.

Example 6a:

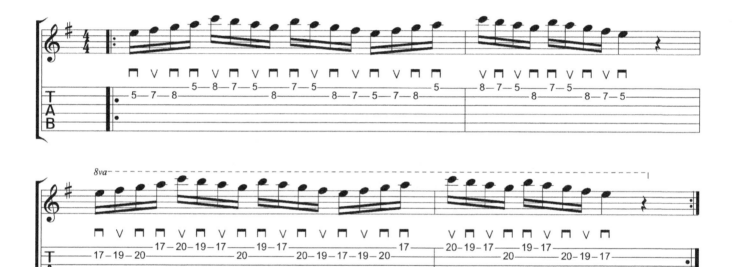

Example 6b, also in E minor, features three beats of descending fours or a 4-3-2-1 sequence, followed by one beat of four ascending 1/16th notes. The technical execution of this loop is a vital facet of the lick because it introduces the idea of a slur and a *crosspicking* stroke to pave the way for the lone note application in the 3rd beat of the bar. The lone note strategy and its setup play a big part in the sequences that follow.

Study this drill by working on beats 3 and 4 at first. This is the more natural half of the lick and a typical way of using the lone note on the high E string. Next, add at the last two 1/16th notes of beat 2 comprised of downstroke on the 10th fret of the B string with a pull-off to the 8th fret.

A subtle crosspicking motion will be required to get on the right side of the high E string for beat 3 by stealthily lifting the hand at the wrist joint (wrist extension). Crosspicking is a movement created by flexion and extension of the wrist to go over a string. It's common in styles like Bluegrass and Country where string changes can be required after single notes per string, but a rarely-detected occurrence in Yngwie's style.

The hammer-on just before the string change allows enough time to get into position without the need to overtly hop over the first string. Enough movement to clear the string is all it takes to preserve the other components of the drill and keep it flowing.

Example 6b:

Since you've done all that hard work, let's apply the same form to another loop, this time in E harmonic minor.

Example 6c:

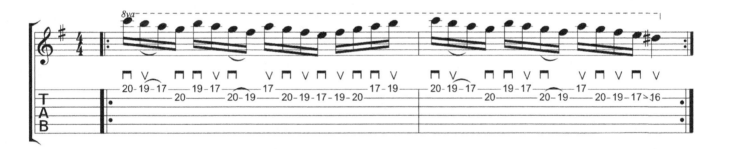

Loops can be a great start to a descending scale, as shown in Example 6f, which takes the drill from Example 6b and adds a descending E minor pattern in bar two where the loop would have otherwise repeated.

Example 6d:

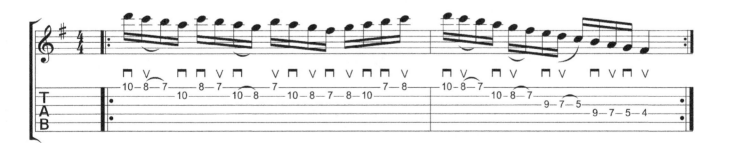

When a descending fours sequence is played all the way through a positional scale pattern like that of Example 6e, it's useful to first take note of three things:

1. There is a repeated layout of notes on each string pair: three notes and one note, two notes and two notes, one note and three notes. After these three steps take place, the layout repeats on the next string pair (starting on the 4th beat of the first bar in this case).

2. The first cycle of three descending fours starts on a downstroke (beats 1-3 of bar one).

3. The ensuing cycles of three descending fours start on upstrokes.

Example 6e:

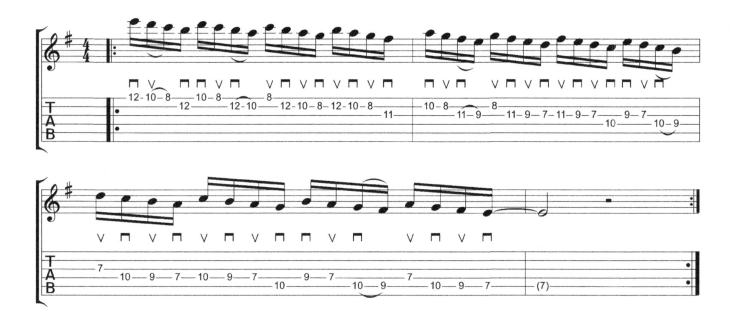

For the sake of uniformity, the previous example could also start with *up, down, up* to bring in line with the subsequent repeats of the sequence (see beat 4 of bar one). However, doing so won't always be an option depending on the licks leading into such a sequence, as Example 6g will reinforce.

Yngwie favours fretboard patterns that don't require finger rolling or awkward position shifts in sequencing. Don't we all? To thwart fingering inconveniences, Yngwie uses single-string descending fours to locate and descend in his preferred patterns. Example 6f uses one such inconvenient pattern, remedied in Example 6g with a more finger-friendly pattern using the same notes.

Example 6f:

Instead, let's use single-string position shifts to locate a familiar shape in Example 6g. The single-string descending fours in beats 1 and 2 of the first bar again dictate that the positional element of the sequence on beat 3 begins on a downstroke.

Example 6g:

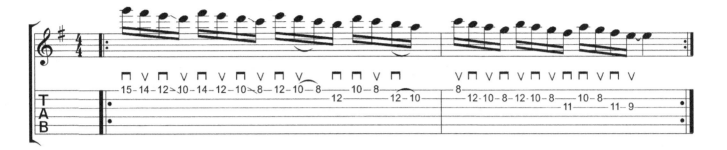

Ascending Sequences

Some of the most commonly used ascending sequences in Yngwie's playing are the 1-2-3-1 and 3-1-2-3 forms, both of which are permutations of the ascending fours or 1-2-3-4 sequence, as the next few drills highlight.

Example 6h uses the 1-2-3-1 sequence, meaning that each unit of four notes contains three ascending notes, followed by a return to the first note. The sequence then moves up to the second degree of the scale from which the 1-2-3-1 unit is reiterated and so on.

The lone note exception occurs in ascending sequences just like it does in descending examples, handled with an upstroke and preceded this time by a hammer-on. In this drill, the lone note first occurs on the third 1/16th note of beat 2, bar one.

Example 6h:

One of the best payoffs to learning the sequencing aspect of Yngwie's system is the continuity of picking that emerges when learning derivatives of an idea already studied. Examples 6i and 6j are cases in point. At first glance, the 3-1-2-3 layout of Example 6i might seem like a new sequence. It is, in fact, the result of dropping the first two 1/16th notes of Example 6h and starting what remains from the 1st beat of the bar. By removing those notes while leaving the pick strokes as they were, we can form a new musical idea from an existing mechanical template.

Example 6i:

Next, by removing the first *three* 1/16th notes of Example 6h and keeping the applicable pick strokes intact, an ascending fours sequence is revealed.

Example 6j:

While the beginning upstroke of the last example is consistent with its permutation of the previous examples, being able to start it on a downstroke on the fly in improvisation is also a worthwhile option to keep up your sleeve. In your practice, try alternating the first bar of Example 6j with this substitute measure.

Example 6k:

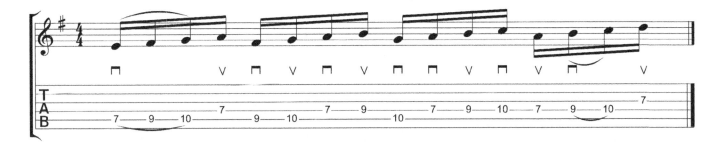

Combining single-string and positional ascending sequences is an excellent way to build an idea beyond the limits of either. Your goal for sequences like Example 6l is to create a seamless ascent as the single-string position-shifts on the third and first strings are brought together by the positional increments in bar two and the first half of bar three. This drill is again in the key of E minor but suits the tonality of C Lydian, built upon the VI degree of E minor or IV degree of G Major.

Example 6l:

Chapter Seven: Picking Decryption

These examples will test your perception of how lines should be executed using The Yng Way. At first, the examples are presented without pick strokes or slurring indicators. Peruse each phrase before reaching for your guitar to see if you can decode the picking solution that matches the principles in this book. Next, test your hypothesis and conclude, or reassess until satisfied.

Example 7a:

Example 7b:

Example 7c:

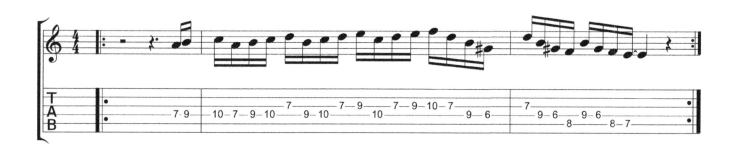

On the next page, the same examples have been decoded with Yngwie-compliant pick strokes and slurs, as well as the decryption keys used.

Solutions for Chapter Seven Examples

Below are the completed versions of Examples 7a, 7b and 7c. Each lick now has picking and slurs indicated, plus the decryption key that corresponds to the decision made with each string change.

Decryption keys:

    EC = Economy-picked string change (ascending strategy)

    PU = Pull-off after an even number of alternate picking strokes (descending strategy)

    LN = Upstroke preceded by a hammer-on or pull-off (lone note exception)

Example 7a Picking Solution:

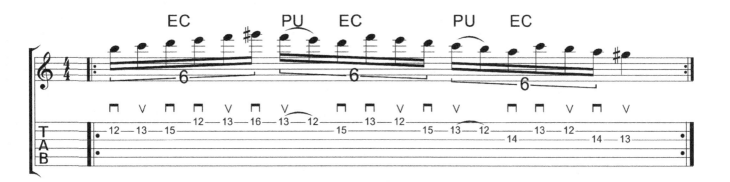

Example 7b Picking Solution:

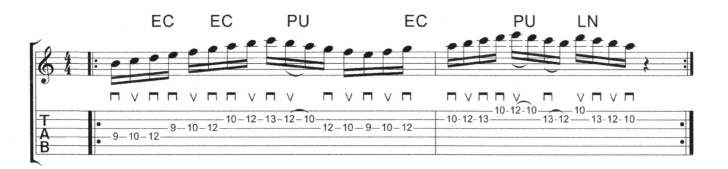

Example 7c Picking Solution:

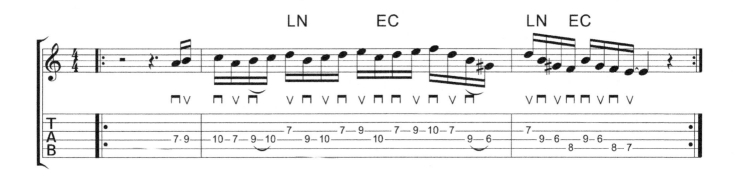

If your intuition served you correctly, you have done well! If not, study the differences between your conclusion and the answers presented. More deductive reasoning awaits you in the transcriptions of Yngwie's music online and in books, so be sure to spend some time on the written medium of his music, outside of studying this book.

Part Three is a collection of authentic-sounding lines in the Malmsteen style that will build upon the skillset you have created throughout Part Two.

Part Three: Advanced Studies

It's time to put all the methods, sounds and expertise you've acquired into more extended passages that would be right at home in an Yngwie-esque solo. While perfect for practice material just as a violinist hones his or her chops on Kreutzer or Paganini themes, it is primarily intended for you to use these phrases in actual music and improvisation.

Each study is discussed in terms relating to:

- *Musical attributes*

- *Pressure points that may require extra attention in practice*

- *Mechanical Sub-concepts that augment ideas covered in previous chapters*

I have grouped these studies according to musical key, but it's essential to your progress a musician that you transpose your favourite ideas to many keys.

Chapter Eight: Studies in E Minor

Study 1 (Example 8a)

The core element in this study is a three-and-a-bit-octave harmonic minor pattern, one of Yngwie's signature *One-Way* layouts. It is only ever used this way in descending. Each octave takes place on two strings, one string containing four notes and the other containing three, except for a position shift on the low E string to access three additional notes.

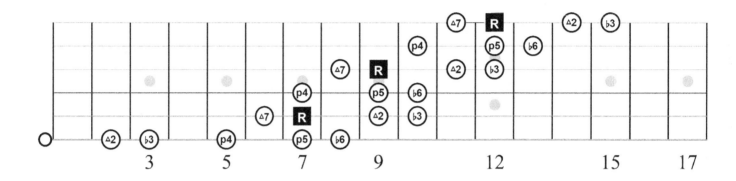

Playing this pattern high to low with alternate picking would result in each octave having opposite pick strokes to the next. The Yng Way enables a consistent approach to the pattern that is not thrown off-course by the interchange of even and odd numbers of notes per string.

In Example 8a, the scale is preceded by a melodic motif that also repeats in octaves, beginning on the third 1/8th note of bar one, beat 3 and ending on the first note of the descending scale in bar three. The index finger should initiate each four-note iteration of the ascending motif. In bars three and four, lead each descending stage with either the third or fourth finger as per your fingering preference. Yngwie uses this pattern over the tonic triad of a minor key.

Example 8a:

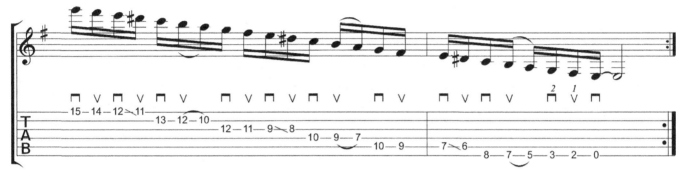

Study 2 (Example 8b)

Being able to re-contextualise your ideas is an important skill to have, and the next two studies provide examples of doing. Using the descending scale portion of the previous study as a fingering framework, Example 8b shifts its tonal emphasis to the B Phrygian dominant mode of E harmonic minor, resolving to a B note on the last 1/16th note of bar two. A short *tail* in bars three and four fills out the remaining bars and emphasises the Phrygian dominant characteristics of bII and III intervals.

The position-shifting ostinato in bar one can be used a drill on its own until you can pick it at the same speed as the rest of the pattern. The index finger takes care of the downward position shifts from frets 12 to 11 and, for most players, the fourth finger will feel the most comfortable handling the upward position changes from frets 14 to 15. Focus on your timing, particularly in taking care not to waver from evenly-picked 1/16th notes on the high E string.

Example 8b:

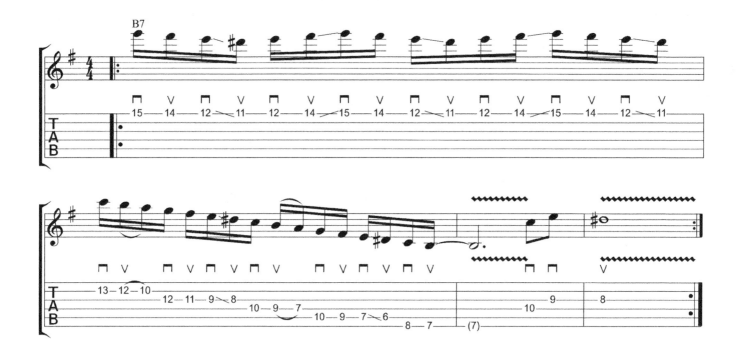

74

Study 3 (Example 8c)

Just as a long stretch of highway has multiple on-ramps and off-ramps, Yngwie's favourite scale shapes form a route that can be entered and exited at various points. Such usage allows both familiarity and variety, maximising the functionality of a pattern without being limited to it.

In this B Phrygian dominant study, a 1-3-2-1 sequence on the high E string steps down from the 17th fret, arriving at the original E minor *highway* in bar two where another two steps of 1-3-2-1 occur. The line travels straight down the B and G strings as usual before hanging on to the D# note that ends bar two.

After the sustaining the D# note into the beginning of bar three, a detour from the highway occurs in the form of another 1-3-2-1 sequence on the G string. The fourth bar sees a return to the familiar descending pattern, concluding on the B note on the 7th fret on the low E string.

Developing detours like these is an excellent way to know your fretboard better while also taking advantage of patterns that work well for you. This run is well-suited to a B7 chord or a B Phrygian Dominant riff like *Now Your Ships Are Burned*.

Example 8c:

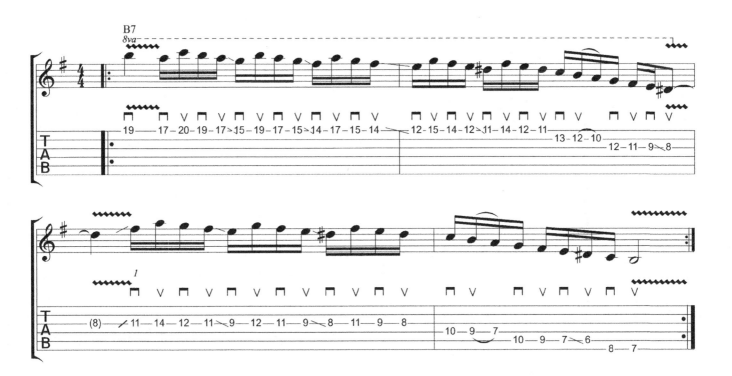

75

Study 4 (Example 8d)

Let's expand on the fretboard coverage with two new patterns. This study combines descending runs that are not only phrased identically in the example but are diatonic 3rds apart, meaning either can function as a harmony line for the other.

Punctuated by *imperfect cadences* (chord I to chord V) in E minor, both runs are based on 1/8th note triplets except for one beat of four 1/16th notes that begin each descent. The triplet rhythm also lends itself to a fast shuffle or 12/8 time signature. Using the faster-starting notes is a standard Yngwie expression tool used to create interest and get things started with a bang. Also characteristic in its delivery is the trait of using a single upstroke followed by legato on the four starter notes, a variation of the lone note exception.

While the fingering of the first descending pattern is yet another integration of four and three notes per string, its counterpart in the fourth bar has four notes on the B string and only two notes on the G string. The difference in layout is because Yngwie always sources the VII degree of the harmonic minor from the B string this in shape string rather than with the comparatively cumbersome reach for the same note on the G string. Besides being a more user-friendly fingering this way, The Yng Way is set up in such a way that you can play any number of notes per string without breaking the technical systems in place.

Example 8d:

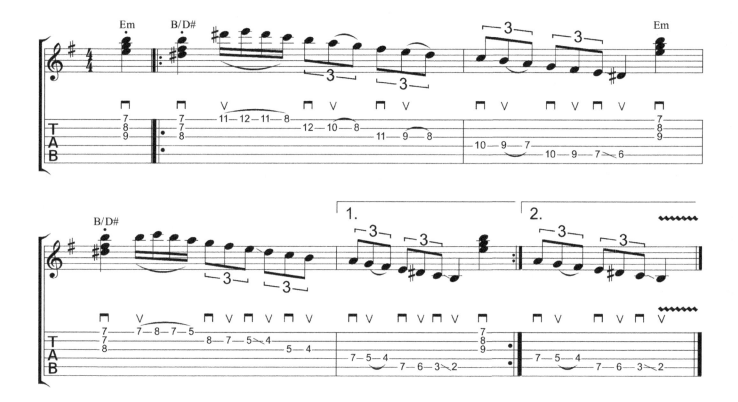

76

Study 5 (Example 8e)

The hybrid minor shape is one of the few patterns that Yngwie uses in both ascending and descending circumstances. The consecutive semitone intervals between the bVII, VII and I degrees create an attention-grabbing chromatic passing tone sound, particularly in sequencing as you travel back and forth through these three scale degrees.

In this study, bar one consists of a looping lick on the first two strings, comprised of three units of descending fours followed by four consecutive ascending notes bringing it back to the 19th fret of the high E string in bar two. Bars two, three and four consist entirely of descending fours from the high E string to the A string. For extra anticipation, bar one can be repeated as many times as you like before releasing the tension in the last bars.

You can use this pattern and sequence over the V or I chord in E minor. If choosing the latter, omit the last D# note at the end of bar four to create resolution over the E minor chord, or swap the order of the D# and the E notes on the fifth string.

Example 8e:

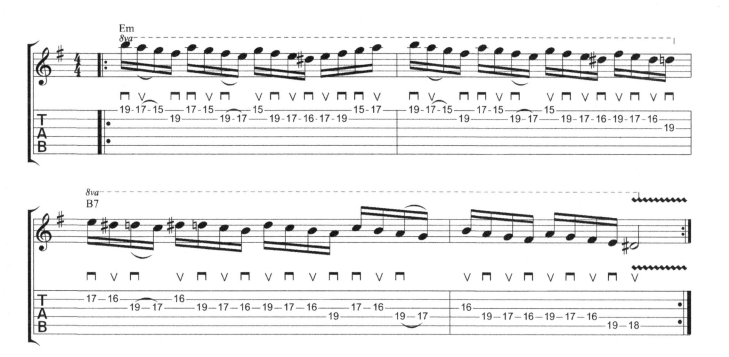

Chapter Nine: Studies in A Minor

Study 6 (Example 9a)

By transposing a couple of previously-featured patterns to the key A minor, this study begins with an ascent of the hybrid minor framework used in Example 8e. It ends with a descent of the harmonic minor pattern from Example 8a and uses a single-string natural minor sequence to connect the two. It is common for Yngwie's lines to combine the attributes of multiple minor scales in extended phrases like this example.

The ascending run in bar one uses the archetypal ascending picking strategy through beats 1, 2 and 3. On beat 4 of the first bar, a 3-1-2-3 sequence traverses positions eight to seventeen along the high E string using notes from the A natural minor scale. In bar three, Yngwie's much-used sixes ostinato takes places between the 17th and 20th frets and again between the 16th and 19th frets. Complying with the sequence numbering system in this book, I think of the sixes ostinato as 3-1-2-3-2-1.

The descending harmonic minor pattern used from the 4th beat of bar three to the end of bar four should feel very familiar by now, having used its E minor version in Studies 1, 2 and 3.

Example 9a:

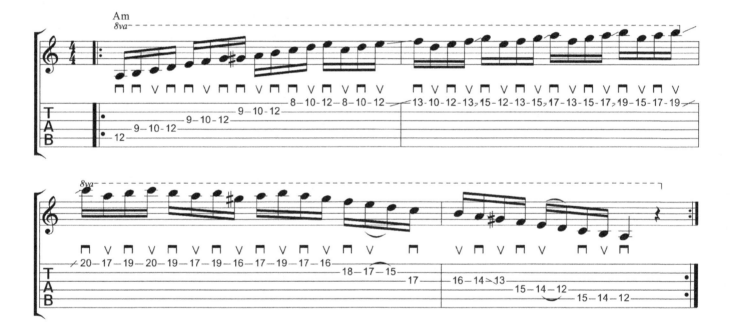

Study 7 (Example 9b)

This E Phrygian dominant study is a rapid-fire exercise in alternate picking, enabled by even numbers of notes per string that allow you to pick every note with ferocity. Yngwie has been known to shred this kind of run on both acoustic and electric to good effect. When played over backings that have a half-time feel, the run will create the effect of 1/32nd notes, which Yngwie uses for drama and contrast over slower backings.

The tremolo-picked high E note in the first half of bar one allows you to set the picking hand in motion before hitting the three-octave descending pattern that covers all strings and concludes on the open low E string. Like the three-octave harmonic minor map used in previous examples, this shape contains seven notes between each string pair. This time, however, it's three notes on the higher string and four notes on the lower. For consistency, start the E note in each octave with the same finger. For Yngwie, that means the second finger.

Example 9b:

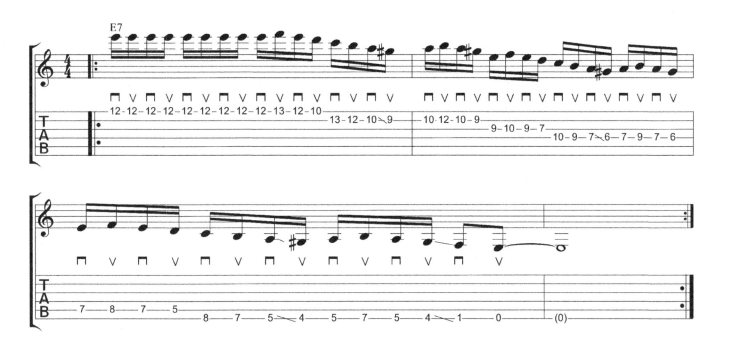

Study 8 (Example 9c)

Something to remember when picking within the system of this book is that string layout determines what pick strokes are used rather than the rhythmic location of notes within the bars or beats. Some examples might create a temporary sense of displacement as a result, but the benefits of mechanical consistency will soon replace it. This study is a case in point.

As a result of the nine pick-up notes in bar one, upstrokes are brought about on the first 1/8th note triplet of each subsequent bar, which might seem like an odd proposition at first. Taking into account the last of those pick-up notes (the 12th fret high E note at the end of bar one), what we have is the same picking sequence as Example 9b, reconfigured from 1/16th notes to 1/8th note triplets.

The task, therefore, is to get your brain aligned with the way the existing mechanics apply to different beat divisions and starting points. The only change for your fretting hand is the position shift from the last pick-up note to the first note of bar two.

Example 9c:

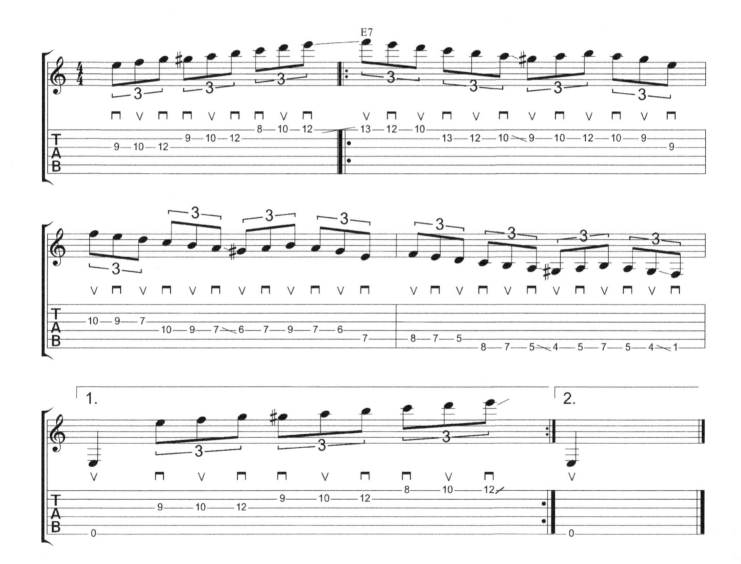

Study 9 (Example 9d)

After the descending even numbers in the last two examples, this alternate-picked study uses the sixes ostinato across all six strings. It begins with three occurrences of the ostinato on the high E string in bar one but replaces the initial F note with a G# on the first sextuplet of beats 2 and 3. For ease of fingering on this first-string portion, assign your third finger to the 13th fret of the E string and fourth finger to the 16th fret rather than using the fourth finger to jump back and forth three frets at a time.

Example 9d:

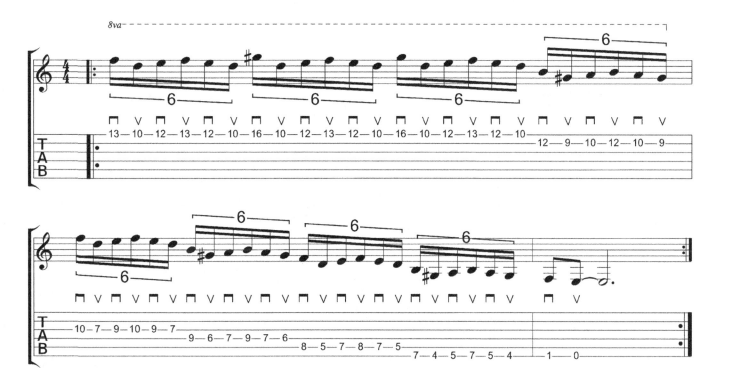

Study 10 (Example 9e)

This ascending study, which fits nicely into any three NPS layout, makes good use of what I call the *swoop and loop*. Consisting of six-note units in string pairs and phrased in 1/16th notes, the sequence in bars one and two contain three notes on the lower string of each pair, two notes on the higher string and one more note on the lower string before a new unit begins a string higher. The swoop and loop term refers to the string-changing pattern which entails an ascending sweep, an outside pick stroke, and another ascending sweep.

After the first two 1/16th notes of bar one, the picking sequence is a repetition of *down, down, up* until the end of bar two. Bar three features two units of ascending fours in beats 1 and 2, followed by two groups of descending fours in beats 3 and 4. Bar four contains a simple ascending phrase to pad out the line.

Given the six-note span of each repeating unit in this sequence, you should also experiment with playing these notes as 1/8th note triplets and 1/16th note triplets or sextuplets.

Example 9e:

Study 11 (Example 9f)

While not sequentially an *exact* reversal of the previous study, this example begins with a sequence in bars one and two that can serve as a great descending companion to the ascending line that starts Example 9e.

Articulated here in an A harmonic minor / E Phrygian dominant shape spanning frets 10 to 17, this sequence again extends over all six strings using a six-note melodic figure in string pairs. Each six notes are played *down, up, pull-off, down, down, up*. The position shift on the 3rd beat of bar two bypasses the sequence for just one 1/4 note value but beat 4 of the bar sees another occurrence of the six-note figure carrying over into the first two notes in bar three.

For the sake of variation, bars three and four complete the study with a series of 1/8th note triplets and straightforward melodic content from the low E string back up to the G string. You can reconfigure the 1/16th notes of bars one and two to triplet groupings for variation, so experiment!

Example 9f:

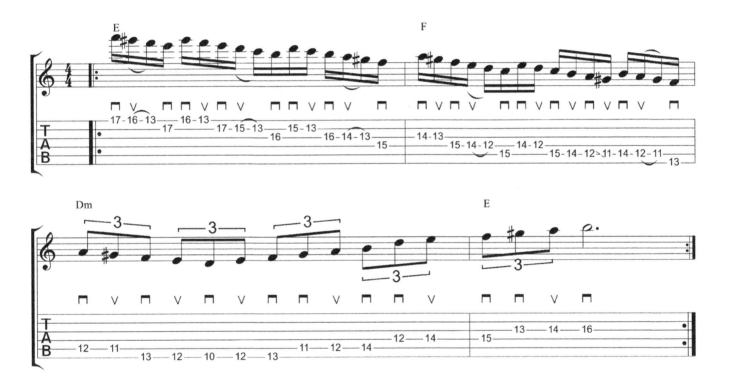

83

Study 12 (Example 9g)

The ascending portion of this A minor study is all about the application of a sideways position-shifting device I call the *Fives Turnaround*. Yngwie connects various three NPS patterns with this device by dropping a note from an otherwise six-note pattern each time he switches positions. It sets up the picking motion so that the position-shift can take place after an upstroke and begin the next position on a downstroke.

Bar one of this example starts in the A natural minor scale, fifth position. After the upstroke that occurs on the first 1/16th note of beat 2, shift your fretting hand back to the 7th fret of the low E string with the index finger. Doing so is the standard move in the fives turnaround.

You can continue to ascend three notes per string and apply the turnaround strategy each time you wish to switch positions on the same string pair. In this study, two more position shifts are set up with groups of five on the D and G strings, and B and E strings as indicated. A descending fours sequence completes the study in bars three and four.

Example 9g:

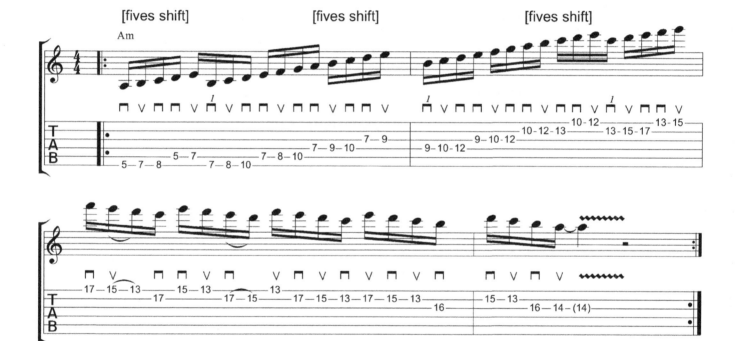

Study 13 (Example 9h)

A downward position-shifting habit of Yngwie's is what I call *Lateral Tens*. He will play ten notes up and down a pair of strings (usually the high E and B strings), but instead of returning to the starting note, a new set of ten begins one diatonic position lower. The Lateral Tens can occur in a standalone lick, or in the case of this study, appear after an ascending lead-up.

Ignoring the note groupings for a moment, take a look at the B string and high E string portions of the first bar in Example 9h. Here is an isolated lateral ten unit that can be practised as a loop to get accustomed to the combination of the ascending sweep, hammer-ons and pull-offs, and two alternate-picked notes back on the B string that is sequenced in units.

After spending some time looping the first lateral ten, proceed to the remaining tens. The second group begins on beat 1 of bar two. The third group begins mid-way through bar two on the 12th fret of the second string, and the last set starts at the beginning of bar three.

Next, it is time to consider the use of tuplets in phrasing. Many of Yngwie's lines contain what may feel like *extra notes* when your experience has thus far been the use of conventional divisions of beats like 1/8th notes, 1/16th notes and triplets thereof. In phrasing examples like *this* study, the focus is not necessarily upon how many notes to squeeze into a beat, but on starting ideas at particular target points within the bars.

The aim here, therefore, is to have a series of motifs that begin on beats 1 and 3 of each bar and apply the necessary acceleration to arrive at the next idea on the target beat. So, the nine ascending 1/16th notes at the beginning of the first bar fit in the space of beats 1 and 2, the first lateral ten (with a couple of extra-rushed legato notes) will be played in beats 3 and 4, and so on.

From beat 3 of the third bar, the phrasing eases into regular 1/16th notes as the line descends and shifts positions towards the A note on the 5th fret of the low E string in bar four. It can take a little time to get used to the *push and pull* of this study, but if care is taken to start each idea on its target beat, you can become accustomed to it. Play each portion at whatever rate of acceleration is required to get to the next on time.

Example 9h:

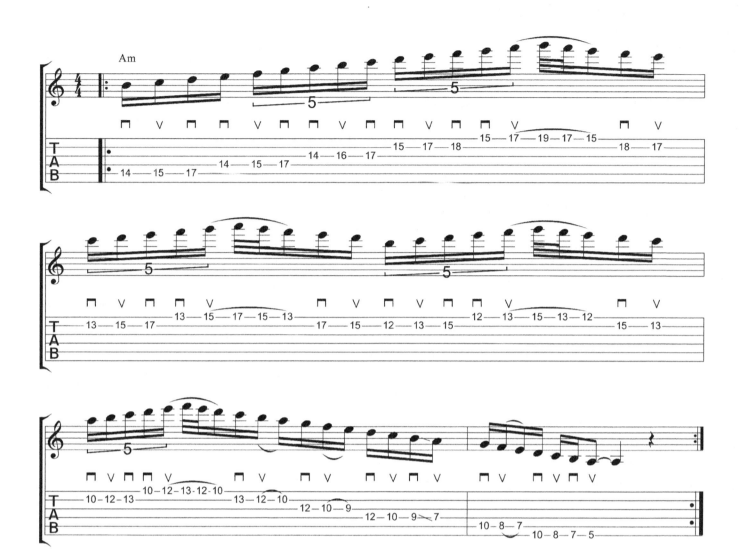

Chapter Ten: Studies in B Minor

Study 14 (Example 10a)

Ascending fours should feel like quite a fixture in your picking repertoire by now, which will be put to use in the B hybrid minor pattern in bars one, two and the first three beats of bar three. It leads to the discussion point of this study.

The pedal-point lick that extends from the 4th beat of bar three to the end of bar four is a point of focus in this example. Single pick strokes go back and forth between the high E string and B string without the pre-emptive hammer-on or pull-off that you have seen in descending and ascending fours sequences. As the 15th fret, high E string pedal-tone stays put, and the alternating notes travel down the B harmonic minor scale, consecutive outside-picked strokes are required when the lower notes move down to the B string in bar four.

Yngwie's picking motion for multi-string pedal-point always subtly incorporates the crosspicking approach discussed in connection with the lone note strategy, or the more mechanically-accurate description: wrist extension and flexion. Crosspicking was covered in Chapter Six, but for instances that require you to pick each note (like this example), there is only half the time to move the pick to either side of the string pair without any preparatory slur notes.

To build your crosspicking chops, take the four notes that occur in beat 2 of the fourth bar, and create a repeating drill from them. When later combined with the rest of Example 10a, your goal is to be able to pick the pedal-point element without any hindrance to the flow or tempo you establish in the first three measures.

Example 10a

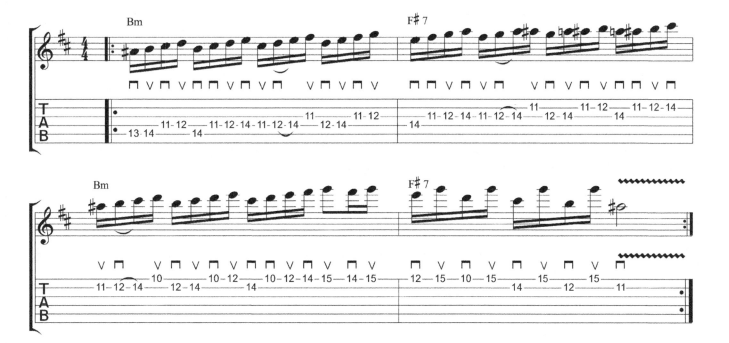

Study 15 (Example 10b)

Similar to the way the *Fives Turnaround* was used to switch positions after an even number (in an otherwise odd number of notes per string), the *Sevens Slide* adds a note to a group of six ascending notes via a slide at the end of the higher string in a pair.

In this study, an ascending B natural minor pattern in bar one has an extension slide on the high E string from the 12th fret to the 14th fret going to beat 4. This 14th fret F# note, while being a part of the Sevens Slide that began on beat 3, is also now the highest note in a new set of six beginning on the B string, 10th fret. Going into bar two of the example, the slide to the 15th fret of the E string is another occurrence of the Sevens Slide, so each time a slide occurs, the slid note becomes the sixth of a new group as the positions travel up the string pair.

Regarding notation, I have again interpreted Yngwie's tendency to rush the last four notes of bar one to allow the new position to begin in bar two. This rushing occurs in each instance of the Sevens Slide so that it need not take more time to play seven ascending notes than six would have. You can also experiment with playing each note with the same duration as the next, keeping in mind that as a result, you push back the sequence one 1/16th note for each occurrence of the Sevens Slide.

Example 10b:

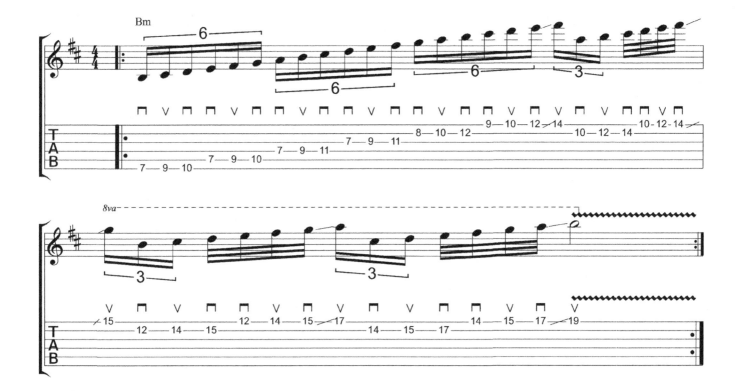

Study 16 (Example 10c)

The Sevens Slide can occur on other string pairs too, despite Yngwie's favouring of the B and high E strings. This natural minor scale example wanders up the A and D strings, beginning on the highest note in a six-string pattern, with slides occurring on the D string until the index finger arrives at the 7th fret of the A string. The B minor pattern from Example 10b is used to go from the fifth string to the first string, with a small legato burst occurring on the 2nd beat of bar two before returning to the B string to end the lick.

With all of the examples involving rushed-sounding timing, keep in mind that these speed bursts needn't be as stiff and precise as notated. One of the things that make Yngwie stand out as a creative and intuitive player is his knack for sounding a little loose even while executing some highly technical mechanics. Time feel is just as crucial in rock as it is in jazz, so find your groove as you develop this material.

Example 10c

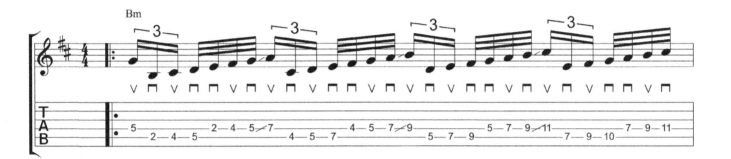

Study 17 (Example 10d)

The Switchblade is a name I gave to a descending position shift that I first noticed on Yngwie's *Live In Leningrad* concert on the track *Crystal Ball* back in 1989. The reason for the name was because of how quickly the high E string notes popped out from what would otherwise be a single-string descending fours sequence on the B string. This pattern occurs in bars one and two of Example 10d.

Relocating the first of each four-note group to a higher string has an intervallic appeal, but it also requires an upstroke on the higher string, and *down, up, down* on the lower string of a pair - a reversal of what would occur in descending fours on one string only. Crosspicking facilitates the transitions from the B string back to the high E string.

I have witnessed Yngwie playing this kind of pattern with a couple of different approaches over the years, but the one notated is the most technically consistent with his picking style. In situations where a more legato sound is desired, the upstroke on the E string and downstroke on the B string can be picked, and a pull-off and legato slide can initiate the remaining two notes of each four.

Example 10d

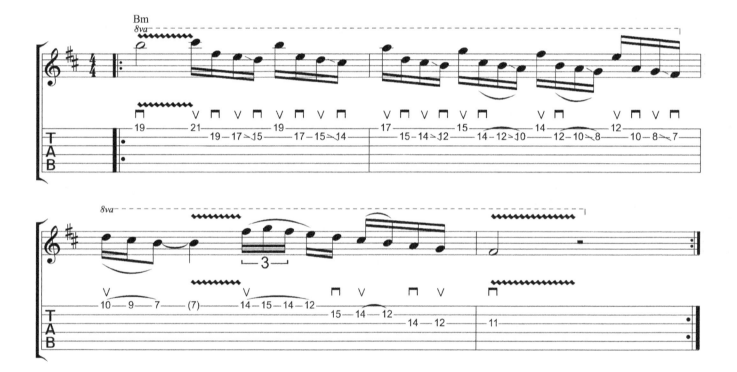

Study 18 (Example 10e)

For the last study piece, let's take Yngwie's version of crosspicking to its extreme with a lick that sandwiches it between two economy picking ideas using B harmonic minor. How Yngwie approaches sequences when his go-to system doesn't appear to fit, is one of the most common things I get asked. Riffs like *I Am A Viking* and *Anguish and Fear* raise questions because they challenge what we think we can or cannot do within the Yngwie system.

Two-string pedal-point licks have already shown us that playing the higher string on an upstroke and the lower string on a downstroke is the most *Yngwie* thing to do in the situation, so with the *thirds* descending sequence portion of Example 10e, it is a matter of applying that solution on a larger scale.

Cast your eyes to the third 1/16th note of beat 2, bar one. Here, the A# note on the 18th fret of the E string leads to the F# on the 19th fret of the B string using *up, down* pick strokes as per the pedal-point approach. The same applies to the next two notes. The rest of the descending sequence intersperses odds and evens as four notes per string are played *down, up, down, up*, and single notes occur with outside, alternating pick strokes. Doing so is, of course, alternate picking, but by leading with upstrokes, inside picking pathways are avoided and therefore as consistent with The Yng Way as possible. Spend some time on this portion of the study before adding the musical bookends on either side.

Leading into the thirds sequences is an ascending B minor (major VII) arpeggio on beat 1 of the first bar, executed with a sweep and one upstroke. The B and G notes that begin Beat 2 are, melodically speaking, the beginning of the thirds sequences downward, but are executed with a downstroke and a pull-off to set up the lone note upstroke on the 18th fret of the E string.

In bar two, a textbook economy-picked B harmonic minor pattern begins on the second 1/16th note of the 4th beat, which continues through bar three. At this point, you should raise one fist in the air and scream *I have mastered The Yng Way!*

Example 10e:

Conclusion

In my studies on this fantastic instrument, it has always been the concepts, motivations and systems behind things that have kept me picking up the guitar every day; to find the idea behind the ideas. So too, through your studies of this book and into the future, I hope that you enjoy the processes of understanding, working at, and applying its material to both Yngwie's music and your own.

From these pages, you have worked through a complex combination of strategies, which speaks to not only the genius of Yngwie Malmsteen's unique approach to the guitar but to your quest for knowledge and mastery. So, congratulations on getting this far!

This book is the kind that I expect that you'll need to re-read, backtrack and cross-reference multiple times, so I encourage you to do so, and not feel overly pressured to absorb everything on the first read through. I also urge you to use this book as a companion piece to Yngwie songs and solos you study or transcribe. Keep it close by and consult it anytime your intuition doesn't immediately provide a solution.

Some critics accuse Yngwie of being a repetitive player. I've always said that, rather than have a hundred tricks in his bag, Yngwie is a player who knows how to use five skills in twenty different ways each. As the concepts in this book manifest in your studies of the Malmsteen catalogue, they will become re-enforced through the very repetition that detractors would use to discredit his style.

In practice, divide your routine into portions just as the chapters in the book have. You won't likely have time to work on every lick every day but try to address your target areas of improvement with a selection of examples that focus on the relevant skill.

Play with gusto, and be relentless in your pursuits. That is The Yng Way!

Chris

Glossary of Terms

Active principle	A fundamental aspect of how motion will be carried out
Alternate picking	Picking that uses consistently opposing pick strokes, down and up
Anchoring	Placing of the picking hand on the guitar bridge
Anguish and Fear	Track 7 from the Yngwie Malmsteen album *Marching Out*
Anti-clockwise offset	Turning the pick anti-clockwise from the neutral position
Arpeggio	The notes of a chord, sounded individually either in rhythm or melody
Ascending fours	A scale sequence that moves upward in steps using four consecutive scale notes each time, e.g., A B C D, B C D E, C D E F etc
Auxiliary mechanics	Motions that occur because of or as a supplement to the primary function
Biomechanics	The laws relating to the study of movement and structure
Caprices, 24	A collection of compositions by Romantic-era violinist Niccolo Paganini
Clockwise offset	Turning the pick clockwise from the neutral position
Crosspicking	An alternate picking style that uses wrist flexion and extension to reposition the pick from string to string
Crotchet	A quarter note with a value of one beat in a 4/4 bar
Demisemi quaver	A thirty-second note with a value of an eighth of a beat in a 4/4 bar
Descending fours	A scale sequence that moves downwards in steps using four consecutive scale notes each time, e.g., A G F E, G F E D, F E D C etc
D-grip	Holding the pick in the shape of an uppercase D letter with the thumb and finger
Diatonic	Belonging to or derived from a key
Diminished 7th	An arpeggio consisting of degrees I, bIII, bV, bbVII
Downward pick slant	Tilting the back end of the pick downward so that downstrokes push in towards the guitar body
DPO	Downward picking orientation
Economy picking	Directional motion that results in a string starting with a continuation of the pick stroke that completed the previous string
Fireball	An album by the band Deep Purple
Fives Turnaround	A two-string pattern consisting of three notes on a string and two notes on a higher string, used to launch the fretting hand into another position
Forearm rotation	Picking hand motion that originates the from inwards and outwards movement of the forearm muscles rather than the wrist or elbow joints
Harmonic Minor Scale	A scale consisting of degrees I, II, bIII, IV, V, bVI, VII or natural minor with a major VII degree
Horizontal axis	In line with the guitar strings
Hybrid Minor Scale	A synthetic minor scale that includes both the bVII and VII degrees consecutively
Hybrid picking	Using the plectrum and picking hand fingers to pick notes
I am A Viking	Track 5 from the Yngwie Malmsteen album *Marching Out*
Imperfect Cadence	Harmonic tension created by concluding a passage with a I chord moving to a V chord in a major or minor key

Inside picking	A path along which the pick travels directly between the strings with the shortest distance
Lateral Tens	Ten-note melodic units moved sideways on a pair of strings
Legato	Tied together, smooth, consisting of hammer-ons and pull-offs
Lone note exception	The way of handling a single note on a string when other strategies do not apply
Natural Minor Scale	A scale consisting of degrees I, II, bIII, IV, V, bVI, bVII
Newtonian	Relating to the discoveries of Isaac Newton
Now Your Ships Are Burned	Track 3 from the Yngwie Malmsteen album *Rising Force*
NPS	An abbreviation of Notes Per String
Ostinato	A continually repeated phrase or rhythm
Outside picking	A path along which the pick travels the longest distance around the strings
Palm-muting	Using the picking hand to dull or silence the sound of strings
Parallel picking	Downstrokes and upstrokes that move parallel to the guitar body
Pedal-point	A melodic device in which a note is repeated while other notes alternately proceed without reference to it
Perfect Cadence	Harmonic resolution created by a V chord moving to a I chord in a major or minor key
Phrygian Dominant	A mode created from the notes of harmonic minor, arranged from the V degree and used over the V chord
Pick grip	Relating to how the hand and fingers position the guitar pick for playing
Pick orientation	The ongoing tendency to favour one kind of pick slant over the other
Pick edge offset	The state of having one edge of the pick positioned to contact the string first
Pick-gato	A portmanteau meaning to combine picking and slurs in a single phrase
Picking pathway	The route created by the motion of the pick
Pick slant	Leaning the pick forward or backwards along the vertical axis instead of at a 90-degree angle to the guitar body
Positional scale	A scale pattern that does not require sliding to more than one position
Pronation	Inward rotation of the forearm so that the surface of the hand faces downward
1/8th note	An eighth note with a value of half a beat in a 4/4 bar
Relative minor scale	The natural minor scale when referred to its formation from the VI degree of a major scale
Rest stroke	When the pick comes to a stop on a string before executing the next note
Rested principle	A fundamental aspect of preparing for motion in an optimum way
Semiquaver	A sixteenth note with a value of a quarter of a beat in a 4/4 bar
Sevens Slide	A two-string pattern consisting of three notes on one string and four notes on a higher string that includes a position shift
Slurs, slurring	Hammer-ons, pull-offs and legato-slides
Supination, active	Rotation of the forearm so that the surface of the hand faces outward
Supination, rested	A resting point already biased in favour of supination before motion has occurred

Supination bias	Downward picking orientation
Tapping	A two-handed technique using hammer-ons and pull-offs from fingers of the picking hand on the fretboard
Tonal Sequence	A melodic device in which a motif is repeated in a higher or lower pitch and subsequent repetitions are diatonic transpositions of the original idea
Tremolo picking	Picking the same note repeatedly at high speed
Triplet	Three notes played in the space that two of the same would typically occupy, e.g., a 1/8th note triplet played within the duration of two 1/8th notes
UPO	Upward picking orientation
Upward pick slant	Tilting the back end of the pick upward so that downstrokes move away from the guitar body
Vertical axis	Perpendicular to the guitar strings; parallel to the guitar body
Wrist deviation, radial	Sideways movement at the wrist joint towards the radius
Wrist deviation, ulnar	Sideways movement at the wrist joint towards the ulna
Wrist extension	Bending the wrist outwards from the neutral position
Wrist flexion	Bending at the wrist joint inwards from the neutral position
Yng Way, the	The state of playing within the principles contained in Yngwie's style

SPEEDSTRATEGIES
FORGUITAR

Essential Guitar Techniques, Arpeggios and Licks for Total Fretboard Mastery

CHRIS**BROOKS**

FUNDAMENTAL**CHANGES**

Introduction

While there are a few books that do a decent job of teaching sweep picking on guitar, in my 25 years of teaching I've come across hundreds of students who understand the concept but still fail to get the sound they want.

While the concept of brushing the pick through *arpeggios* or *broken chords* with single downstrokes or upstrokes seems straightforward enough, it's only one piece of the puzzle. It's time for a method that develops an all-encompassing approach to creating efficient arpeggio lines and incorporates all the necessary bio-mechanics and nuance of pick control.

As a teacher, I'm constantly asked the following:

How do I make it sound good?

How do I control the noise?

Why does one direction feel easier than the other?

What should I do when there's more than one note on a string?

How do I change direction?

How do I get beyond triads?

Why don't I sound as good as Jason Becker, Frank Gambale or Vinnie Moore?

Questions like these warrant a more comprehensive approach than a book of drills, so rather than cutting straight to the licks, this book will get you thinking about the quantum of factors affecting your results, and how to make them all work for you. From rudiments to extensive fretboard coverage, this book outlines a whole system you can use to become an incredible sweep picker.

Beyond laying out the essential principles of sweeping technique and the tools for developing it, this method presents you with options, explain the outcomes of the choices you make along the way, and encourage you to systemise your strengths into a personalised approach.

To get the most out of this book, invest some reading time with and without your guitar in hand. You'll find that without the temptation to plug in and jump straight to the licks, you will absorb more information. When it's time to practise, be diligent with correctly repeating the examples before speed is applied. When the best methods become habit, challenge yourself by pushing things to the edge of your ability, assessing the results and attending to any issues that appear.

Most of the chapters conclude with practice or goals to accomplish before moving ahead. Practice methods will vary significantly from player to player, but these summaries will tell you what to expect in each of the stages of learning, and how to approach your workout sessions for the best results.

There is a lot of information on offer – so much so that the writing of my second book on this topic is already underway. Be patient with yourself as you develop the skills covered in this volume, because this material lays the foundation for what comes next.

Thanks for once again entrusting me to be your guide, and enjoy the process of building speed strategies for arpeggios.

Chris Brooks

Chapter One: Rudiments of Flow

Regardless of your musical style or experience, there are elements that all players can incorporate into sweep picking to increase efficiency, flow, tone and timing. As readers of my previous book, *Neoclassical Speed Strategies for Guitar* will note, there are commonalities between the biomechanics of that system and the ones required for good sweep picking.

I break the development of sweep picking into six rudiments:

1. Pick edge offset

2. Rest strokes

3. Directional pick slants

4. Turning mechanics

5. Fretting hand timing

6. String control

You may already have some of these in place, but let's progress through each in the suggested order.

Pick Edge Offset

Creating a flowing sweep starts from the moment the pick approaches the string. Angling the pick horizontally (or Pick edge offsetting) allows either the outer or inner edge of the pick to lead the contact with the string, avoiding friction that might be created by using its full flat face. (*on-axis*).

Pick edge offsets are *off*-axis positions created by both your wrist placement and pick grip. While there is no right or wrong way to angle the pick off axis to the string, some approaches are more common than others.

If your pick grip uses the pad of the thumb and the side of the index finger, *outer edge offset* (Figure 1a) might feel like the most natural offset for you. This means that the edge of the pick that faces away from the hand is what contacts the strings first on downstrokes.

Notable sweep pickers with this grip and offset include Vinnie Moore, Paul Gilbert, Michael Romeo, Yngwie Malmsteen, Jason Becker and Frank Gambale. Among these players, you might see varying degrees of bending in the joints of the thumb and index finger, so do your homework on your favourite pickers. Examine and emulate!

If your pick is held with more pad of the index finger than the previous description, *inner edge offset* (Figure 1b) is the most likely to occur, with the inside edge of the pick contacting first a downstroke. You might also see some concave bending of the thumb.

Right-handed players can also consider outer and inner edge-leading to be *clockwise* and *anti-clockwise* offsets respectively, with the opposite being true for left-handed players.

Some players have an unusual mix and match of approaches (Marty Friedman and John Norum, for example), so don't feel pressured to fit into one category or the other. The point of order is to examine the amount of friction your pick creates against the string and incorporate a degree of pick edge offset to minimise it.

Figure 1a: Clockwise edge offset   **Figure 1b: Anti-clockwise edge offset**

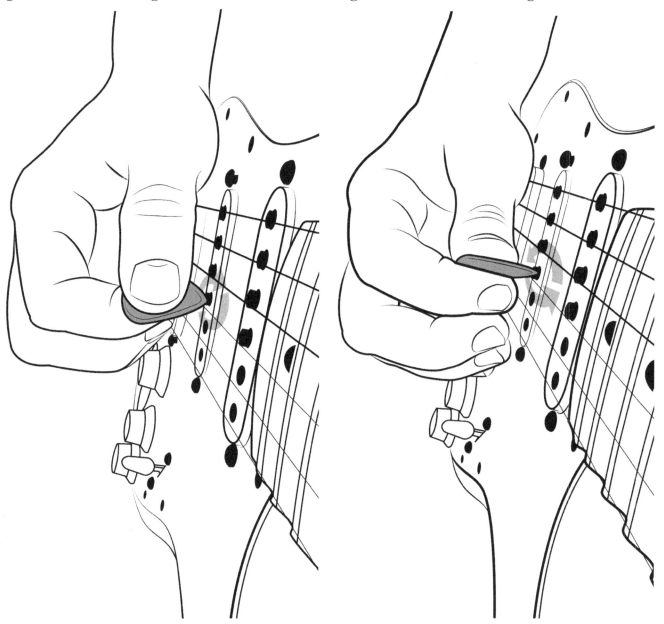

Rest Strokes

As you know, sweep picking is the technique of playing multiple notes with the same pick stroke. However, incorporating the *rest stroke* is the difference between a real sweep and a series of successive free strokes.

The rest stroke or *Apoyando* was popularised as a fingerstyle technique in the nineteenth-century and used for scale and melody work. When applying Apoyando, the guitarist plucks upward with the fingers or downward with the thumb so that each stroke simultaneously lands and rests on the adjacent string. You have probably noticed that bass players do the same thing to this day. The angled picking pathway created by this technique is arguably the precursor to today's modern pick slant.

When using a pick, the rest stroke involves following each pick stroke through to the next string, sounding the following note when leaving a new string rather than when arriving at it.

During a downward sweep, upstrokes between notes are therefore eliminated, as a single downstroke steps down to each new string. In an upward sweep the reverse occurs. Combined with directional pick slants and pick edge offsets, rest strokes enable economical, smooth and dynamically-consistent sweep picking.

Directional Pick Slants

In the Apoyando rest stroke technique, slanted lines of picking motion are formed by the tips of the fingers or thumb (Figure 1c) as they snap from the original string to the *rest string*. In both cases, the picking pathways are angled *into* the guitar body rather than parallel to it. These pathways are called *pick slants*, with the angle of the thumb creating a *downward pick slant* and the angle of the fingers creating an *upward pick slant*.

Figure 1c: the thumb plucks the low E string and pushes into the A string; the index finger plucks the B string and pushes into the G string.

With a guitar pick, a pick slant is easily established using rotation of the forearm muscles, resulting in the picking hand turning outward or inward (Figure 1d).

A downward slant is the result of outward rotation (supination) from the perpendicular or neutral position.

An upward slant is the result of inward rotation (pronation) from the neutral position. Both slants push towards the guitar body on their way to the rest string.

Neoclassical Speed Strategies covers pick slant and picking orientation in great detail, but for the purpose of sweep picking arpeggios, the concept of slanting can be condensed into two applications:

• Downward sweeping is done with a downward pick slant.

• Upward sweeping is done with an upward pick slant.

Slants work with rest strokes to create smooth contact with new strings and make directional changes possible without getting the pick trapped on the wrong side of a string.

Figure 1d: downward and upward pick slants

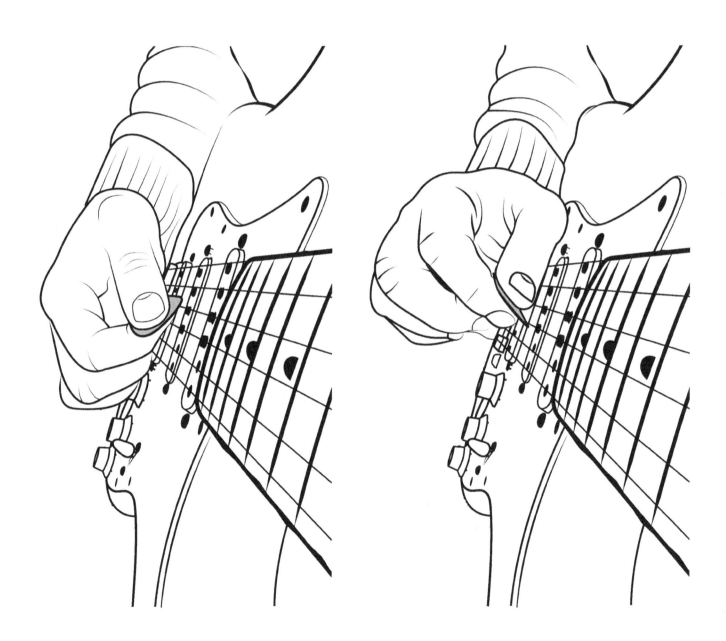

Understanding the Pick Slant Indicators in This Book

I've devised two markers to show pick slant directions for examples in this book:

\ **p.s.** for downward pick slant

/ **p.s.** for upward pick slant

When you can associate either sweeping direction with the applicable pick slant, you will no longer require the indicators.

It's important to keep in mind that the locations of pick slant indicators are approximate. The re-orienting of the pick occurs smoothly just before the point it's notated. Avoid any robotic, jolting switches.

When reaching moderate and high speeds with Example 1a, you'll most likely feel yourself anticipating each new pick slant as you leave the previous note, so that the fully formed upward pick slant on beats 2 and 4 can be initiated coming out of the last 1/8th notes of beats 1 and 3. You can develop your own style for this, so long as your pick avoids getting trapped between strings when changing picking direction.

Example 1a:

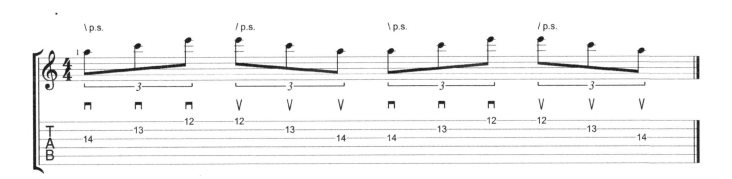

To develop your pick slant and rest stroke technique, start with Example 1b which uses muted strings on the fretting hand to allow complete focus on the picking hand. Ensure that there are no free strokes between strings, meaning that each pick stroke should land on a new string the moment it leaves the previous one (excluding the final string in either direction, of course). The 1/8th rests allow time to change the pick slant in anticipation of the next sweep.

Example 1b:

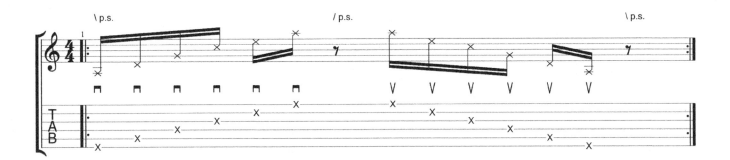

Turning Mechanics

Turning mechanics are the strategies that come into effect when an idea changes direction, repeats, skips strings, or any other factor that interrupts the directional flow of a sweep picking form.

The most common of these are the *outside turn* and the *inside turn*, which refer to picking around the strings in question (*outside picking*) or between them (*inside picking*). Despite the notion that sweep picking is about *always* choosing the shortest distance between two points, there are situations in which the effects of picking orientation produce some logical options worth considering.

Two terms I've created to help you relate turning mechanics to pick slants are *Upscaping* and *Downscaping*. Both refer to how we 'escape' the strings when changing direction.

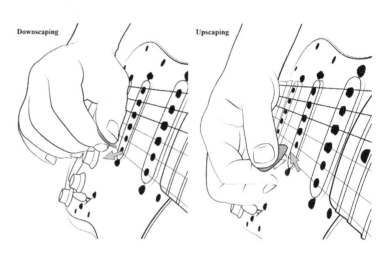

Upscaping is escaping the strings with an upstroke in a downward pick slant. You'll be using that a lot in Chapter Two for repeating ascending sweeps.

Downscaping is the opposite: using a downstroke in an upward pick slant to escape the strings. You'll be using that in descending and bidirectional sweeps.

Fretting Hand Timing

Given that arpeggios are used to create melody in this book it's essential to develop clean, separated notes that neither overlap nor sound too choppy (staccato) when sweep picking. Fretting hand timing plays a role in this endeavour.

The two elements to be considered are synchronisation and duration. It's a common pitfall of the keen entry-level sweep picker to articulate the notes at the beginning and end of a broad arpeggio yet have a bunch of unarticulated mush in the middle! Hey, we've all been that kid in the music store on a Saturday!

Synchronisation must be a key goal, making sure that each pick stroke has a matching fretted note. Considering that the rest stroke technique sees the pick landing on each new string as soon as it leaves the previous string, the aim is not necessarily to have a fretted note ready on the rest string at that precise nanosecond, but by the moment the pick *leaves* the string. Remember that each note is articulated by the exit, not the entry to each step of the sweep.

If synchronisation is about *when* to arrive at a note, then duration is about *how long* to stay. Notes that overlap will sound chordal and perhaps unpleasant to the ear when play with distortion. In the opposite spectrum, notes changed too hastily may lose their fluid effect and seem disjointed. Unless otherwise intended as a musical choice, aim for arpeggios that sound smooth and pleasing to the ear.

String Control

The final rudiment of good sweep picking is string control which is achieved through a trio of *palm muting*, *palm rolling* and *fretting hand muting*. Mastering this three-pronged approach will help you create the desired articulation for the notes you play, and prevent unwelcome noise and sympathetic vibration from the other strings.

Existing in real performance, but difficult to represent in tablature alone, string control takes place in Example 1c across all strings, even for a small triad like this. On the low E and A strings (and any other bass strings if you play an extended-range guitar), picking hand palm muting is used to silence the strings placed geographically above the picking region.

Adjacent strings tend to elicit the most noise when sweep-picking arpeggios, so when fretting the C note on the 10th fret of the D string, use the pad of your second finger to contact and mute the G string below (Figure 1e). Do not apply pressure on that string in a barre form since you do not wish to sound a double-stop.

When you pick the 9th fret and 12th fret notes on the G string, the pads of the index and fourth fingers will mute the B string (and high E string if necessary). Depending on the size of your index finger, the very tip of the index finger may serve as a muting device for the D string at this point as well. Because of the cyclical nature of this lick, you may prefer to leave your index finger in place throughout the repeats.

Example 1c:

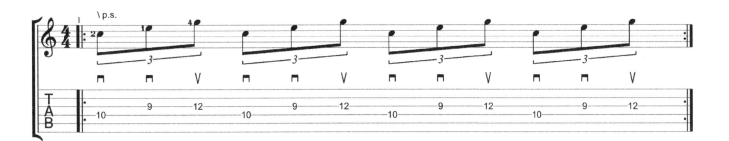

Figure 1e: the second finger frets the 4th string while muting the 3rd string.

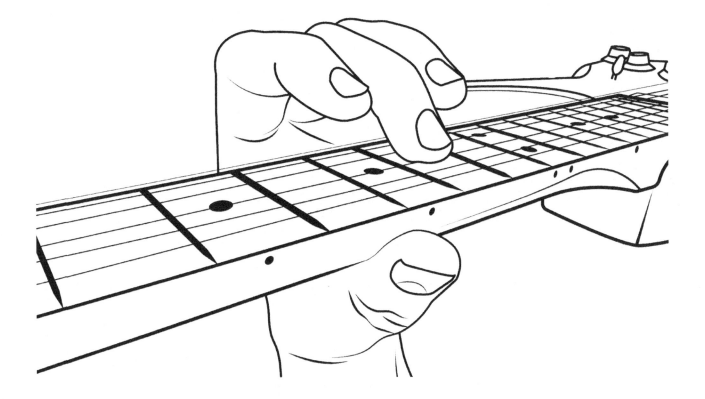

Applying the Picking Hand Palm Roll

Sweep picking across many strings requires great co-operation between picking hand and fretting hand muting. Expanding Example 1c by repeating the same fingering and picking form through three octaves, Example 1d requires the hands to work in opposites when muting.

In the lowest octave, apply no palm muting. Instead, use the underside of your fretting index finger to gently mute the higher strings (known as *across the board* muting). In the middle octave, a palm mute should fall into place on the A and E strings as the pick makes its way to the D string. In the highest octave, roll the palm muting to silence everything but the B and high E strings.

Practise this example with and without overdrive and listen out for any noise that needs to be addressed.

Example 1d:

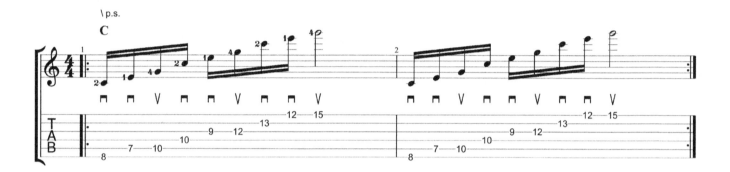

Palm rolling can also be used to add dynamic variation. In Example 1e, the G Major triad is articulated with alternating palm-muted and open sounds by rolling the mute on and away from the D and G strings. Listen to the audio to hear the contrast between open and muted picking.

Example 1e:

As with anything musical, the arbiter of success is in what you hear. As you build your sweep picking chops progressively through the chapters that follow, keep a critical ear on the sound of your arpeggios, and revise the fundamentals in this section whenever something does not sound clean and articulate.

Chapter Two: Ascending Strategy

In this chapter we will focus on the development and application of four components:

• Downward (ascending) sweep picking technique

• Downward rest stroke

• Downward pick slant

• Outside turning mechanic and upscaping

Using an A Minor triad (1, b3, 5), the ascending drills progress from two-string to six-string sweeps in an expanding shape that will cover more than two octaves by the end of the chapter. Students of the CAGED system might recognise this pattern as a hybrid of the D and C shapes of CAGED (covered in Chapter Eight).

Shown below are two diagrams: the first shows the notes of the triad; the second indicates the fingers to be used throughout. Before sweeping, place the suggested fretting hand fingers on each of the notes, one at a time. Do so four to six times before you engage the picking hand in the first example.

A Minor

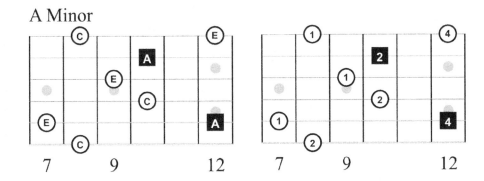

Example 2a starts with a downward sweep from the B string to the high E string using a downward pick slant and a rest stroke. After pushing through the C note on the E string, a high E note on the same string is played with an upstroke. Palm muting must be used on strings three to six.

By maintaining one pick slant throughout, the upstroke will pull the pick away from the guitar, upscaping back to the second string without any need to hop around it.

Example 2a:

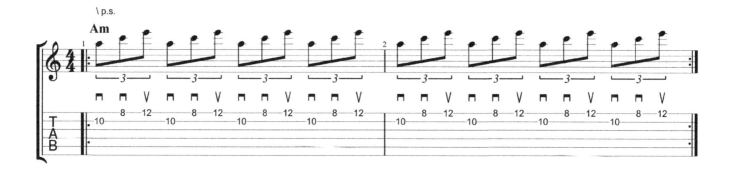

If the pick slant is ignored, the upstroke from the third note will trap the pick between the strings, creating the need for a secondary movement to bring the pick back to the starting point. The purpose of the pick slant is to avoid this problem.

An economy picker who encounters a triad like the above may bypass the outside turn mechanic from the high E string back to the B string, instead using an upward inside turn mechanic to use an up pick on the repeats.

This change creates a different picking form after the first downward sweep and is shown in Example 2b. This example is included to give you a broader sense of the options of sweep picking. This is covered in detail when we look at the descending approach in Chapter Four.

Example 2b (examine but don't practise just yet):

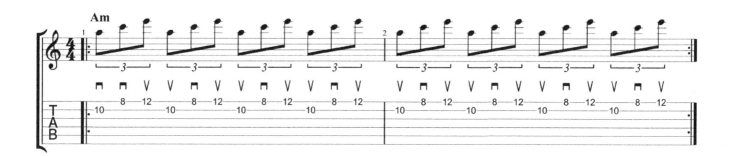

The looping nature of Example 2a means that the phrase can be melodically displaced without affecting picking mechanics, as demonstrated in Examples 2c and 2d. Displacement means that the same group of notes can be moved to different parts of the beat without affecting the optimal picking form.

Example 2c starts from the second note of the A Minor triad, and Example 2d begins on the third note.

For tidy notation, you'll often see examples like this written in 12/8 time rather than 4/4 with a constant stream of triplets. If you count aloud when you play, you can still vocalise the rhythm with *one-and-ah, two-and-ah* etc., as you would in 4/4.

Example 2c:

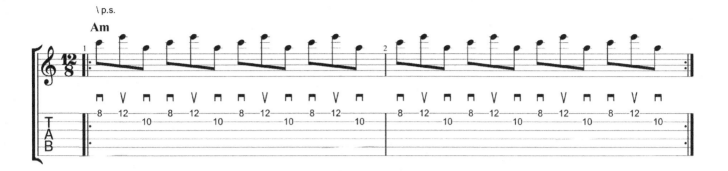

Beginning the next example with an upstroke might seem unusual at first, particularly if you've only ever alternate-picked things. However, with some practise, the benefits of mechanical consistency will pay off, negating the need for separate picking forms for each variation of the lick.

Example 2d:

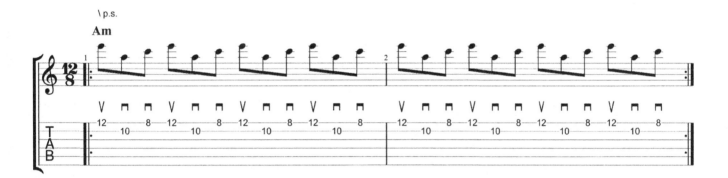

Expanding the arpeggio and sweep mechanic is merely a matter of adding an extra string. Example 2e sees the addition of an E note to the 9th fret of the G string.

Example 2e:

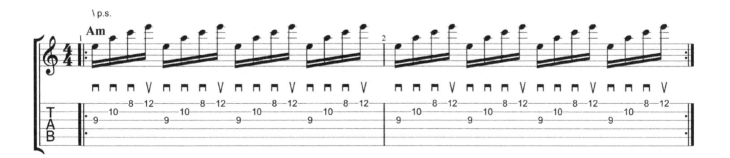

Displacing the previous example to start on the highest note of the triad with its associated upstroke, you may once again feel a little disorientation until you get the hang of it. Begin Example 2f very slowly, avoiding any timing discrepancies that might arise from having an extra downstroke note as the shape grows.

Example 2f:

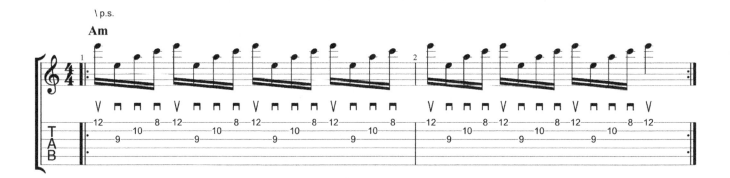

Extending the shape into the sweep pattern in Example 2g isn't very common due to the melodic displacement and the extended string leaps that occur in the repetition. Example 2h remedies this with a figure that provides more time to get from the high E string back to the D string.

Example 2g:

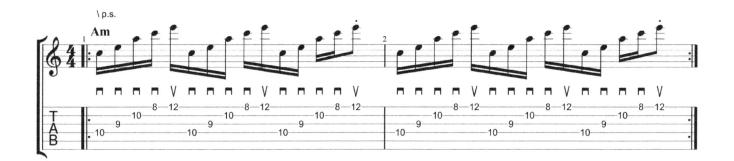

Example 2h:

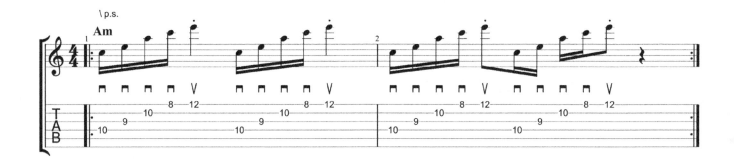

Example 2i consolidates the mechanics that you've acquired so far and the challenge is to maintain stable timing despite the distance of string jumps increasing as you work through each bar. Remember that any lick should only be played as fast as the most challenging part of it, so avoid rushing through beats 1 and 2 if it means slowing down in beats 3 and 4.

The two-string and three-string triads begin on beats 1 and 2 respectively but the four-string version starts on the second triplet of beat 3.

Example 2i:

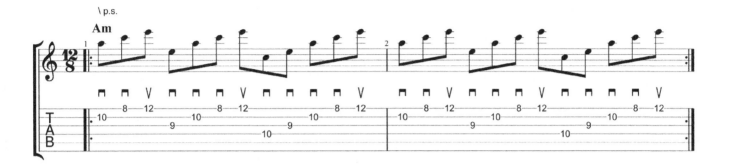

Since the five-string pattern uses the fourth finger for both the A root note on the A string and the E note on the high E string, it isn't feasible to launch into straight repeats with this shape. Instead, try integrating some other string groups, as outlined in Example 2j, which uses two and three string patterns.

With larger shapes, sweep picking can feel like trying to control a ball rolling down a hill. Avoid letting the timing get away from you as you mix sweeps in this drill.

Example 2j:

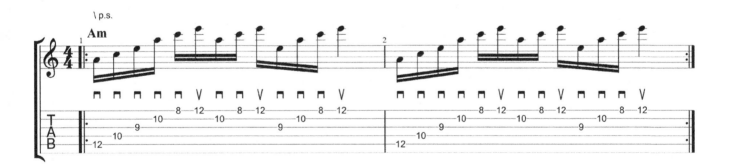

Musically, the next logical note to add to the A Minor triad is an E note below the A root. While the E note could be sourced from the 12th fret of the low E string, placing it on the 7th fret of the A string removes any fourth finger rolling that would have been necessary.

The shape now has two notes per string at either end, on the fifth and first strings, with three options for dealing with the A string, as spelt out in each bar of Example 2k.

1. Pick the two notes on the A string *down, up* and continue sweeping from the D string.

2. Pick the 7th fret of the A string with a downstroke, hammer on to the 12th fret and continue sweeping

3. Pick the two notes on the A string *up, down* with the downstroke sweeping through

Example 2k:

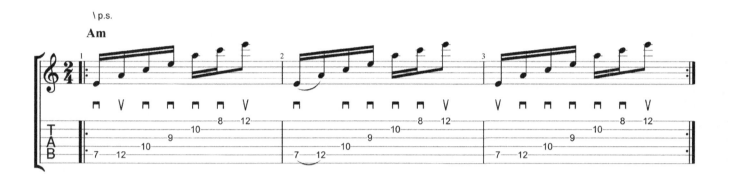

Which one is the best? For the sake of versatility, test all three and see what fits naturally into your style. I tend to alternate between the first two options. Option One has a consistent dynamic, being all picked, but Option Two is perhaps the least disruptive to pick stroke flow and involves the same number of strokes as the five-string ascent used in Example 2j. The rest stroke occurs between the first two downstrokes while the hammer-on takes place.

You can mix and match approaches according to the situation. For example, pick all the notes when staying within five strings, or use a hammer-on in the six-string form that you will see shortly in Example 2m.

The five-string two at each end shape works well in triplet rhythms like the one in Example 2l. This drill ascends through strings five to one, then doubles back for a two-string iteration in the second bar.

Example 2l:

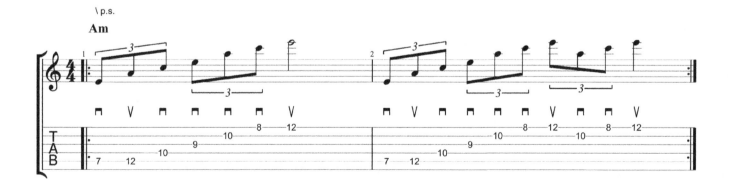

112

Another advantage of the layout used in Examples 2k and 2l is the finger-friendly extension now available on the low E string. By adding a C note on the 8th fret using the second finger, Example 2m extends from the low E string to the high E string with a single downstroke, using the hammer-on and an extended rest stroke on the A string to maximise the directional potential of the pick.

Example 2m:

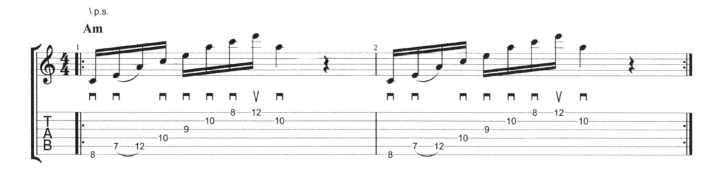

Practice and the Three Stages of Motor Learning

We have now built a method for growing two-string triads into six-string sweeps while applying the technical fundamentals listed at the beginning of the chapter.

To solidify the examples taught so far, create a practice routine appropriate to your playing experience. If sweep picking is new to you, spend more developmental time on the smaller examples before adding strings.

Play each example in this chapter in free time a few times as an overview before adding the metronome. If you really need to focus on the picking hand, mute the strings with the fretting hand and try the picking pattern for each drill percussively at first, adding the pitched notes after a few runs through.

This is the *cognitive stage* of learning, where movements are slow and given much mental focus. In the cognitive stage, it's normal to feel like every aspect of a new skill is laborious. You are activating neural pathways that become strengthened through repetition. Ensure you're applying all the rudiments described in Chapter One.

On an average practice day, you might choose to work on three or four sweep picking drills in one session. Aim for at least twenty good repeats of an exercise before moving to the next. Do a few sets of twenty if you're keen. Forego the metronome just a little longer, since you should be focused on getting the motions fluid, efficient and consistent. When you can do this you have reached the *associative stage*.

In the associative stage, tasks take less time to complete, require less conscious thought, and allow the multitasking of other elements of playing. You will notice that you have more freedom to consider what you are playing rather than simply how you are playing it. For example, you might find yourself focusing less on how to get the pick from one string to the next, and more about improving your tone and timing as you go. Everything you've learned on guitar so far has gone through this stage on its way from the cognitive process to autonomous freedom.

In the associative stage, you shouldn't be aiming for maximum speed (yet), but you will gain a useful insight into your progress by trying a burst of faster repeats, to see if your technique is ready to withstand some acceleration. If it's not, go back to *development speed*, but keep working those bursts from time to time.

As the first few drills get easier, shift your focus to new exercises, relegating accomplished material to warm-ups. For example, if you spent twenty minutes working on Examples 2a, 2c, 2d and 2e on Monday and Tuesday, spend five minutes revising them on Wednesday before having a focused session based on Examples 2f to 2i.

When you can play through each of the examples comfortably, take out the metronome and determine your *edge of ability* tempo (EOA). Your EOA tempo is the speed at which you can hold the lick together, just before the point of disintegration. Next, drop the metronome back to half of your EOA tempo and progressively work back up to maximum. For example, if your top speed for a lick is 100bpm, drop the metronome back to 50bpm, then work upwards in 10bpm increments when you can accurately play about ten repeats. At the end of the session, play in free time to the edge of your ability and see if your EOA tempo has increased against the metronome.

When you can play something fast in an almost automatic fashion, this is the *autonomous* stage. Your movements will be accurate and consistent. People refer to this as *muscle memory*, but muscles don't have a consciousness. It just means that your motor skills have reached an independent level.

Don't be discouraged if you can only bite off a few drills at a time, or if it takes weeks rather than days to see some gains. Practice is like physical exercise: a consistent program is the one that is likely to bring results. Trust and enjoy the process!

It's normal to have different drills spread simultaneously across the cognitive, associative and autonomous categories as you improve old drills while learning new ones. In general, however, getting better at even a few sweeping licks can advance the progress of other exercises that are in each stage of learning.

To mix things up for your ears, apply the ideas from this chapter to the major triad form (1, 3, 5) and practise each, adhering to the same picking patterns as the A Minor examples. This will allow you to start outlining common chord progressions involving major and minor sounds. The extended major triad looks like this:

A Major

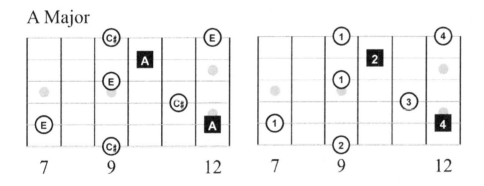

In the next section, you will be able to apply your new sweep chops to a range of etudes that are way more musical than static triads and will challenge your ability to change chords in time with the music.

Chapter Three: Ascending Etudes

In this section, the mechanical patterns of Chapter Two are applied to different chords and inversions to challenge the fretting hand and entertain the ears. Most of these have a somewhat Neoclassical Rock styling, but you can later apply the same picking forms to any chord progression or genre of your choice.

All shapes used are taken in part or whole from the Fretboard Coverage material in Chapter Eight. For now, just learn any new fingerings as they occur in each etude. There is nothing too complicated to worry about regarding fingering.

In these examples, the brain has to work harder as you move to the correct positions and notes within each triad, so be sure not to neglect the fundamental principles when practising the drills from a slow pace to a brisk EOA tempo. In each example, apply your own preferences for muting and picking dynamics, and feel free to emulate my approaches from the audio. All the examples in this chapter use a downward pick slant.

To begin, Example 3a use the two-string mechanic. The etude contains triads that start on either the root or 5th of the chord – the latter involving some index finger rolling across string pairs. Be careful not to play position rolls in a barre chord fashion with the notes audibly overlapping.

Bars one to four use the two-string mechanic on the D and G strings, changing octaves and strings to the B and high E strings in bars five to eight.

Example 3a:

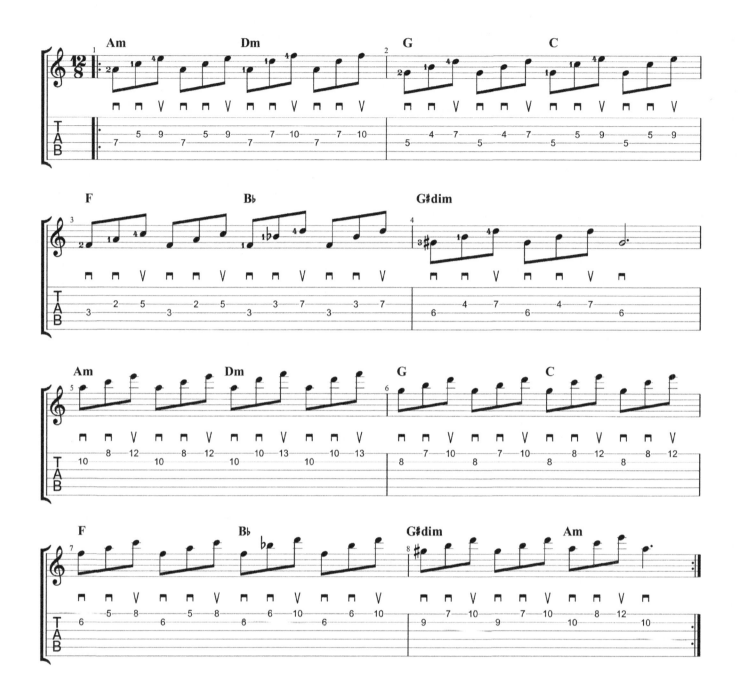

Advancing to three strings in Example 3b, a new shape is introduced at beat 3 of the first bar. This is an inversion of the previous A Minor triad and derived from the A shape of the CAGED system. The second bar introduces a diminished triad shape which is a variation of the C shape but with b3 and b5 degrees.

Example 3b:

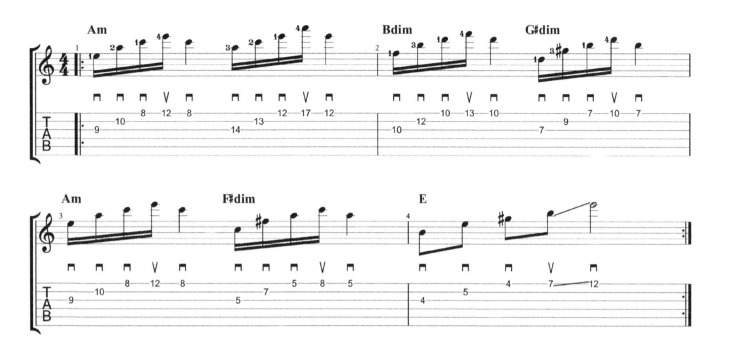

Example 3c uses a 12/8 feel and brings together triads from the keys of C Major and C Minor. It's important to keep the *up, down, up* pick strokes in the second note grouping of each bar at the same speed as the downward sweeping that occurs within the beats on either side.

Example 3c:

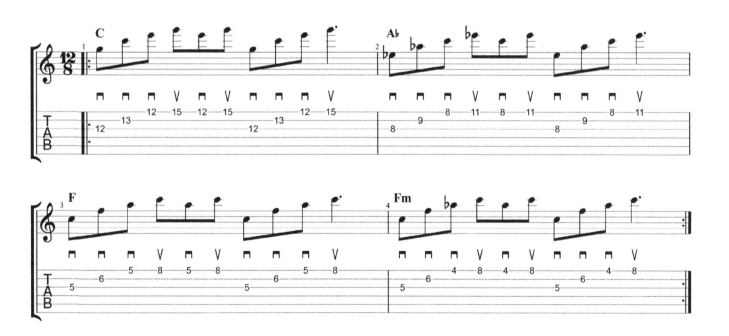

Example 3d begins and ends each bar on the D string, with two-string and three-string sweeps interwoven.

Example 3d:

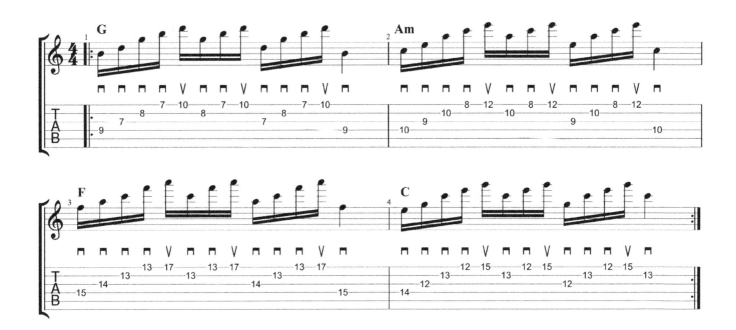

On five strings, Example 3e will put you through your paces with the extended C Shape triads. Be sure that the timing of the hammer-ons does not waver.

Example 3e:

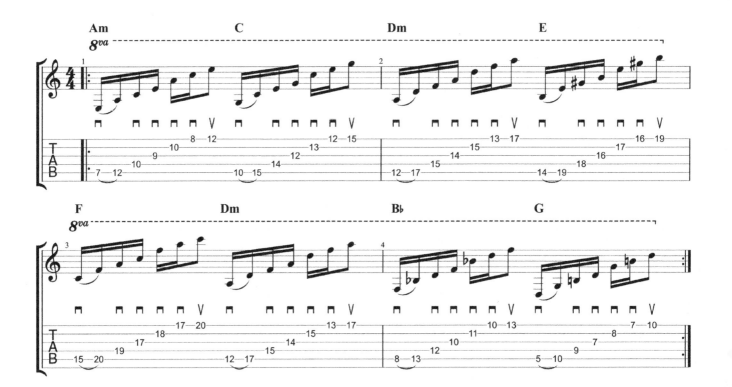

Example 3f applies the full six-string shape mapped out at the end of Chapter Two through an ascending progression. Passing through the chords C Major, Eb Major, F Major and F Minor, the first three notes of each bar are executed with *down, down, up* pick strokes with an outside string change back to the low E string. As the same three notes reappear, the two downstrokes and hammer-on applied previously in Example 2l are employed.

Example 3f:

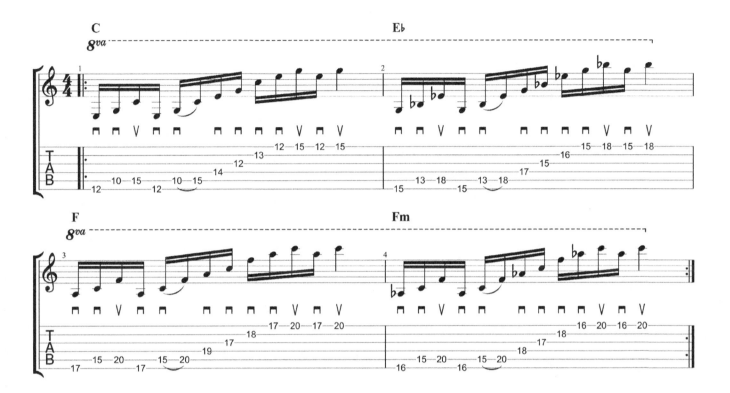

How to Practise Chapter Three

Since the picking hand requirements of these etudes each correspond to a development drill in Chapter Two, I suggest switching your focus to the musical applications and fingering hand requirements presented in this chapter. If you're confident enough with the material in the previous chapter, you might choose to replace it altogether with these etudes. If you feel you're not quite there yet, drill the appropriate exercise from Chapter Two as a warm-up for its linked etude in Chapter Three.

You could, for example, warm-up your picking hand with Example 2a from slow to EOA a couple of times, then run Example 3a through the three stages of development discussed in the conclusion of Chapter Two.

As soon as any exercise serves little to no developmental gain, replace it with one that is more advanced so that your practice time is not eaten up playing things you can already do (unless it's for enjoyment, of course). As your volume of practice material increases, your time may not. If you only have thirty to sixty minutes to practice, make it count with material that stretches you as a player.

Begin each practice session with a plan of what you'd like to achieve. Doing so is more likely to produce a feeling of accomplishment, even if you take just a few steps down a long road.

Chapter Four: Descending Strategy

In this section, shapes from Chapter Two will be used to build your descending sweep picking technique. Working in the opposite direction to the previous two chapters necessitates a few crucial changes to the method. The modified components of descending sweeping are:

• Upward (descending) sweep picking technique

• Upward rest stroke

• Upward pick slant with a couple of forced downward exceptions

• Inside turning mechanic, upscaping and downscaping

Sweeping in the upward direction feels slightly unnatural to many players at first, so don't be discouraged if your technique requires a little more attention in this area. Since picking with a downward slant is arguably the most common natural orientation among guitarists, creating a mirrored version of your technique can take time. Another potential hurdle in this endeavour stems from the fact that descending within common forms like the C shape triad involves alternating the pick slants at either end.

In isolation, upward sweep picking drills like Example 4a can be executed with an upward pick slant throughout, but in more realistic usage (like that of Example 4b) changes to the direction and pick slant will occur. In such cases, it's essential to keep the sweep as logical as possible and minimise the effect of the directional changes.

Example 4a:

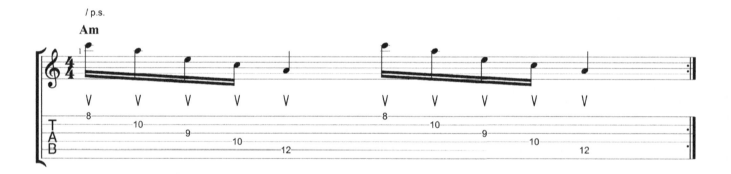

While many players will naturally head to the first note of Example 4b with a downward pick slant, downscaping needs to occur between the two notes on the high E string to set up the upward pick slant required for descending sweep picking. When arriving at the 12th fret of the A string via the rest stroke from the D string, upscaping occurs coming out of the A note to set up the necessary downward pick slant for the subsequent notes on the D and G strings, as well as the return to the high E string on repeats.

Example 4b:

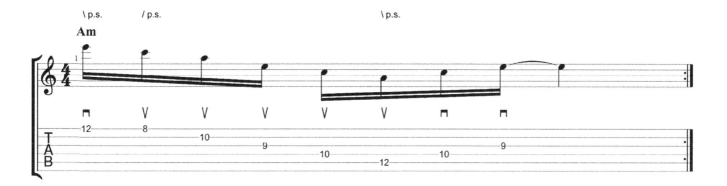

Set the two previous examples aside for the time being and progress through the following drills to incrementally develop the descending approach.

As a two-string drill, Example 4c contains only one sweep picking stroke. The primary objective is to become accustomed to the constant changes in pick slant. The first note of the loop occurs on a downstroke with downward pick slant, switching to an upward pick slant for the sweep back through the 8th fret of the high E string to the 10th fret of the B string.

After landing on the B string via the rest stroke, adjust into downward pick slant so that the pick is not caught between the B and G strings, and has clear passage back to the high E string. It is somewhat like flicking into downward pick slant out of the upstroke and will occur on whichever note is lowest as the triad expands across more strings.

On the first downstroke of bar one, the downward pick slant is not mandatory, but since it will be on the repeats, it has been indicated as such for continuity. The degree of pick slant does not need to be extreme in any of the examples, since exaggerated leaning can cost you time and energy. Enough slant to enable clean string changes without overt hopping is all that is necessary. At speed, the pick might even look neutral with this kind of pattern or create an illusion akin to a bending spoon trick. The pick slant changes will occur on the same notes each time.

Example 4c:

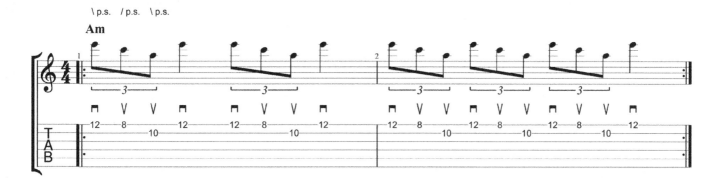

As the size of the triad is increased, the picking mechanic merely requires an extra upstroke and rest stroke per new string, shifting the inside turning mechanic to the final string before the turnaround. The larger the triad, the more you can take advantage of the directional flow of the notes, as Example 4d demonstrates.

Example 4d:

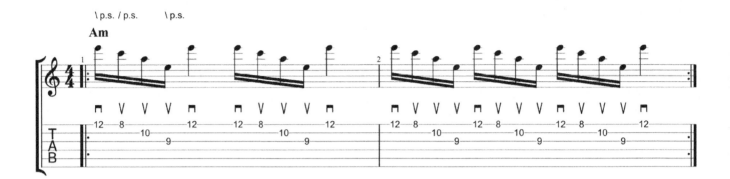

Permutations of the previous example do not change the placement of pick strokes and slants. Example 4e starts on an upstroke but is effectively the same pattern used in bar two of the last drill.

Example 4e:

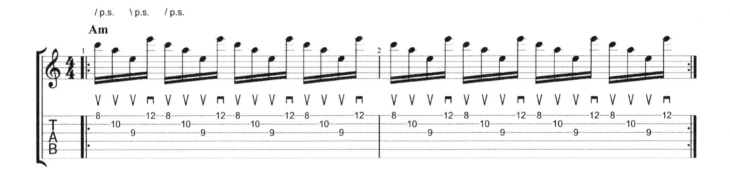

As Example 4f spans four strings, the directional flow of upward sweeping becomes more apparent. The rhythm of this example uses 1/16th and 1/8th notes so that speed and accuracy can be targeted within a single pattern.

Example 4f:

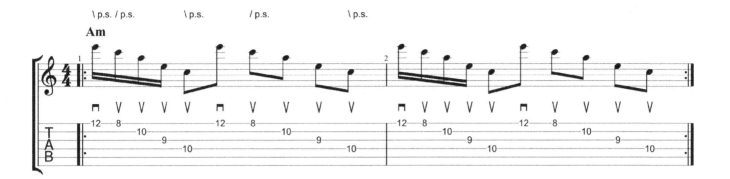

Approaching the two notes located on the A string, Example 4g uses all picked notes to maintain definition, whereas Example 4h uses a pull-off from the 12th fret to the 7th fret to allow flow as the pick continues in the upward direction to the low E string. It then ends with an inside turn back to the A string.

Example 4g:

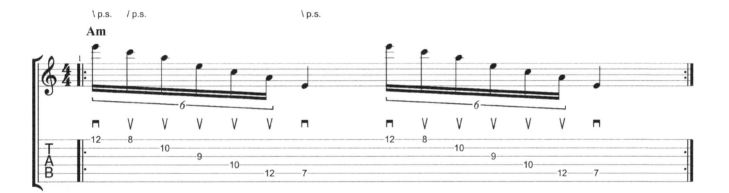

Example 4h:

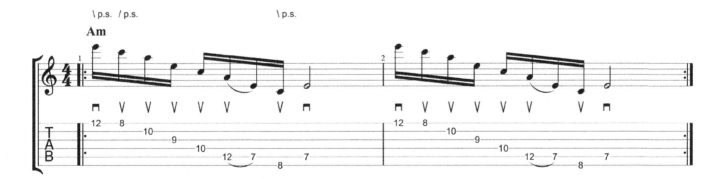

Before moving on to the descending etudes in Chapter Five, it's again recommended that you apply all the examples in this chapter to an A Major triad. It will be essential to weave together major and minor shapes with equal dexterity and, in the chapters that follow, to be as comfortable with descending sweeps as ascending sweeps.

How to Practise Chapter Four

If you're anything like me, more time might be spent in the cognitive stage of learning this descending technique than the ascending approach.

Your goal for this chapter is to perform descending sweeps with the same accuracy and confidence as their ascending counterparts. One way to track your progress during the associative stage is to play ascending and descending triads side by side within the same string groups. An example of this would be to alternate between Example 2m and Example 4h. Compare them in free time at first, then bring in the metronome for some analytical comparison.

As with the ascending approach, the descending approach will be applied musically in the etudes that follow.

Chapter Five: Descending Etudes

You should now have a sound knowledge of the implications and applications of pick slant in descending sweep picking. For that reason, pick slant indicators have been omitted from the following examples since they are the same as the descending drills in the previous chapter, e.g. the two-string exercises in Chapter Four use the same mechanics as two-string etudes in this chapter, and so on.

Example 5a is based on the picking of Example 4c but with six different triads across the four bars of the etude. Avoid letting position shifts affect your timing and work at speeds you can maintain all the way through before accelerating.

Example 5a:

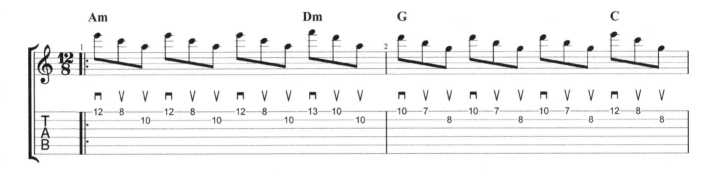

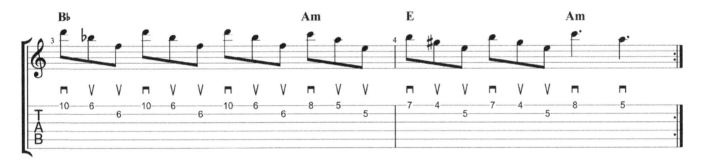

Example 5b is in 3/4 time and uses three-string minor and diminished triads and inversions. Alternate between clean and distorted tones as you practise etudes such as this, to ensure that your technique is clean and no string noise occurs.

While the diminished triads are named according to their C shape forms, each one functions harmonically as a dominant V chord (E7b9) to form a perfect cadence with the A Minor triad.

In the D Diminished triad (D F Ab) in bar three, the G# note is enharmonically equivalent to the Ab note in the triad. G# is used in the notation because it best represents the function of the 7th degree of the A Harmonic Minor scale.

Example 5b:

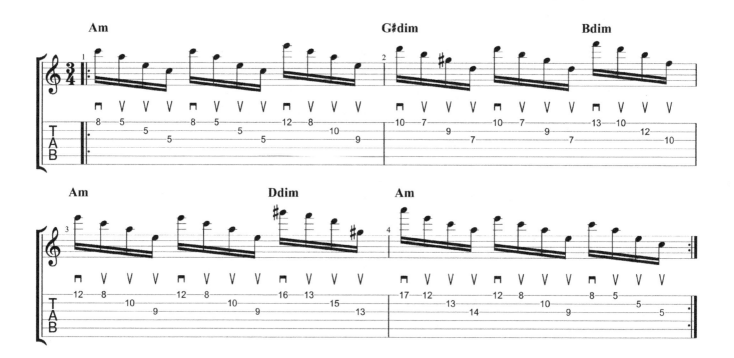

Example 5c uses major, minor and diminished triads exclusively in the C shape. Since several of the triads start halfway through beats of the bar, take care to ensure that you execute them according to the rhythms and pick strokes indicated.

Example 5c:

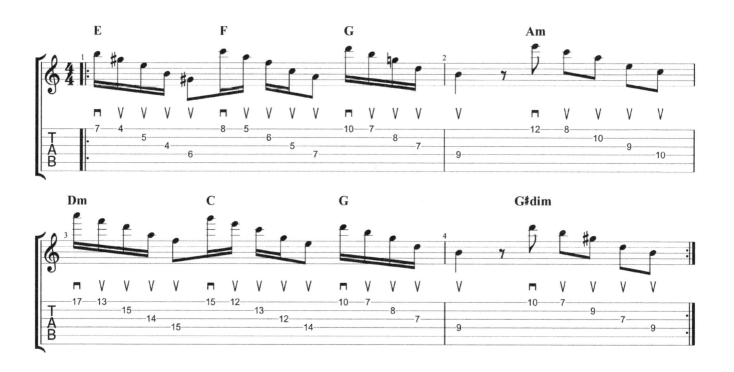

Example 5d uses two minor and two major triads, all beginning after a 1/4 rest in each bar. This is just a musical choice for the etude, but in the six-string etude of Example 5e, you will see the previously rested portion of each first beat filled out with two alternate-picked notes.

Example 5d:

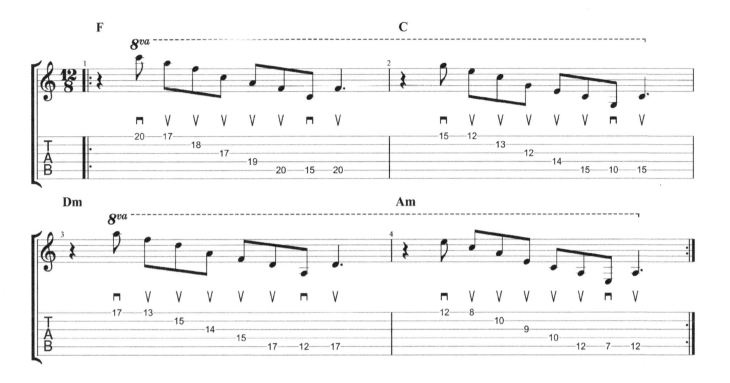

The final descending etude (Example 5e), is the most complicated example in the book so far and will test your ability to combine alternate picking and sweep picking with consistent timing and tidy execution.

How to Practise Chapter Five

Your goals here are much the same as in Chapter Three: apply the mechanics in a musical way using the previous drills for development and warm-up purposes. You should recall the shapes quite easily by now, and an associative stage of mechanical development should allow for time to focus on where each upcoming arpeggio will be located on the fretboard.

Example 5e:

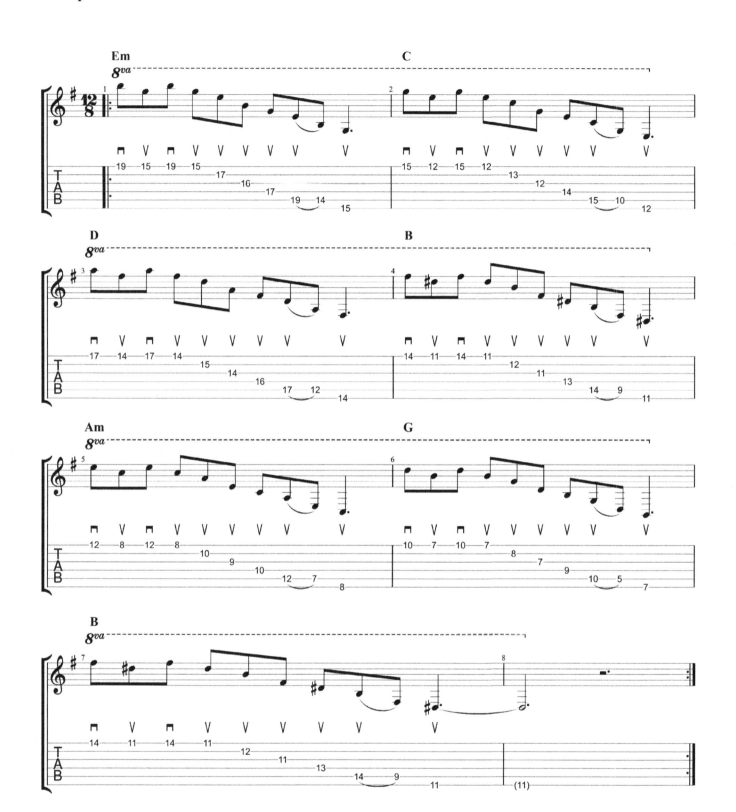

Chapter Six: Bidirectional Strategies

Now that you have systemised ascending and descending sweep picking in isolation, it's time to combine them and consider some options that arise from directional changes. The bidirectional strategies allow for a lot of personalisation.

Mechanics used in this section include:

- Double and single turnarounds

- Downward and upward sweep picking technique

- Rest strokes in both directions

- Alternating pick slant

- Inside and outside turning mechanics (upscaping and downscaping)

- Hammer-ons and pull-offs

Double Turnarounds

When an ascending picking form is combined with its equal but opposite descent, it produces something I call the *Double Turnaround*. The term refers to the use of repeated notes at either end of a triad, so that both sweep directions begin on down strokes, as shown in the next three drills.

Each triad uses an even number of pick strokes to change direction, regardless of how many single-note strings appear between the turnaround points. With swift direction changes, it's important to remember that changes to pick slant can occur slightly before or after the points noted. Changes that are too forced and abrupt might even impact your potential speed.

If it flows and you're avoiding getting the pick stuck between strings, you're doing it right!

Example 6a:

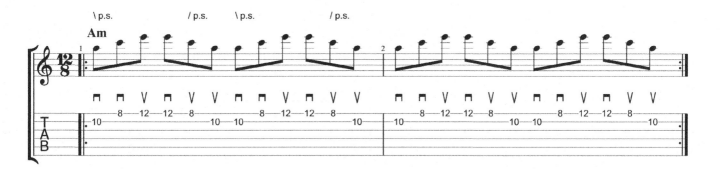

Example 6b:

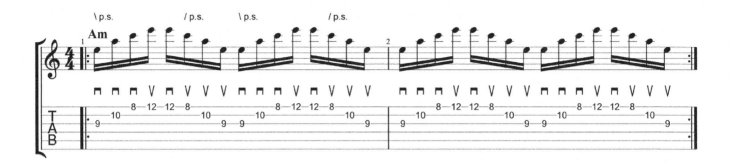

Example 6c:

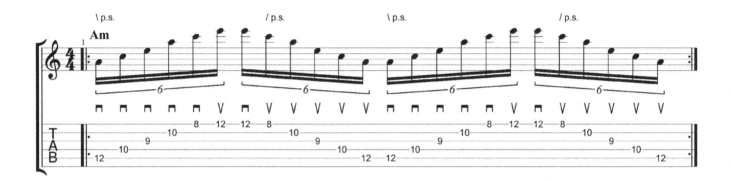

To avoid repeating the same pitch at either end of a double turnaround sweep, the picking mechanics can be applied to progressions of triads that change after each ascent or descent. Examples 6d, 6e, and 6f correspond to the two-, three- and five-string triad forms with a four-chord progression applied.

Example 6d:

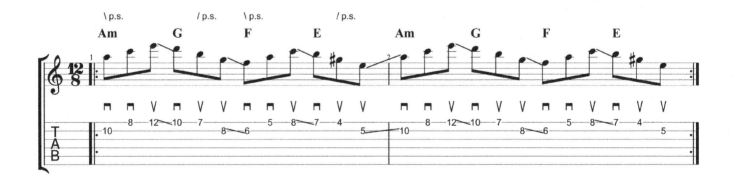

Example 6e:

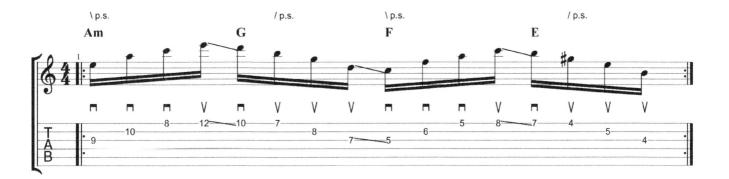

Example 6f:

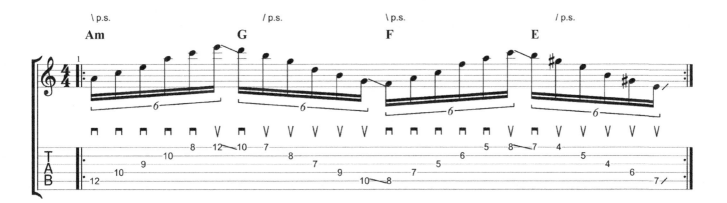

Single Turnarounds

Looping a sweep picking pattern without duplicating the top or bottom notes is a *single turnaround*. The highest or lowest note is not played twice merely for ease of changing direction, and the turnaround does not require an even number of notes.

The extended five-string triad in Example 6g works as a single turnaround lick. The pick strokes used in beats 1 and 2 naturally reoccur on the repeat of the phrase in beats 3 and 4. The ease of repetition undoubtedly accounts for the frequent use of this sweeping form in various inversions.

Example 6g:

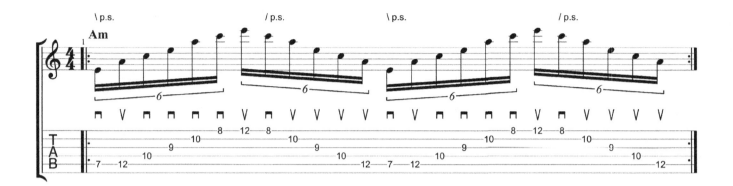

With the addition of a hammer-on in the ascent and a pull-off in the descent for a smoother ride, this form works even better. Example 6h offers an etude for this approach, moving through the triads A Minor, C Major, A Minor and G Major. With only two picked notes on the high E string, it makes sense to adjust the pick slant coming out of the ascending half of each arpeggio and into the descending half.

Example 6h:

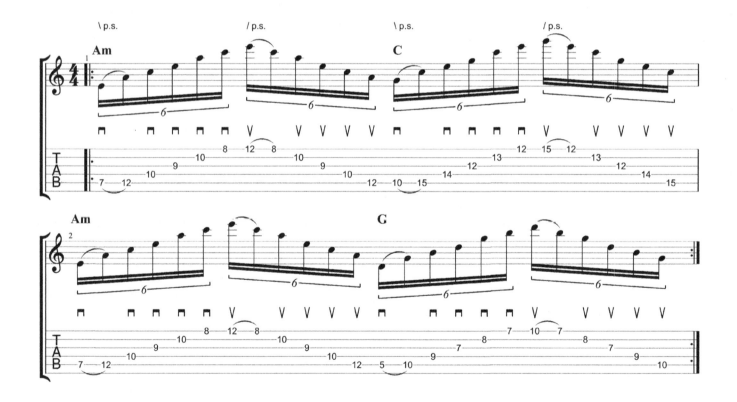

Groups where the lowest string of each shape contains only a single note can be less intuitive than previous examples, raising questions about inside picking versus outside picking, and using one set of mechanics the first time versus a different version on the repeats. Some patterns may also create confusion due to unique approaches used by various famous sweep pickers. Let's demystify that.

To strategize your personal approach and remove all uncertainty from the options, let's run through the string groups progressively.

Two-string Single Turnarounds

Ascending and descending within the two-string A Minor triad presents a problem early on if all notes are picked. Evident in Example 6i, an ascending sweep only occurs the first time since the drill is soon forced into an inside alternate picking form upon repeating.

Example 6i:

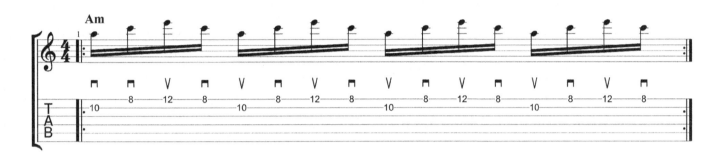

The most straightforward remedy is to maintain the downward pick slant of the ascending approach in Chapter Two and use a pull-off between the E and C notes on the high E string. Doing so facilitates endless repeats of the pattern without changes to pick strokes or pick slant and ensures no more than two picked notes on the turnaround string.

Example 6j:

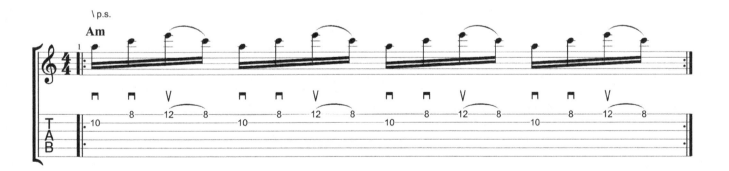

Starting the loop from a different point still requires no change to pick strokes or slant. The sweep just occurs at the end of each beat instead of the beginning.

Example 6k:

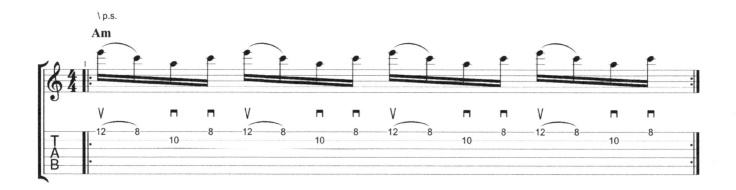

Three-, Four- and Five-String Single Turnarounds

Limiting the number of picked notes on the high E string to two helps form a smooth looping strategy for larger string groups. *Down, up, pull-off* will be the go-to approach for single turnaround triads unless you specifically desire the effect of picking every note.

Expanding Example 6j to ascending three-, four- and five-string groups is simple. Add a new lower string each time, with another downstroke and rest stroke for each.

Example 6l:

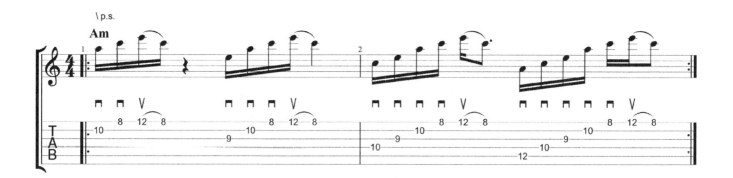

Let's deal with single notes at the bottom of triads next. In the following line, should the C note (10th fret on the D string) in beat 3 of the first bar be played as a continuation of the upward sweep from beat 2, or with a downstroke as the beginning of a new ascending sweep?

Example 6m:

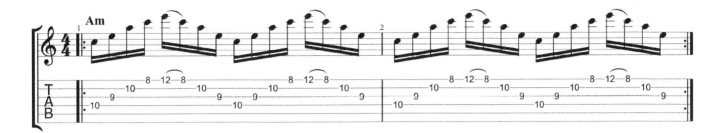

Like the glass half empty / half full scenario, the truth is that it depends on how you look at it.

Example 6n treats the C as part of the descending upstroke sweep at the beginning of the 3rd beat of bar one. Note that pick slant changes coming out of the C note in preparation for the inside turn mechanic that begins the next ascending downstroke sweep.

Example 6n:

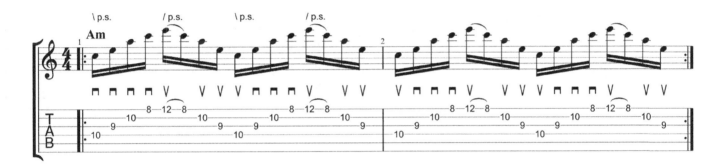

Example 6o presents the other option whereby each C note on the D string is considered the start of a new ascending downstroke sweep. For the outside turn mechanic to work, the pick slant needs to change coming out of the E note on the 9th fret of the G string before each repeat.

Example 6o:

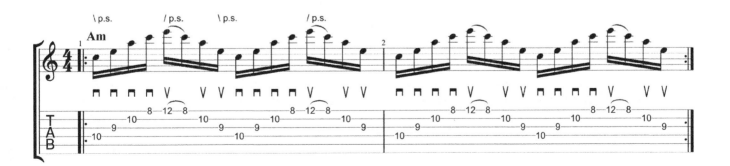

It's OK to have a mechanical or tonal preference for either, and you're still capable of mastering both with your knowledge of pick slants. The trick is to decide, have an opinion about both, and make the most of the option you prefer, keeping the other up your sleeve for any instances in which it makes sense to use.

Example 6p applies an inside turnaround in a five-string pattern that recalls the style of Jason Becker. Note the pull-off that is employed in the second iteration of the pattern.

Example 6p:

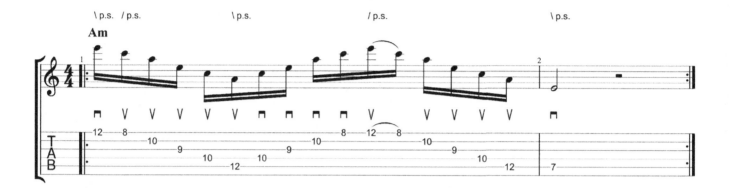

Example 6q is a case in point where a different player will opt for a downstroke on the lowest note and uses the outside mechanic typical of players like Yngwie Malmsteen. It starts on an upstroke and is followed by a pull-off to mimic what naturally occurs in the repeats. Malmsteen maintains a downward pick slant for this kind of pattern throughout, going into the upstroke on the B string with a cross-picking motion.

Example 6q:

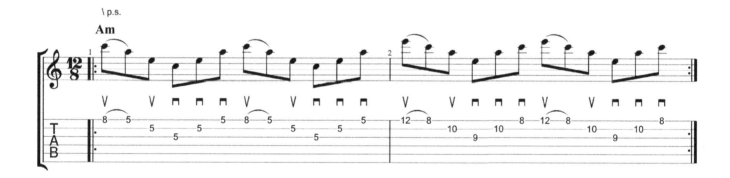

Contrasting that method with an upward pick slant and an inside turn mechanic (Example 6r) also makes a lot of sense, so experiment with both approaches and choose the one for you. In Malmsteen's case, the outward downstroke for repeats is the go-to approach for just about any sweep picking line.

Example 6r:

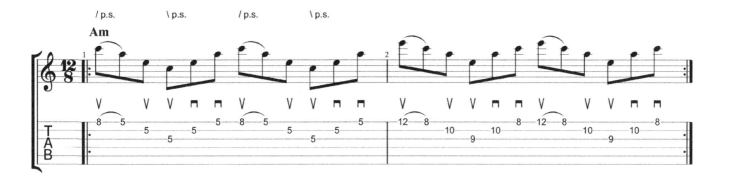

Six-String Single Turnarounds

Six-string sweeping within the shapes used so far also uses a single note on the lowest string – the low E. This single note can once again be repeated with an upstroke as part of the descending sweep (Example 6s), or with a downstroke as the beginning of a new ascending sweep (Example 6t). In either case, the inclusion of slurs on the A string will most likely give you the smoothest sounding loop, regardless of which directional change you choose.

To use the outside turn mechanic on the low E string, adjust the pick slant a little earlier as indicated.

Example 6s:

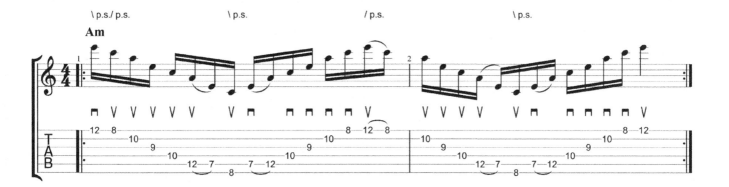

Example 6t:

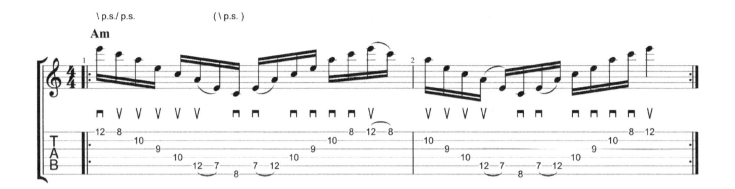

Mid-air Changes in Direction

To get creative with bidirectional sweeping, you can change direction at any point within a triad instead of waiting to arrive at the top or bottom of a range of notes. The next couple of examples mimic the effect that a harpist or pianist would create when cascading through arpeggios.

Example 6u begins on the lowest C note of an A Minor triad, cascading back and forth as it reaches new high points throughout. For the direction changes occurring at the 3rd beat of bar one and the 2nd and 3rd beats of bar two, it's necessary to use the inside turning mechanic.

On the 2nd and 4th beats of bar one I've opted for outside picking from the A string back to the low E string since those points within the drill can make use of the two-string mechanic developed back in Example 6j. Choosing this option provides two more opportunities to sweep pick rather than force an inside turn and pick slant reversal.

Example 6u:

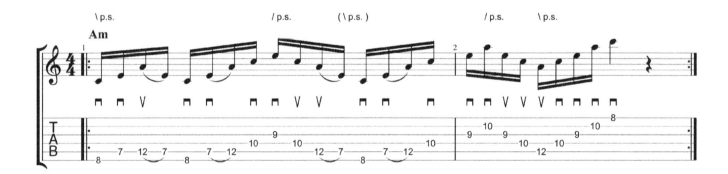

Contrasting the previous approach, Example 6v uses an inside turn between the A string and low E string in beat 4 of the first bar to extend the upward sweep that precedes the directional switch. You still have the option of the outside turn if you prefer it.

Example 6v:

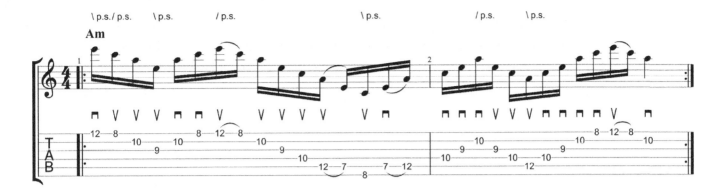

How to Practise Chapter Six

In most cases where things can be done in multiple ways, I tell those who study with me to *put it through the speed test*. What immediately feels best in the cognitive stage of learning might not always be the method that advances to the autonomous stage.

For a time, you may have to let competing strategies do battle during your practice time, assessing the benefits and applications of each until one stands out as a true preference, capable of helping you deliver your ideas at the desired tempo. To that end, try directional changes in all the ways discussed in this chapter, eventually putting most energy into the choices that produce the most results.

With the bidirectional etudes that follow in Chapter Eight, you will have many chances to put all the sweeping chops you've acquired to use in examples that most reflect *real-world* usage of technique.

Chapter Seven: Bidirectional Etudes

Since Chapter Six outlines various options for two-way sweep picking, each etude in this chapter will reference a related mechanical approach from the previous section.

Example 7a is built around a *circle of fourths* chord progression typical of baroque-influenced rock. The single turnaround picking mechanic from Example 6k is used throughout. This etude can also be moved to different keys and strings by using the same frets on the third and fourth strings as well as the fifth and sixth strings. In bar seven, the G# note is enharmonically equivalent to the Ab note in the D Diminished triad.

Example 7a:

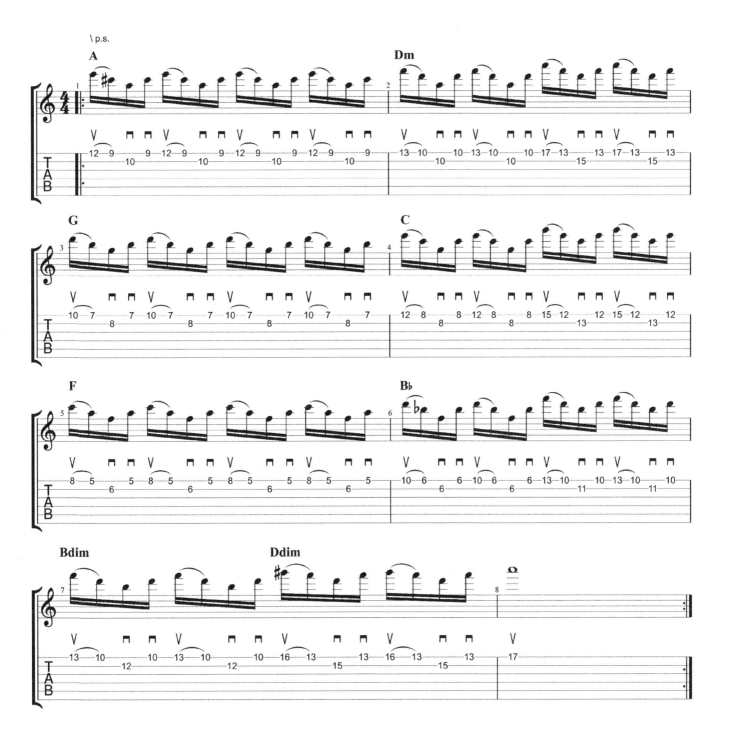

Example 7b uses the double turnaround mechanic from Example 6a on the D and G strings in a progression sourced from the key of G Major. Bars one and two ascend and descend within each position before changing triads, while bars three and four split up the picking mechanic between ascending and descending triads.

Example 7b:

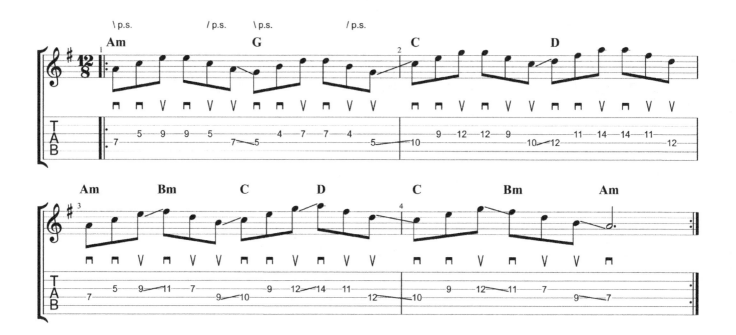

With the same harmonic progression as the previous etude, Example 7c is written for three string triads with double turnarounds throughout.

Example 7c:

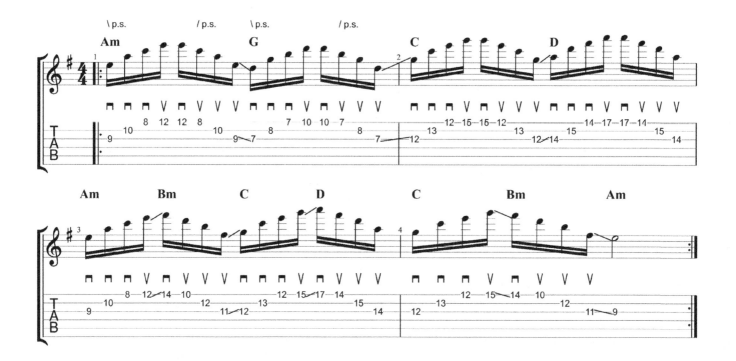

Built with the inside turn mechanic and alternating pick slant of drills like Example 6s in mind, this etude expands and contracts within each triad, using three, five and four strings for each chord in the progression. Practise each bar separately at first, reconnecting the parts when you've memorised all four shapes. Ensure that your transitions are in time with the beat when putting it back together.

Example 7d:

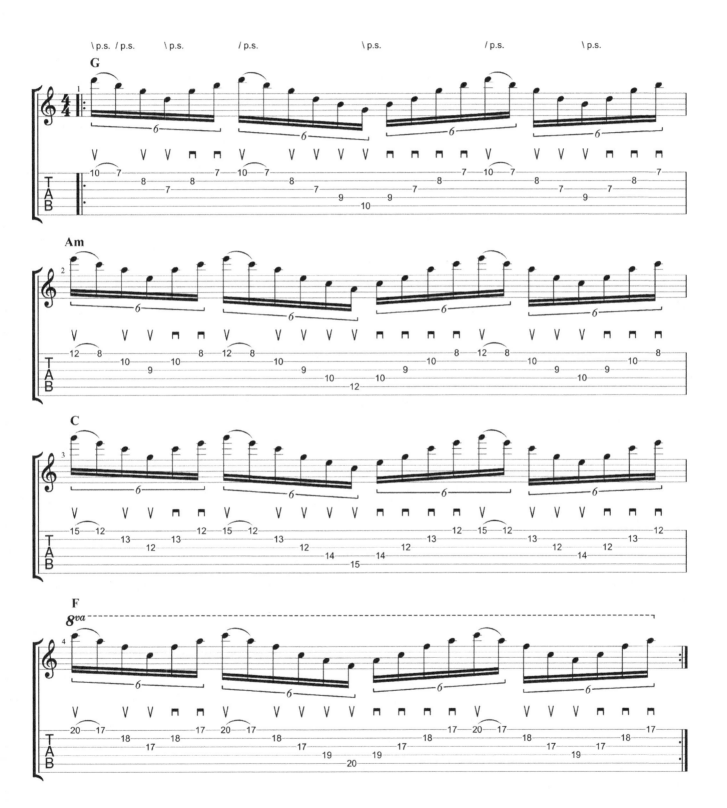

In Example 7e, the A Major triad in bar one initially turns around at the A note on the 10th fret of the B string. In the second ascent, the triad extends to the top, within position. In bar two, the C triad gives way to an early switch to the D triad in anticipation of the fourth bar.

The C triad can begin on either a downstroke or upstroke, but I've chosen a downstroke in this instance to duplicate the picking of bars one and two in bars three and four.

Example 7e:

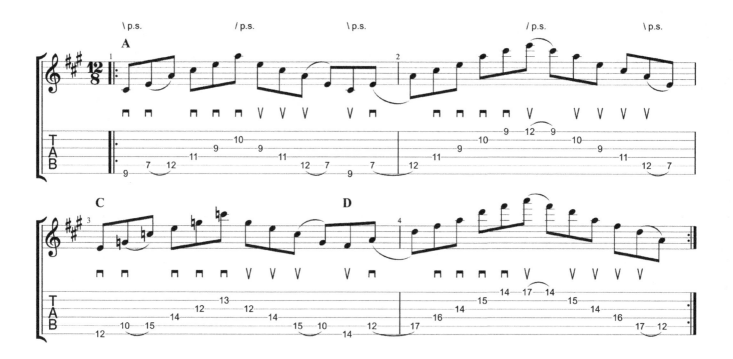

To complete the chapter, Example 7f is designed to work the inside turn mechanic at several points within one triad. Timing is crucial as you switch between 1/16th notes and 1/16th note triplets, with direction changes occurring on most strings at various points. When you can play this example, apply the sequence used to other chord progressions.

Example 7f:

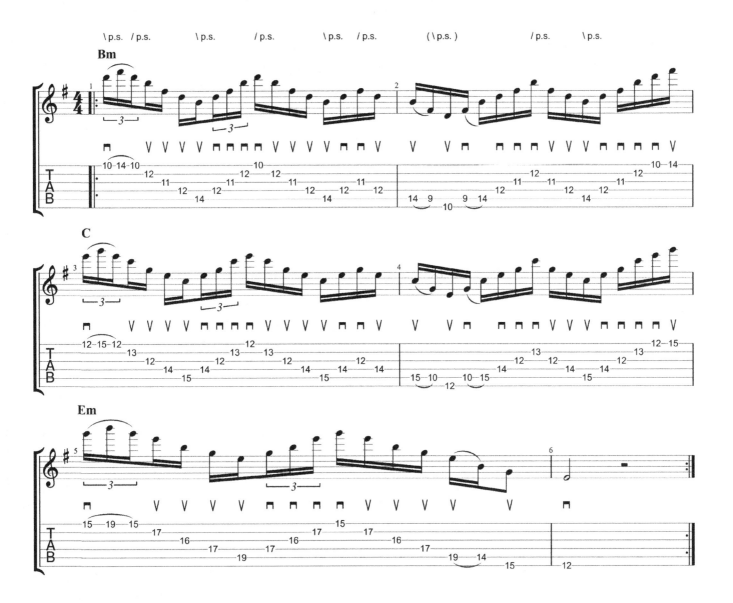

How to Practise Chapter Seven

Moving forward, it's vital that you take the ideas presented in these etudes and make them your own with different chord progressions, styles, phrasing and tempi.

Having studied all that you have so far, you'll probably notice that etudes like the ones in this chapter become associative and autonomous quicker than the drills from which they are derived. This is because your motor skills are recognising the application of standard moves. As time passes, you will find new material even more natural to develop, allowing more emphasis on the musical delivery of your sweep picking lines.

Your focus in this chapter (besides playing neatly and in time) is to enjoy the music. Hopefully, the journey is enjoyable already, but with some much cooler material up your sleeve, the joy factor increases as you make actual music, taking you a level above merely *getting it right*.

Recommendations for further study

Here are some pieces to seek out to put your bidirectional sweep picking chops to use in music.

- *Altitudes* – Jason Becker

- *Serrana* – Jason Becker

- *Race with Destiny* – Vinnie Moore

- *Demon Driver* – Yngwie Malmsteen

- *Overture* – Yngwie Malmsteen

- *Liar* – Yngwie Malmsteen

- *No Boundaries* – Michael Angelo Batio

- *Requiem for the Living* – Jeff Loomis

Chapter Eight: Fretboard Coverage - Triads

With the mechanics of ascending, descending and bidirectional sweep picking at your disposal, it's time to expand the vocabulary of triads and arpeggios using various systems for fretboard coverage. With so many chord tones available across the neck, it's essential to examine the best ways to structure the options into manageable chunks that allow you to make music. To that end, this gargantuan chapter delves into the following:

- CAGED system triads

- Speed shape triads

- Major, Minor, Diminished and Augmented triad mapping

- Suspended 2nd and Suspended 4th chord mapping

CAGED System Triad Overview

Many guitarists learn the location of chord tones within the CAGED system, a method of visualising and zoning the fretboard according to the open chord shapes of C Major, A Major, G Major, E Major and D Major and the location of the root notes of each.

While valuable for improvisation and the integration of scales and chord tones, the tonal overlap and irregular layouts mean that this system of coverage might not provide the mechanical consistency one expects for a technique like sweep picking. However, understanding the use of triads within the CAGED system will help you understand the refinements that are used in the *speed shape* approach.

The following five patterns highlight the A Major triad notes (A, C#, E) within the CAGED scale patterns in the key of A Major, beginning with what many of us learn as the *old faithful* major scale pattern (E shape).

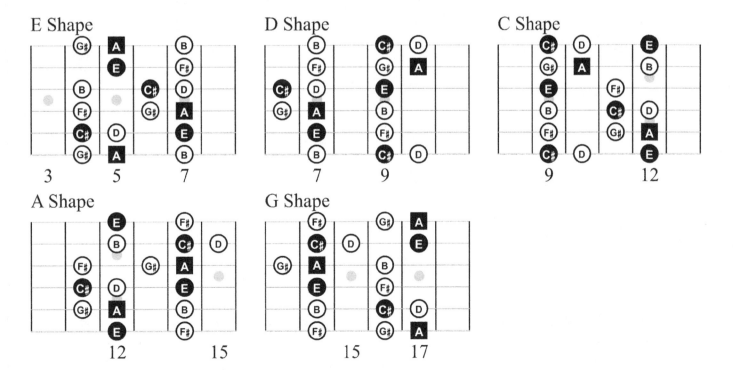

147

The IV and V chords of major scale harmony, which are also major triads, can be found using the same five shapes but from different starting points using their relevant notes. Check out these two diagrams which map the D Major (D, F# A) and E Major (E, G#, B) triads within the A Major scale patterns:

D Major triads in A Major

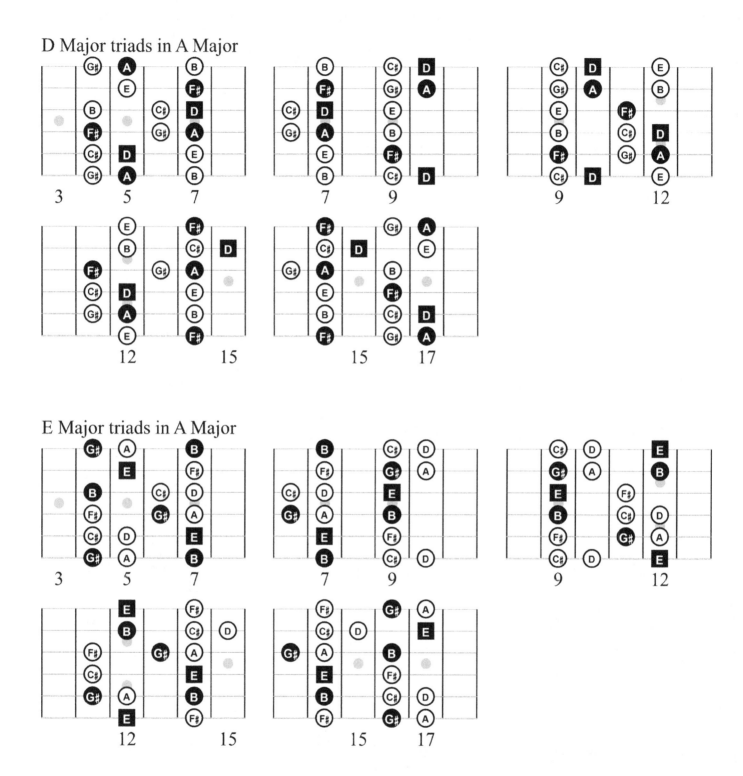

E Major triads in A Major

Example 8a uses my personal fingerings for the CAGED major triads, including any slurs or slides I use for either functionality or styling. These fingerings deviate from the notion of playing all CAGED ideas with a 1-2-3-4 fretting approach.

Example 8a:

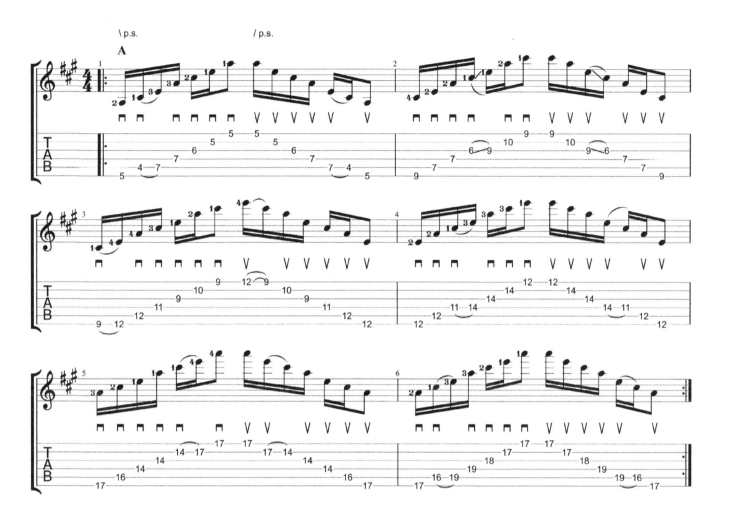

Minor triads (1, b3, 5) also exist within the CAGED system and are allocated shape names that correspond to the location of their root notes. For example, the G shape Minor triad is so named because, regardless of the pitch of the chord, the root notes share the same location as they do in a G chord. The G, E and A shapes of CAGED minor triads are arguably the most sweep-friendly and the D and C shapes are often hybridised into one usable shape which we first used in Chapter Two.

In the key of A Major, three minor chords are found at degrees II, III and VI of the scale. Those are B Minor (B, D, F#, as mapped in the diagrams that follow), C# Minor (C#, E, G#) and F# Minor (F#, A, C#). Feel free to be as conventional or experimental with the fingerings as you want, until you find what works best for you.

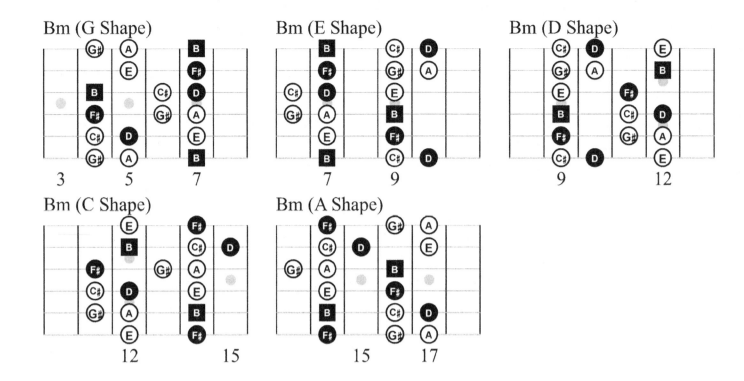

The final triad type of major scale harmony, occurring at the VII degree of the scale, is the diminished triad (1, b3, b5). Diminished triads can also be found within the CAGED system and, as you can see from the following diagrams, each pattern contains one skipped string. Hopping over one string might feel unusual if you have not done so before, but give it some time.

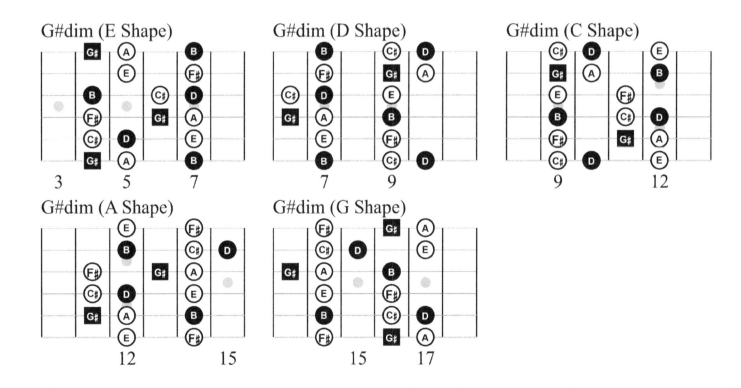

Speed Shapes for Major Triads

Fast arpeggio lines are often aided by the implementation of systemised fingering and picking templates that can be applied to a variety of chords and inversions. By eliminating some of the positional and tonal overlaps of the CAGED patterns and tweaking the layout so that identical picking forms can be applied, the *Speed Shapes* cover an octave of horizontal fretboard real estate with just three patterns. The three patterns connect with any number of strings for extensive fretboard coverage and can be modified for each chord type.

Based on hybrids of CAGED shapes (E/D, D/C and A/G), an A Major triad and its two inversions can be played using a number system layout of 1-2-1-1-1-2. The numbers refer to how many notes appear on each string from the low E string to the high E string. All picking drills used in Chapters Two, Four and Six can be applied to each of these speed shapes, which will be referred to as *Speed Shape 1, Speed Shape 2* and *Speed Shape 3* herein.

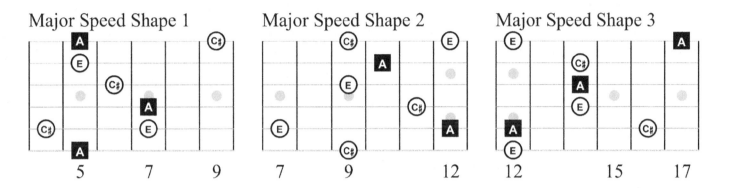

Major Speed Shape 1   Major Speed Shape 2   Major Speed Shape 3

My suggested fingerings and execution for the A Major speed shapes are offered in Example 8b and should remain consistent throughout Examples 8c to 8f as the number of strings decreases each time. Each example retains the mechanics applicable to that portion of the complete patterns.

The rhythms in the notation of these examples differ from drill to drill using a variety of note values, so listen to the audio examples available if the notation is beyond your rhythmic reading level. You can also begin by playing each with even rhythms like constant 1/8th or 1/16th notes before applying the transcribed rhythms which were chosen to fit within bars of 4/4 time.

Example 8b – Major triad speed shapes across six strings:

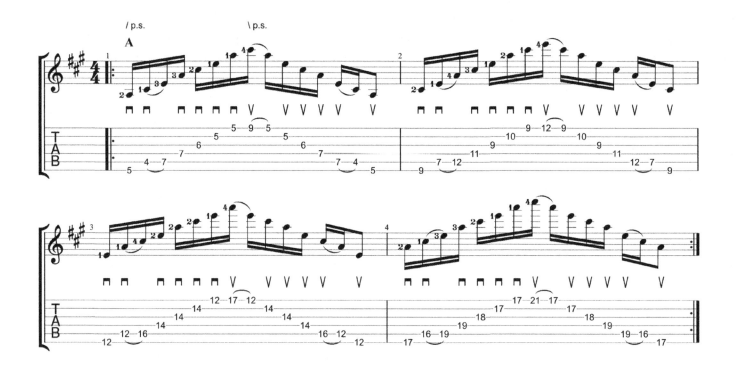

Example 8c – Major triad speed shapes across five strings:

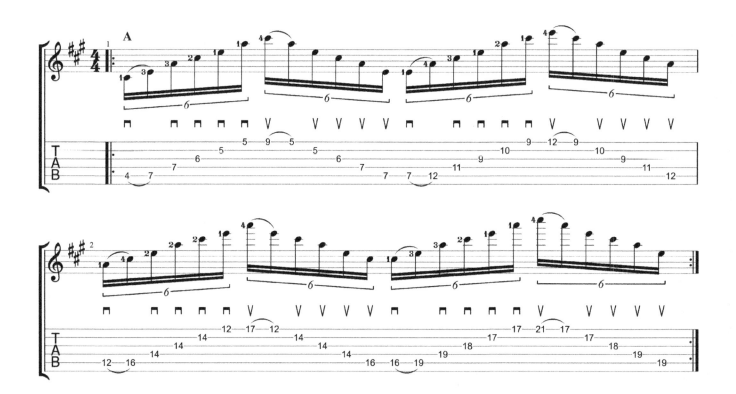

Example 8d – Major triad speed shapes across four strings:

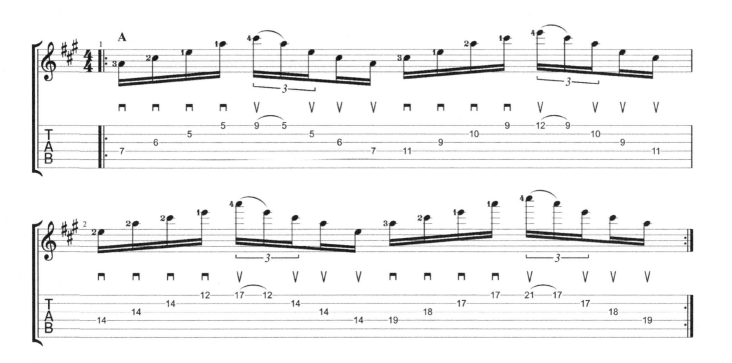

Example 8e – Major triad speed shapes across three strings:

Example 8f – Major triad speed shapes across two strings:

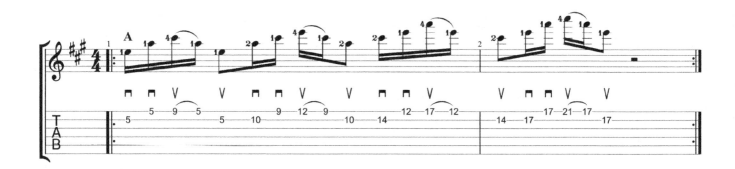

Using a mix of ascending and descending directions with whole and partial patterns can make for an exciting and seemingly endless flow of chord tones. Example 8g creates such an effect as it ascends using Speed Shape 1, descends and ascends using Speed Shape 2 and a three-string portion of Speed Shape 3, and concludes with five strings of descending using Speed Shape 1, an octave higher.

Example 8g:

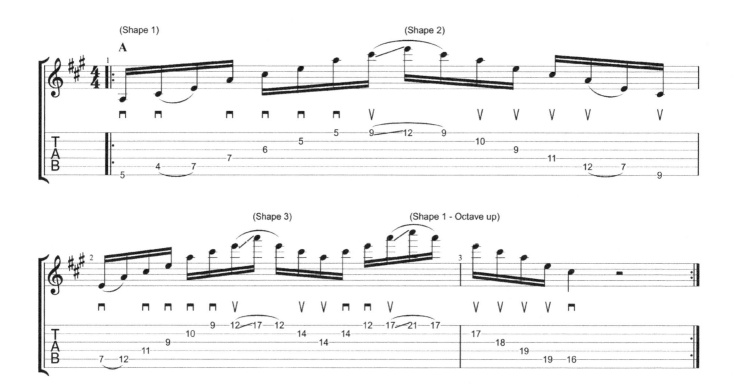

Shape Your Own Path

Any time a shape comes along that isn't to your liking, creating alternatives is just a matter of consulting the fretboard map for the chord in question, relocating notes with problematic fingerings or forming new patterns from scratch.

A Major triad across the fretboard

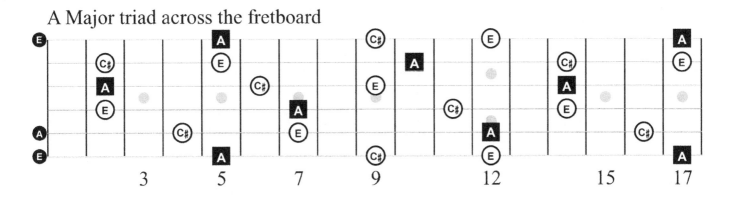

Speed Shapes for Minor Triads

The transition from major to minor triads involves merely lowering the 3rd of the former by one semitone within each 1-2-1-1-1-2 picking form, producing the following shapes:

Minor Speed Shape 1   Minor Speed Shape 2   Minor Speed Shape 3

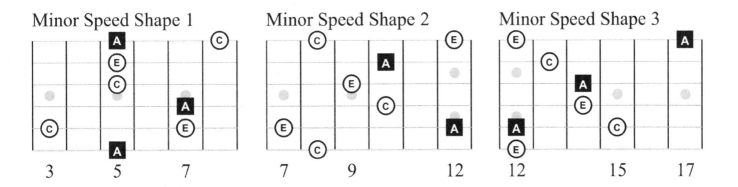

My suggested fingerings for the minor speed shapes (and any part thereof) are detailed in Example 8h. If you develop an alternative approach, ensure that your choices allow for fluid, accurate and consistent execution.

Example 8h:

After learning the minor speed shapes, repeat Examples 8c to 8f using minor triads.

By studying the triad tones across the fretboard, other shapes can be built and used as alternatives to the previous shapes.

A Minor triad across the fretboard

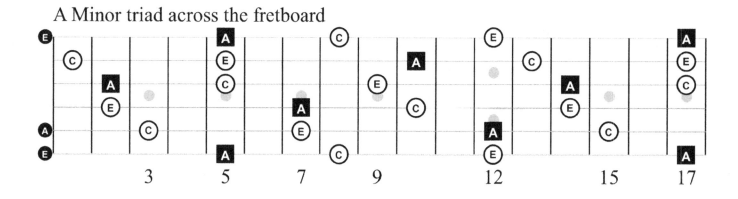

Here are two patterns for Am triads that reduce stretching by moving one note each from the A string to the low E string. The first pattern is straight out of the CAGED system.

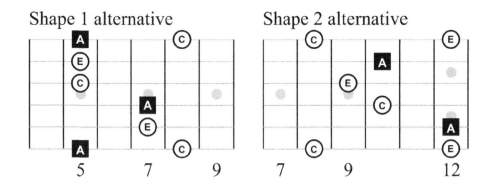

Shape 1 alternative

Shape 2 alternative

Outlining Progressions With Moving Shapes Versus Positional Shapes

Sweeping through chord progressions can be done with a very useful *voice-leading* approach by selecting shapes that occupy similar regions of the fretboard. Consider examples 8i and 8j, which compare position-jumping and voice-leading approaches. In Example 8i, the chords D Major, A Major, E Major and F# Minor each begin on their respective root notes using a moving five-string block sourced from Speed Shape 3.

Example 8i:

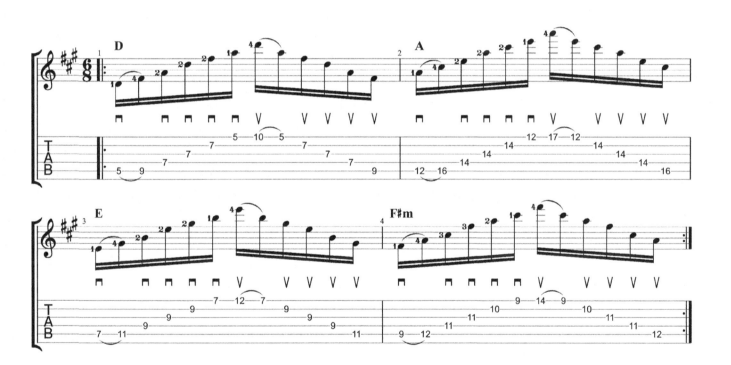

157

The wide position shifts and melodic intervals between each triad in the previous example can sound a little disjointed, even when executed perfectly. Example 8j counters that problem by using five strings of Speed Shape 1 for the D chord, and five strings of Speed Shape 2 for the A chord, resulting in voicings that beginning on either E or F# notes throughout the progression.

Example 8j:

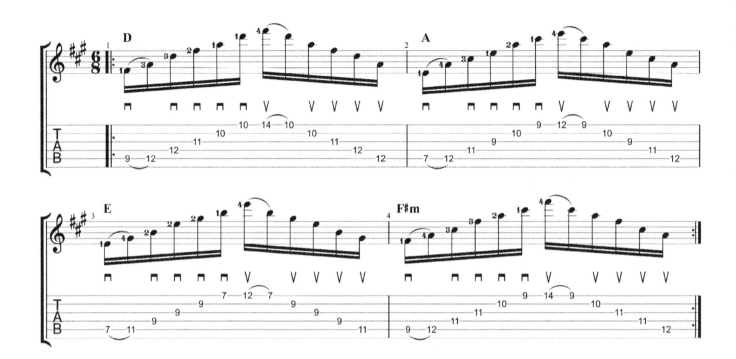

Example 8k provides yet another option for the same sequence of chords. Note how the D Major, A Major and F# Minor triads begin and turnaround on the same A notes, while the E Major begins and ends just a semitone lower on two G# notes. Following a progression within a region of the neck is a great way to create unity and movement simultaneously.

Example 8k:

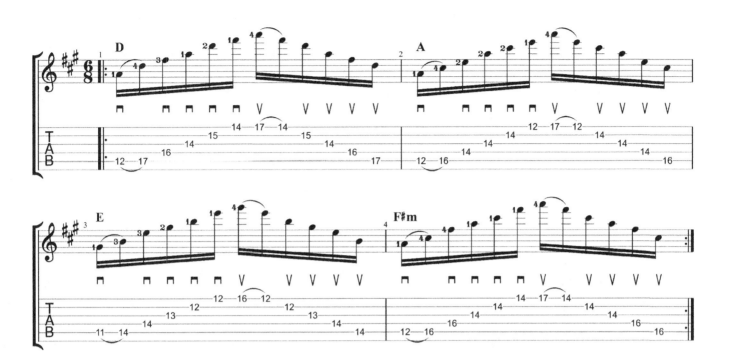

Speed Shapes for Augmented Triads

The augmented triad (1 3 #5) evokes a mysterious sound with its construction of root note, major 3rd and augmented (raised) 5th intervals. Occurring naturally from the III degree of the harmonised *harmonic minor* and *melodic minor* scales and from each degree of the *whole tone scale*, augmented triads can be found by modifying major triad shapes. Doing so results in a single shape that occurs in three locations because the chord consists of consecutive major 3rds.

The symmetrical construction of augmented triads means that Aaug, C#aug and E#aug (Faug, enharmonically) are not only chords unto themselves, but inversions of each other.

Due to the construction formula of the augmented triad (1, 3, #5), it's correct to refer to the 5th of Aaug as E# rather than F.

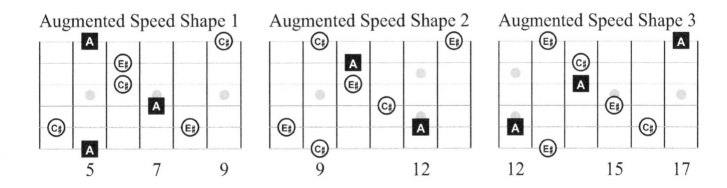

Augmented is one of the few triads for which I will alter the fingering depending on the portion used. The following two patterns illustrate the different fingerings for a six-string shape and an inside four-string pattern, the latter of which is used in Example 81.

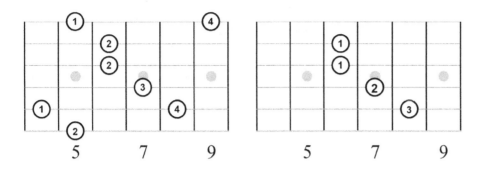

Example 81 is a double turnaround sweeping form that demonstrates the convenience of moving a single shape around the fretboard. At high speed, it's a real attention-grabber!

Example 81:

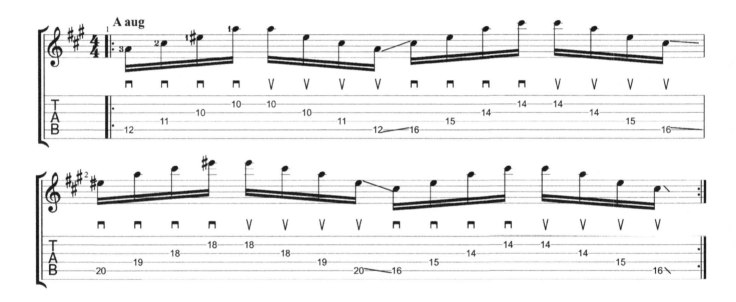

The fretboard map of an augmented triad reveals other possibilities for movable fingerings. See what shapes you can construct from the following diagram and work your ideas through interval jumps of major 3rds.

A Augmented triad across the fretboard

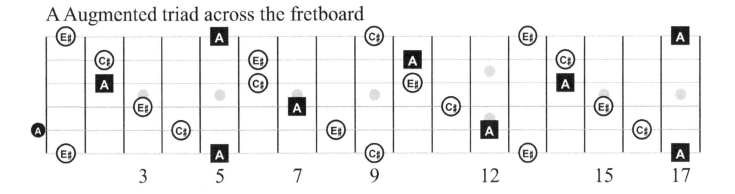

Example 8m takes advantage of the diagonal location of notes from the A root note on the low E string with an ascending sweep to the C# note on the 2nd fret of the B string. The rhythm of this example contrasts a flurry of 1/32nd notes with a staccato 1/8th note in each beat. If the rapid pace of the first four notes of each beat seems daunting, think of each beat as two 1/8th notes, with the first one consisting of an even *rake* starting on the beat, with the goal of reaching the fifth note on the -*and* of each beat.

Example 8m:

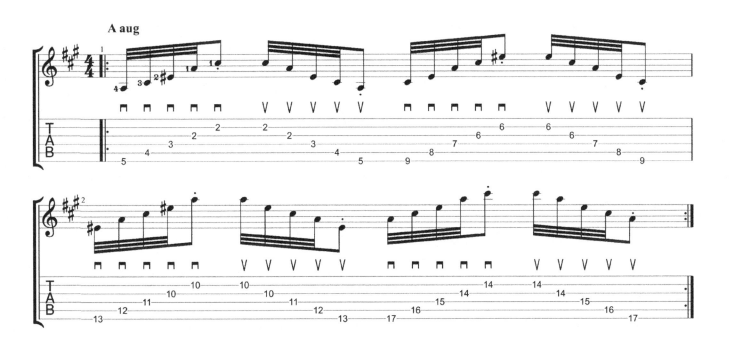

Using a repeated eight-note picking form and ascending in major 3rds, Example 8n climbs through string groups while descending in fretboard position each time. The first two units of eight use the same fingering shape on their respective string groups but are modified in bar two to stay faithful to the augmented triad.

Example 8n:

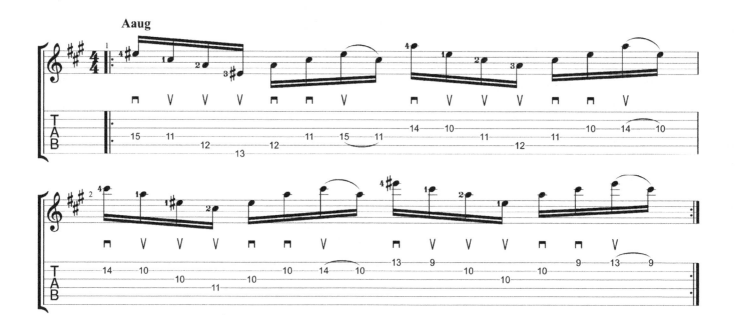

The final augmented example (Example 8o) for this section features a rhythmic palindrome stretched over two beats at a time, meaning the phrasing of beats 2 and 4 are the reverse rhythm of beats 1 and 3. The result is a feeling of acceleration and deceleration over each two-beat group that coincides with the melodic peak of the lick.

Example 8o:

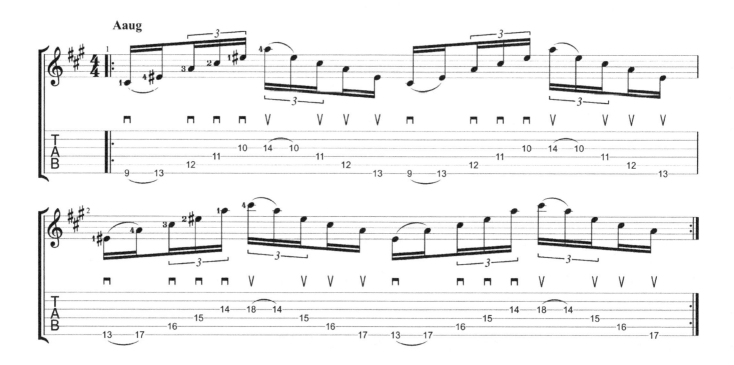

Speed Shapes for Diminished Triads

Unlike the major 3rd stacks used to create an evenly-spaced augmented triad, diminished triads (1 b3 b5) include an extra-large interval of six semitones from the b5 degree up to the next root note. The increased intervallic distance has an impact on the fretting hand layout where 5ths and roots previously lined up nicely on most string pairs in major and minor shapes.

A Diminished triad across the fretboard

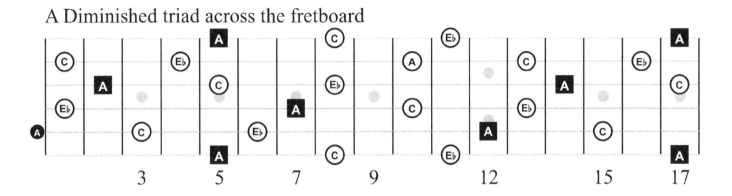

Converting minor triad speed shapes to diminished shapes by lowering all occurrences of the 5th sounds like a reasonable proposition, but the results can be mixed. Let's run through each one and make modifications to optimise flow and speed.

In the first shape, reaching the highest C note on the high E string becomes difficult, since the Eb note on the B string breaks the rolling index finger approach used in the minor speed shape in the same position.

Instead, try reverting to the more compact form derived from the CAGED system. The string skip from the G string to the high E string breaks the sweep in both directions, but is a trade-off between having access to all the same notes in an accessible way or maintaining a sweep with a less feasible fingering.

Diminished Shape 1   String-skipping alternative

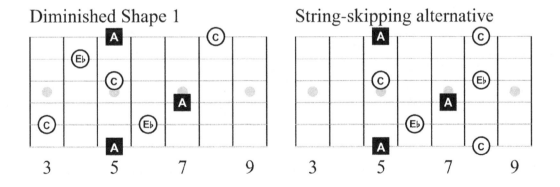

Example 8p:

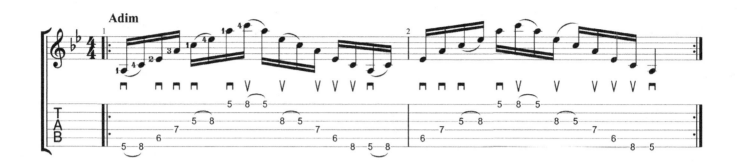

Depending on the fretboard location and key used, Speed Shape 2 can work if you don't mind a big stretch on the fifth string, but there is a more compact shape available in the same region.

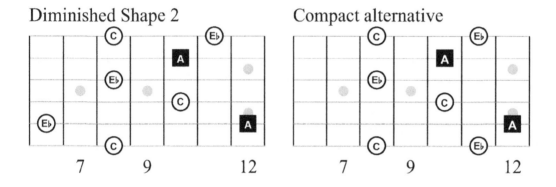

Diminished Shape 2

Compact alternative

Example 8q:

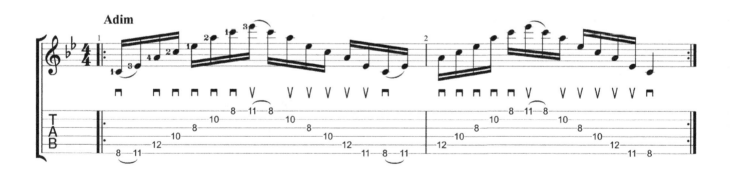

Whichever way you slice it, diminished Speed Shape 3 is quite possibly the most ridiculous proposition you'll find in this book! As daunting as it appears, the absurdity of it creates a crazy-sounding sweep that spans seven frets. My preferred shape, on the right, relocates the lowest A note from the 12th fret of the A string to the 17th fret of the low E string, giving it the same picking mechanic as the alternative to shape two.

Diminished Shape 3

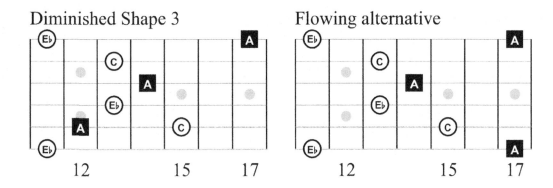

Flowing alternative

To construct the latter shape in bite-sized pieces, first get accustomed to the A note on the low E string, the C note on the A string and the Eb note on the D string using fingers four, two and one. Next, play the same notes one octave higher on the G, B and high E strings using fingers three, two and one. Combine the two elements you have so far before adding the Eb note on the low E string and the highest A note on the high E string.

Keep in mind that if the stretches are too extreme for your fretting hand, you can use any portion of the shape you like to cover the diminished triad in this region of the fretboard. Consider the whole shape a challenge for those with a penchant for the extreme.

Example 8r:

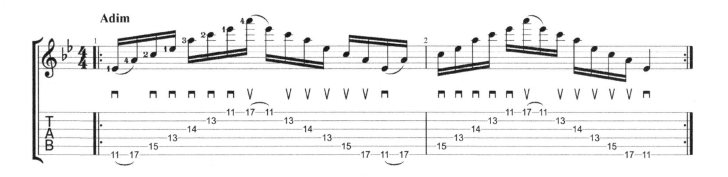

Speed Shapes for Suspended Chords

Being neither major nor minor would exclude the basic suspended 2nd and 4th (*sus2* and *sus4*) chords from inclusion as triads in most theory books. They are included here due to their three-note construction. Suspended chords can resolve to either major or minor chords so long as the major 2nd or perfect 4th degree that replaces the 3rd of the chord fits within the key signature at hand.

Suspended 4th chords occur diatonically at degrees I, II, III, V and VI of the major scale. Suspended 2nd chords can be generated from the I, II, IV, V and VI degrees.

Suspended 2nd and 4th chords can be viewed as inversions of each other from different root notes. For Example, Asus4 (A, D, E) shares the same notes as Dsus2 (D, E, A). Only one set of speed shapes is required as a result, applied according to the chord at hand. In another example of this connecting point of view, an Asus2 chord (A, B, E) contains the same notes as an Esus4 chord (E, A, B).

Asus4 across the fretboard (same notes as Dsus2)

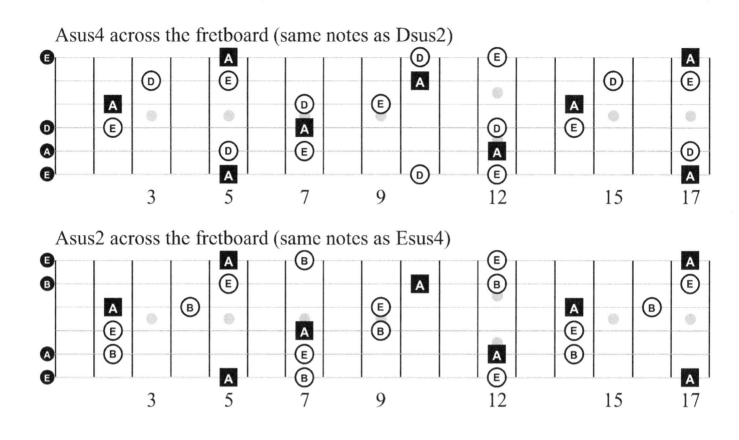

Asus2 across the fretboard (same notes as Esus4)

Using major triad speed shapes as a guide, the suspended fourth can be configured as follows:

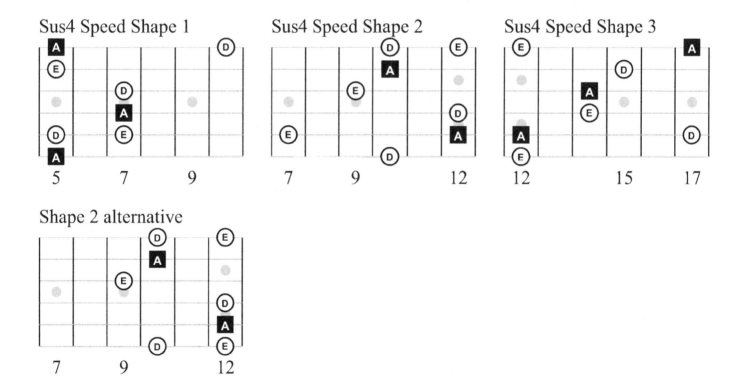

Sus4 Speed Shape 1

Sus4 Speed Shape 2

Sus4 Speed Shape 3

Shape 2 alternative

Example 8s:

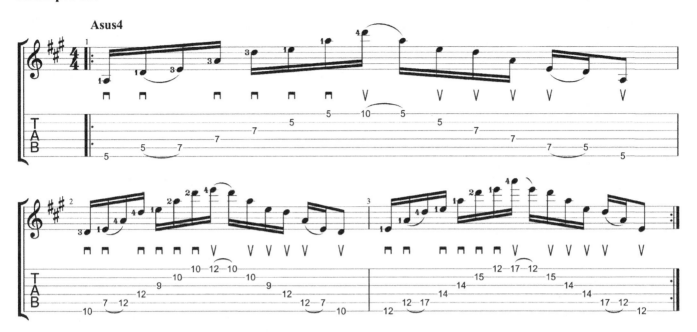

Playing Asus2 using the same shapes is merely a matter of starting with the second shape from an A root note and continuing the patterns in ascending order accordingly. Since the Speed Shape 2 from Example 8u is quite the stretch when moved down five frets, the second note has been sourced from the low E string.

Example 8t:

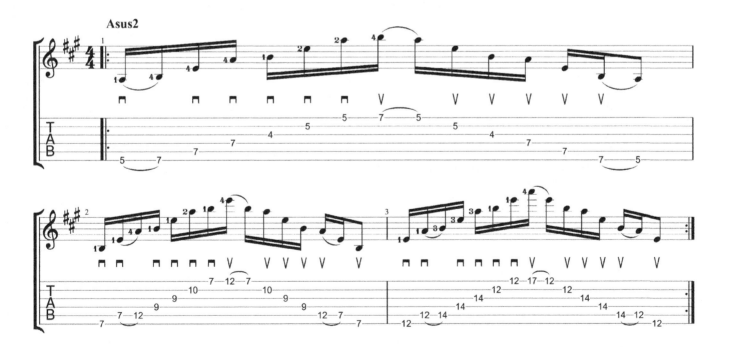

Speed Shape Monster Lick

The last example for this section combines major, augmented, minor and suspended chords in one lick that will test your fluency and ability to switch triads and inversions on the fly.

Example 8u:

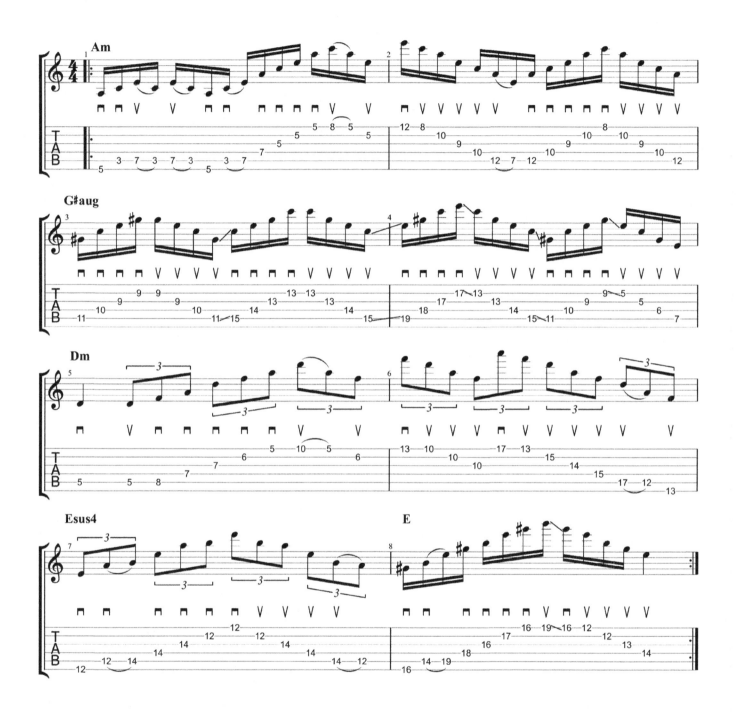

When you can play the above example, there's no excuse not to create your own material based on any chord progression you know or borrow from existing compositions. You have the chops. You have the layouts. It's time to make music!

Goal-setting for Fretboard Coverage

When arriving at the end of an ambitious chapter such as this, it can feel like an arduous task to refine all the information into a routine for development.

Obviously, practise the examples in the chapter, choosing a few at a time without mentally overloading yourself within a single practice session. Since you already have the necessary sweep picking mechanics at your disposal, the area of focus for this chapter should be on memorisation and application of the various chord types and inversions.

Next, ensure that you can complete the list of tasks below. For any areas in which you continue to struggle, refer to the relevant text and examples and then take a second or third attempt at the list.

CAGED

- Play the five CAGED shapes of A Major, D Major and E Major triads from memory (or close to it).

- Play an A Major, D Major and E Major triad in each CAGED box before moving to the next.

- Create your own etude using two major triads and two minor triads from the key of A Major.

Speed Shapes

- Memorise the three speed shapes of the major and minor triads, i.e. six patterns in total.

- Alternate between major and augmented triads in each speed shape before moving to the next, i.e. Speed Shape 1 for major and augmented, Speed Shape 2 for both, and so on.

- Repeat the previous step for minor and diminished triads.

- Play each diatonic triad from the key of A Major using Speed Shape 1: A Major, B Minor, C# Minor, D Major, E Major, F# Minor, G# Diminished.

- Alternate between suspended 2nd and suspended 4th chords in each shape.

- Play each chord type from the same root note, then try the same with each inversion.

Composition

- Create your own etude using the chords A Major, B Minor, Esus4, E Major.

- Create your own etude using the chords F# Minor, F Augmented, A Major, B Major.

- Create your own etude using the chords B Minor, G# Diminished, G Major, D Major.

Chapter Nine: Fretboard Coverage – Sevenths

Triads are great for outlining progressions and, in styles like neo-classical rock, are a stylistic staple of sweep picking repertoire. By contrast, in jazz and particularly in its electrified sub-genre fusion, the simplicity of triads can sound a little ordinary, or perhaps a missed opportunity to expand tonalities.

Arpeggiating beyond triads is a valuable device for adding colour to modal improvisation, outlining upper extensions of basic chords and increasing your palette of sweep picking sounds. This chapter focuses on the addition of the VII degree above the triads discussed in Chapter Eight using CAGED forms and speed shapes. With the addition of a chord tone comes an extra speed shape for seventh chords.

Chords covered in this section include major seventh, dominant seventh, minor seventh, half-diminished, and diminished seventh. Delving into these chords in the prescribed order provides a smooth transition with only one chord tone changing at a time.

Major Seventh Arpeggios - 1, 3, 5, 7

Major seventh chords occur at the I and IV degrees of major scale harmony and contain four notes, the last of which is a major 7th above the root note, or a major 3rd above the 5th.

Amaj7 across the fretboard

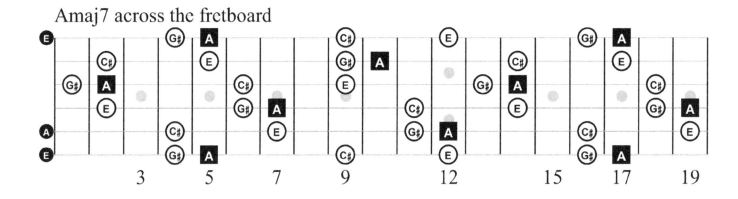

In the CAGED patterns, the most significant hurdles to achieving speed are the locations and proximity of the notes E, G#, A and C# (in the key of A). These clusters of notes can necessitate fingerings that are not always condusive to flow and agility, especially when relying on swift third and fourth finger switching.

Amaj7 (E shape)   Amaj7 (D shape)   Amaj7 (C shape)

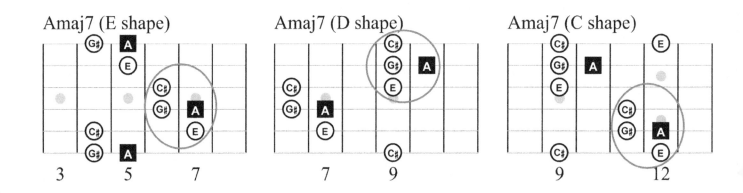

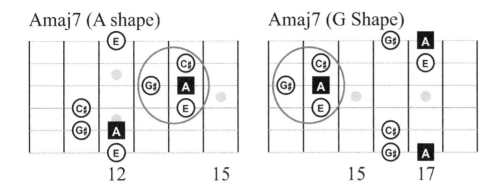

Amaj7 (A shape)

Amaj7 (G Shape)

Speed Shapes for Major Seventh

With the aim of circumventing the technical bottlenecks just described, different portions of the CAGED shapes can be hybridised and optimised for comfort and speed.

Major 7th Speed Shape 1 uses the *root position* and is a hybrid of the CAGED shapes of E and D. It stays in one region of the fretboard, whereas the remaining three shapes contain position slides from the first occurrence of the 7th of the chord up to the next root note.

Speed Shapes 2, 3 and 4 begin on the 3rd, 5th and 7th tones of the chord. Speed Shape 4 is my favourite and is, in my experience, the fastest pattern too, with slurs and slides all positioned in such a way as to create a very slippery-sounding arpeggio.

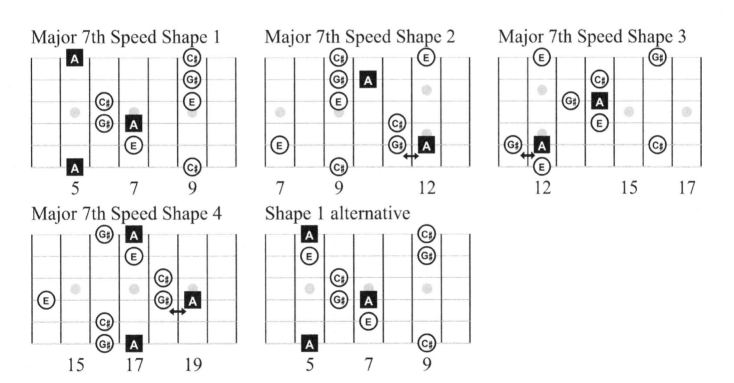

Major 7th Speed Shape 1

Major 7th Speed Shape 2

Major 7th Speed Shape 3

Major 7th Speed Shape 4

Shape 1 alternative

Some guitarists prefer to avoid using the fourth finger for two notes in a row in the root position shape, so an alternative has been provided. Keep in mind that, as a result, the fingering requirements will change according to how much of the shape you decide to use.

Example 9a moves up and down the first octave of the arpeggio before beginning the complete ascent in the 3rd beat of bar one. In bars three and four, the same notes are played using the alternative pattern, requiring different fingerings during the 4th beat of bar three and the 2nd beat of bar four.

Example 9a:

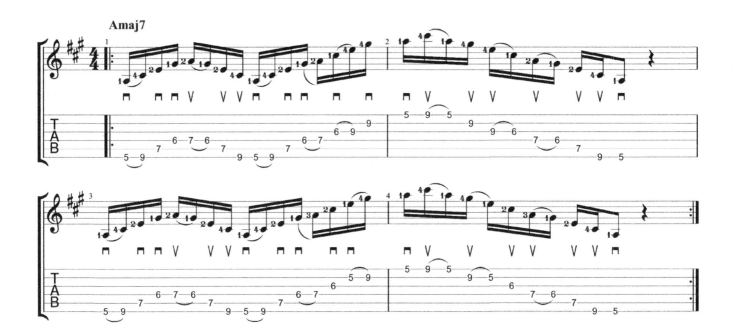

Speed Shape 2 bridges the D and C shapes of CAGED. The inclusion of both a hammer-on and legato slide on the A string gives this lick a running start.

For best results, avoid barring the index finger across the G, B and high E strings at the 9th fret. Instead, roll across the G and B strings in the ascent and vice versa in the descent, using a separate fretting of the index finger on the high E string.

Example 9b:

Once again using a position slide from the first G# note to the A note above it, Speed Shape 3 fuses together notes from the A shape and the next G shape of the CAGED system. While the G# note on the 11th fret of the A string could instead be played on the 16th fret of the low E string, starting the chosen version with two downstrokes gives it more of an authentic sweep picking sound.

Example 9c:

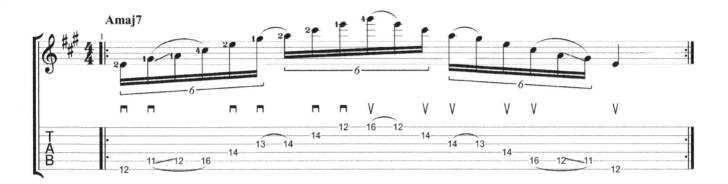

From the diagram of Speed Shape 4, you could be forgiven for assuming that this shape might be the hardest to navigate, but it is comprised of two distinct, easy-to-remember shapes.

To build it, navigate the first five notes which start and finished on the 7th of the chord (G#). With a slide into the 19th fret of the D string, the second part of the pattern is fretted with a very straightforward 4-3-2-1 fingering, with an extra A root note on the 17th fret of the high E string.

For some extra dynamic range, all the notes on the D string can be picked, but for the slippery effect, pick once in either direction and use the suggested execution.

Example 9d:

Dominant Seventh Arpeggios - 1, 3, 5, b7

Occurring on degree V of major, harmonic minor, and melodic minor scale harmony, the dominant seventh chord has a major quality with a minor or flatted 7th. In functional harmony, the 7th of the dominant chord will often resolve down one semitone to the 3rd of the tonic chord. Dominant chords are also extremely popular in modal vamps.

Mapping the dominant seventh chord can be done by lowering the 7th in the major seventh examples by one semitone. A dominant seventh chord with a root note of A has the chord symbol A7.

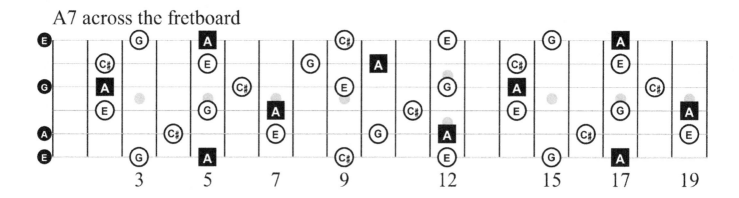

The locations of chord tones in the five CAGED scale patterns arguably produces more finger-friendly arpeggio layouts than in the major seventh chord. Even the somewhat twisted-looking geometry of the D and A shapes of an A7 chord can be navigated nicely with strategic fingering.

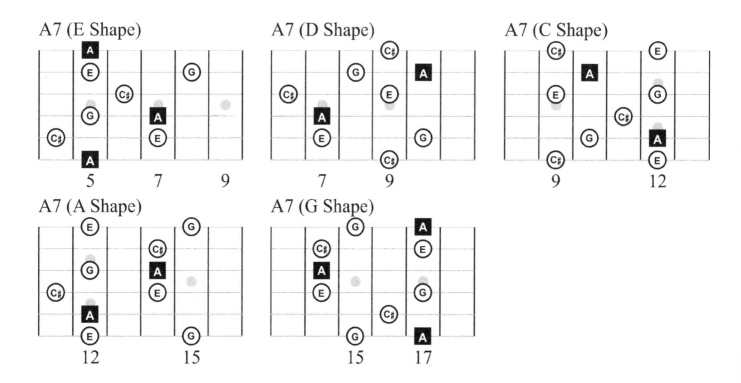

174

Examples 9e to 9i run through each of the CAGED shapes of A7 using my suggested fingerings and pick strokes. Be forewarned that my fingerings are tailored for moderate to high speeds and may, as such, be different from what your classical guitar teacher told you was *the proper way*. If you find a better way for you that passes the speed test, be my guest!

Example 9e:

Example 9f:

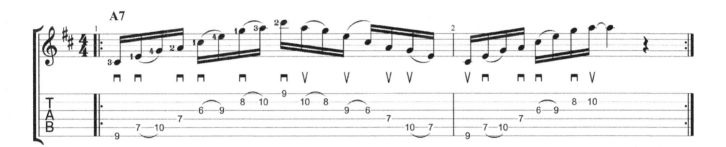

Example 9g:

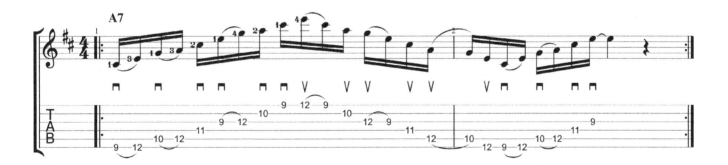

Example 9h:

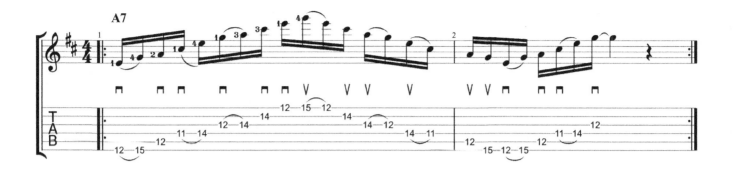

Example 9i:

Speed Shapes for Dominant Seventh

The four speed shapes for dominant 7th arpeggios follow the blueprint of one positional pattern, and three sliding patterns.

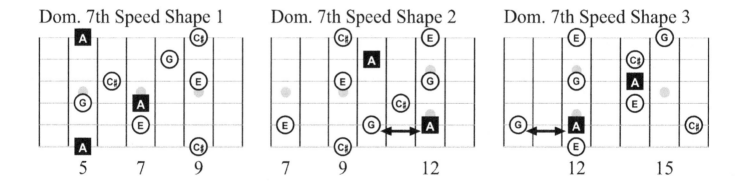

Dom. 7th Speed Shape 4

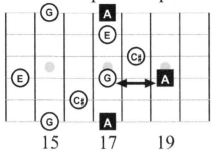

The root position pattern, which once again fuses the E and D shapes of the CAGED system, is more accessible than its major seventh counterpart since it does not require any rolling of the fourth finger between the G and B strings.

Example 9j:

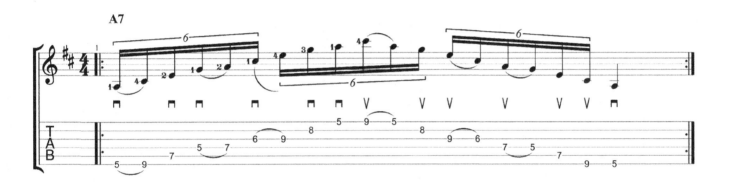

Speed Shape 2 for A7 has just one geometric difference to the C Shape of the CAGED system. By placing the lowest E note of the shape on the A string instead of the low E string, the index finger takes care of the note in place of the fourth finger. Diverging from the corresponding Amaj7 layout, the b7 (G) within the higher octave is on the G string instead of the B string, keeping most of the shape within a three-fret span.

Example 9k:

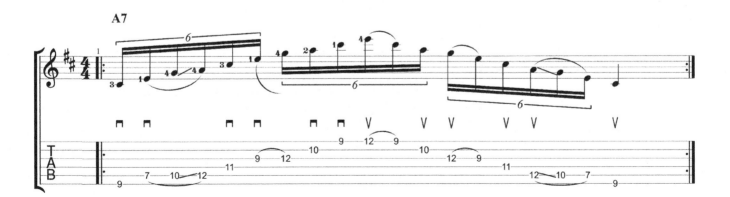

Speed Shape 3 occupies the 12th position, apart from the slide from G to A on the A string which is carried out with the index finger. I think you'll agree that this produces a cleaner fingering option than the CAGED equivalent in Example 9h.

Example 9l:

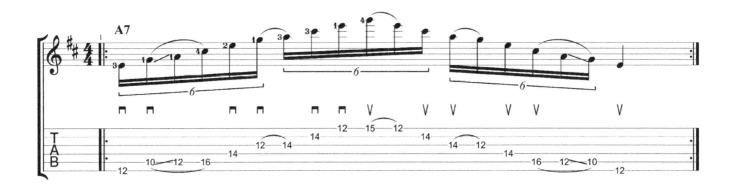

The slur and slide fun of Speed Shape 4 continues with dominant seventh arpeggios in Example 9m. Once again, be reminded that for extra grit, all notes on the D string can be picked down, up, down in the ascent and *up, down, up* in the descent.

Example 9m:

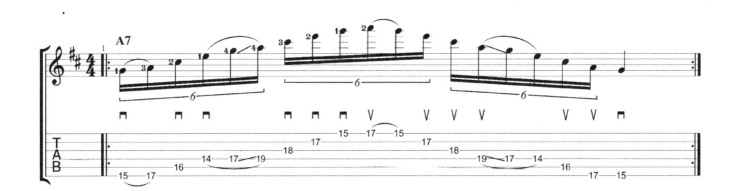

Minor Seventh Arpeggios - 1, b3, 5, b7

Found at the II, III, and VI degrees of major scale harmony, minor seventh chords consist of minor 3rd intervals between the root and 3rd and between the 5th and 7th, in addition to perfect 5th intervals between the root and 5th and between the 3rd and 7th. The first inversion of the minor seventh chord consists of the same notes as a major 6th chord. For example, an Am7 chord (A, C, E, G) contains the same notes as a C6 chord (C, E, G, A).

Am7 across the fretboard

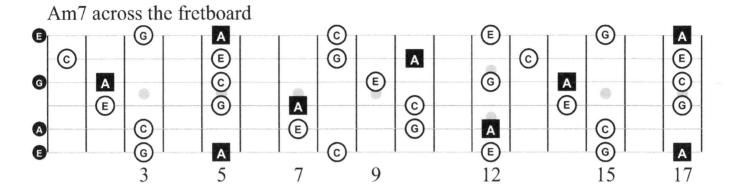

Minor seventh arpeggios are only one note short of a minor pentatonic scale, so there's every chance you'll find the CAGED minor seventh shapes familiar if you've already memorised the five pentatonic boxes.

Matching up each note to its logical finger within a four-fret span is simple for the E and A shapes of CAGED. For the remaining three configurations, the minimal use of the index finger is not particularly indicative of how most of us play in improvisation. For that reason, Examples 9n, 9o and 9p offer alternative fingerings that work for me, along with my reasoning for each deviation from the norm.

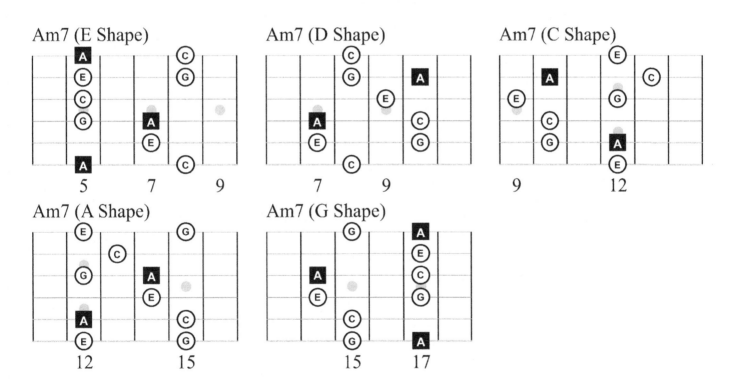

For the D-shaped Am7 arpeggio of Example 9o, removing the cumbersome reliance upon the second and fourth fingers on the B and high E strings aligns the upper octave with the way an isolated C6 arpeggio would be played from the C note of the D string up to the C note of the high E string.

Example 9n:

The C shape of Am7 can be viewed as three string pairs, executed using the most logical finger for each two-string unit.

Example 9o:

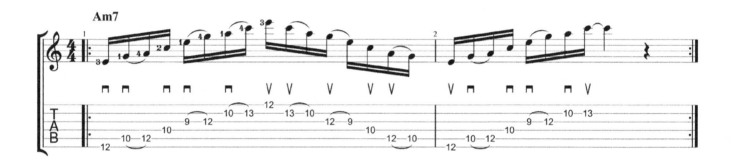

For the G shape of an Am7 chord, I find that fretting the G notes on both E strings with the index finger instead of the second finger can speed things up, especially in the process of turning around for repeats. When using this pattern in a higher octave or key such as this example, the third finger can also replace the fourth finger throughout to avoid cramped fingerings.

Example 9p:

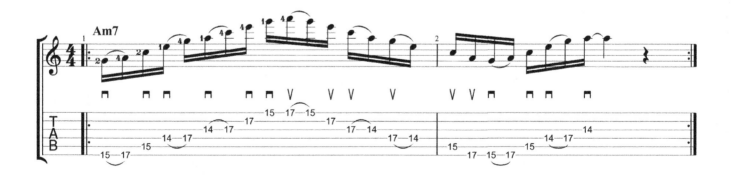

Speed Shapes for Minor Seventh

With the work you have already completed on the speed shapes of the major seventh and dominant seventh arpeggios, you should now be quite familiar with the picking hand mechanics of the four patterns, allowing focus on the fretting hand modifications for each new chord that comes along.

The speed shapes of minor 7th chords flatten the 3rd of each dominant seventh shape used previously.

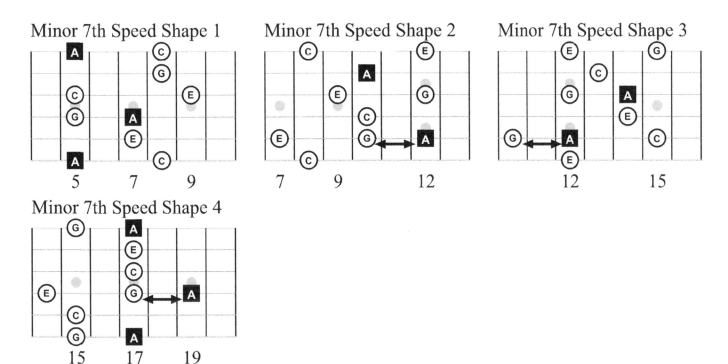

For my fingering suggestions, study Examples 9q to 9t.

Example 9q:

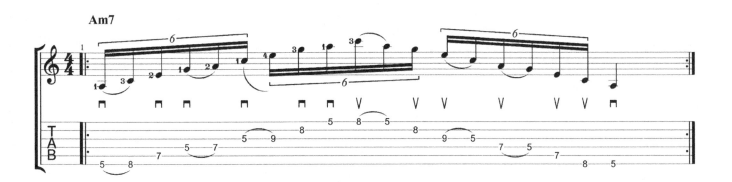

181

Example 9r:

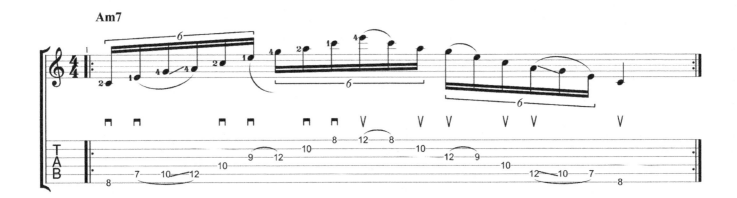

Example 9s:

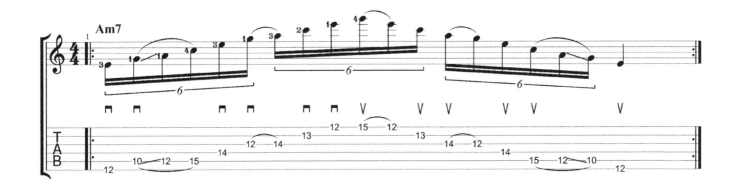

Example 9t:

Half-diminished Arpeggios – 1, b3, b5, b7

The minor seventh (flat five) or *half-diminished* chord occurs in the harmonised major scale (VII), harmonic minor scale (VII) and melodic minor (VI and VII) scales. This chord differs from a minor seventh chord by way of its diminished 5th and is distinct from a *diminished seventh* chord by its b7 (instead of the bb7 of the diminished seventh).

Despite not getting used anywhere near as often as major, dominant and minor seventh arpeggios, these CAGED Am7b5 shapes are user-friendly in both layout and picking mechanics.

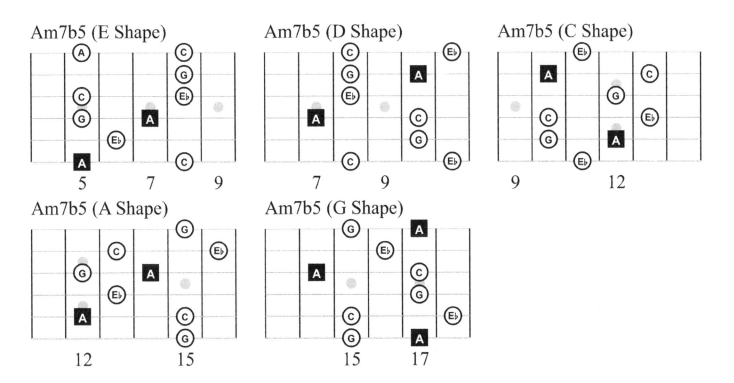

If any of the Am7b5 shapes give you the sense that elements of the C Minor and A Minor triads are being combined, that is because Am7b5 contains the same notes as C Minor Sixth (Cm6).

Example 9u combines the minor seventh flat five CAGED shapes into a single exercise, alternating between ascending and descending.

Example 9u:

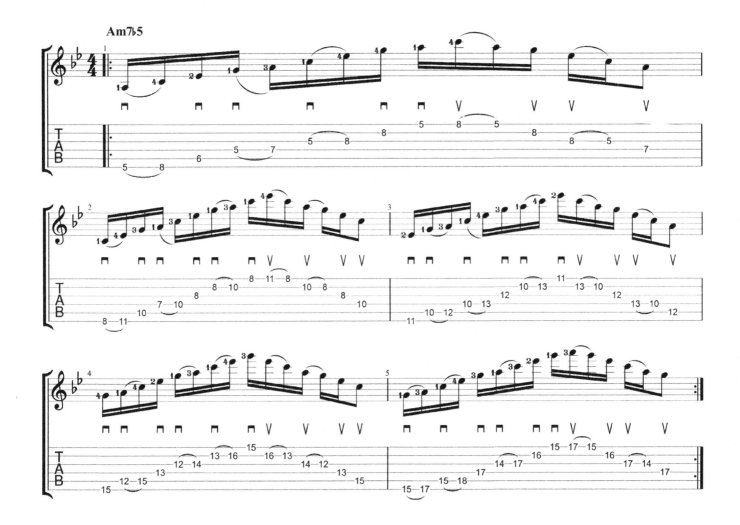

Speed Shapes for Half-Diminished

A couple of interesting things become apparent when altering the minor seventh speed shapes to suit half-diminished arpeggios.

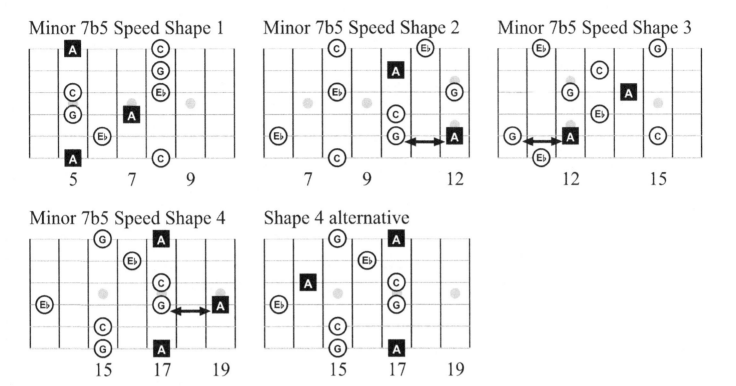

Firstly, Speed Shape 1 generates exactly the same shape as the CAGED system, so you already have one shape ready to go.

Secondly, Speed Shape 4 can be a less viable option for this chord type, depending on the key, due to the whole tone stretch between the 3rd and 4th fingers moving from the D string to the G string.

To circumvent any discomfort, an alternative shape has been provided as another option. This variation works in any position and is a very speed-friendly pattern.

Example 9v:

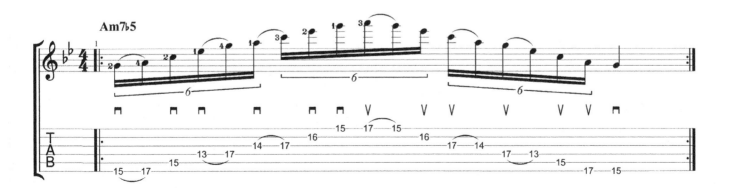

That leaves two patterns left to explore. Both of the remaining shapes adapt well to flattening the 5th of the minor seventh speed shapes. The fingering alterations outlined in Example 9w have little effect on the speed and flow of these inversions.

Example 9w:

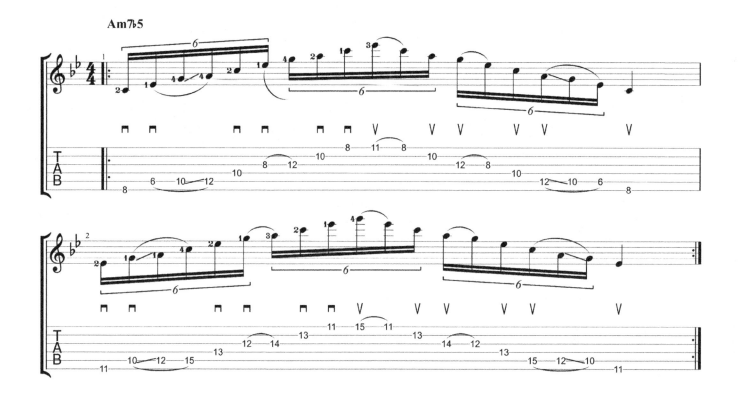

Diminished Seventh Arpeggios – 1, b3, b5, bb7

As covered in my book *Neoclassical Speed Strategies for Guitar*, diminished seventh arpeggios are formed by stacking consecutive minor 3rd intervals. There are also two diminished 5th intervals between the root and 5th, and between the 3rd and 7th of the chord.

Because of the repeated minor 3rd intervals, each inversion of the diminished seventh chord is a new chord in itself. Geometrically, this keeps things very simple since we can choose our favourite shapes and move them up and down in multiples of three frets to cover the fretboard. Even when looking at the entire fretboard of diminished seventh intervals, it's easy to visualise the repeats of any given pattern.

Adim7 across the fretboard

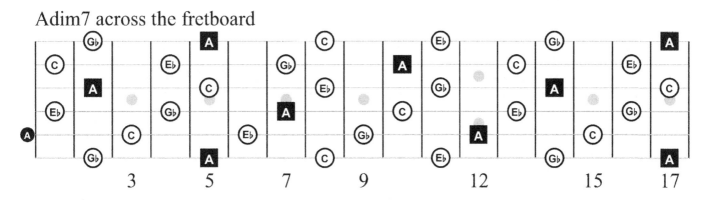

Using the layout of the previous root position patterns, a diminished seventh arpeggio like the following can be moved up and down in accordance with the minor 3rd spacing across the fretboard.

Adim7 (E Shape)

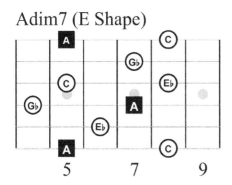

Due to the inversion attributes of diminished 7th chords, the Adim7 examples in this chapter can be used in conjunction with the scales of Bb Harmonic Minor, Db Harmonic Minor, E Harmonic Minor and G Harmonic Minor as a substitute for the V chord in any of those keys.

Other options avail themselves with some exploration of the fretboard, and since the chord tones are so evenly spread across the neck, moving between two specific notes can be like a *Choose Your Own Adventure* book.

Example 9x demonstrates just three ways of moving between the A note on the 5th fret of the low E string and the C note on the 8th fret of the high E string.

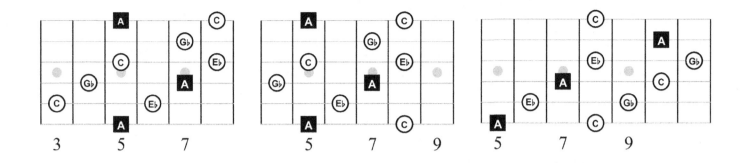

Example 9x:

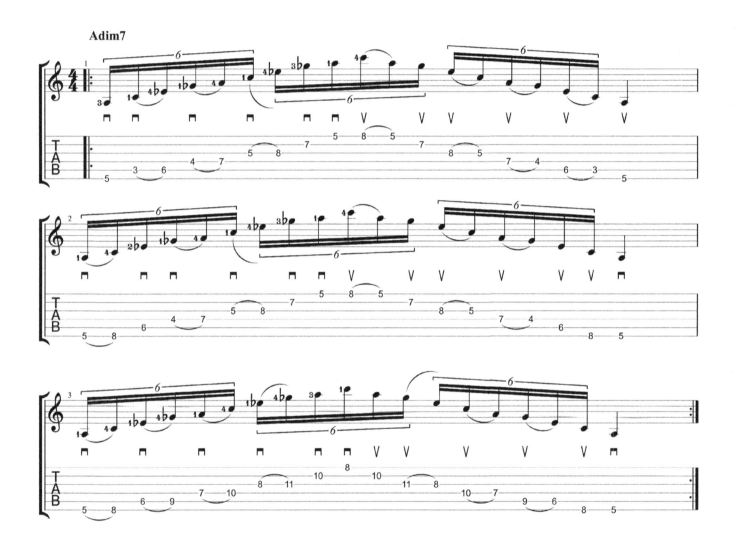

Once you've decided upon your favourite pattern, moving through inversions is done by shifting up and down in minor 3rd leaps. Example 9y demonstrates these jumps using various numbers of strings within the same movable shape.

188

Example 9y:

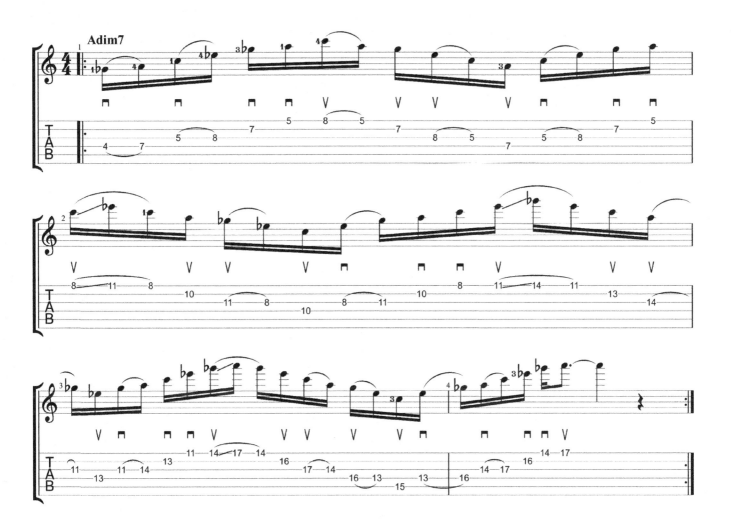

How to Practise Chapter Nine

Notwithstanding the CAGED-based overview of each chord type, the aim of this chapter has been to arm you with speed shapes that have more commonalities than differences. The order of the arpeggios presented has been quite deliberate in the way that each chord type differs from the one before it, and the one after it, by one note each time.

To make the most of the step-by-step approach of modulating from major seventh arpeggios through to diminished arpeggios, I suggest that your practice consists of two initial stages for this material.

1. Practise each arpeggio using its four speed shapes.

2. Practice each speed shape using every chord type before moving to the next shape.

Once you have committed these shapes to memory and have developed the facility to change chord types and inversions at will, the application should progress via the etudes in Chapter Ten.

Chapter Ten: Seventh Arpeggio Etudes

This chapter presents six etudes that explore seventh arpeggios, each with a slightly different objective and style of delivery. On the accompanying audio, each etude is played at full speed with the backing track, then at a slower speed unaccompanied.

The first etude has a prog rock feel and is designed to help you compare different arpeggios from the same root note with the modulation from Gmaj7 to Gm7 and again from Fmaj7 to Fm7.

Example 10a:

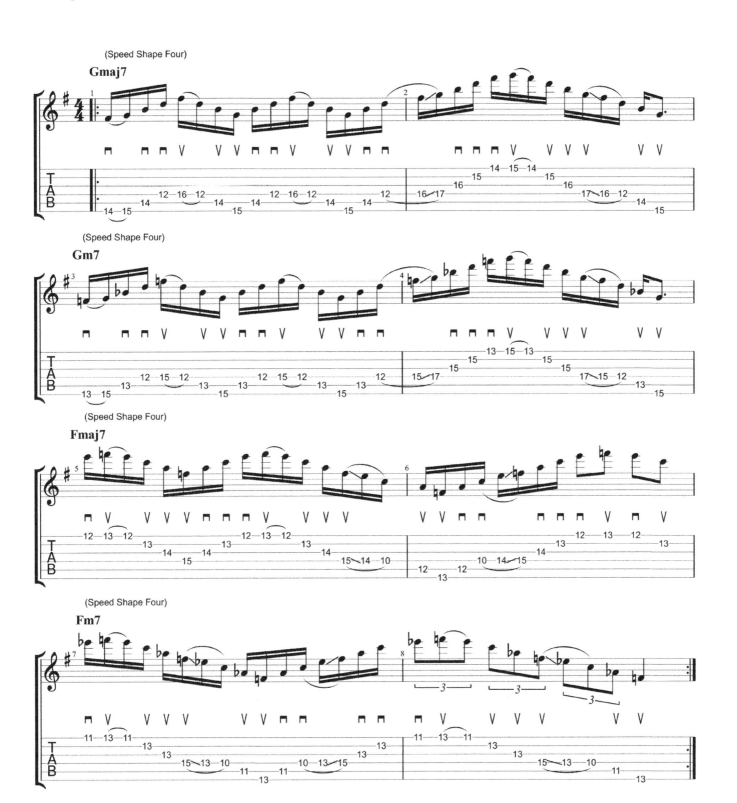

191

Example 10b is in 12/8 time and is written in the style of neoclassical rock players like Vinnie Moore. Using a moving chord progression diatonic to B Minor, this etude uses the same chord sequence twice, but with different inversions for the Gmaj7, Em7 and Bm7 arpeggios each time. The C#dim7 arpeggio in bar four uses an ascending position shift, but is contrasted in bar eight with a descending pattern that works its way down to the low E string.

Example 10b:

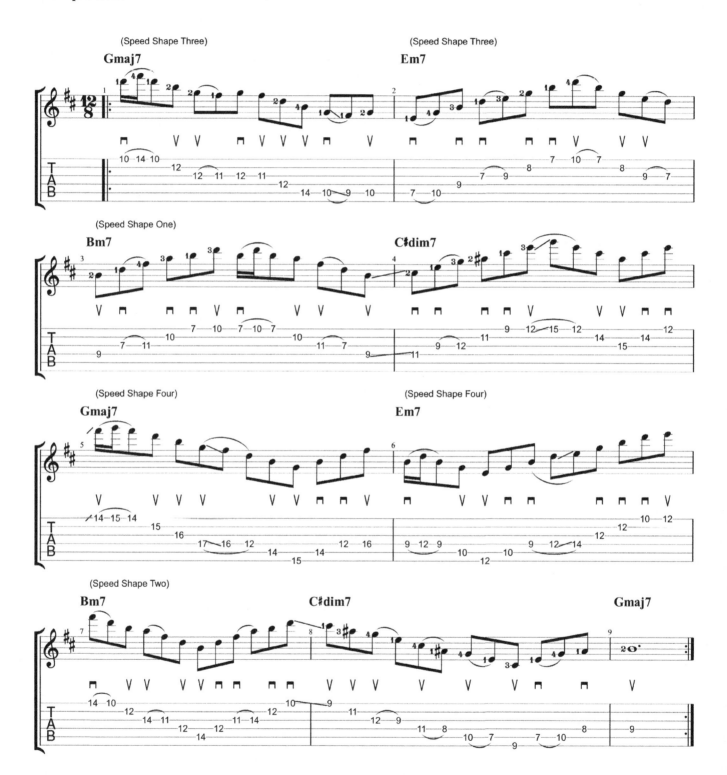

Written with a country feel in mind and comprised solely of dominant seventh chords, the third etude in this chapter will have you switching arpeggios within a smaller range of fretboard space. Primarily occupying the 4th and 5th positions, the chords move through a I, IV, V progression for the first six bars. The seventh and eighth bars feature a turnaround, and it's only at this point that the etude moves into different fretboard positions.

In anticipation of the first chord change from A7 to D7, the last note of bar two is a C natural note. Not only does this make fretting easier for the index finger through the change, it also allows smooth modulation between the tonalities of the two chords.

Example 10c:

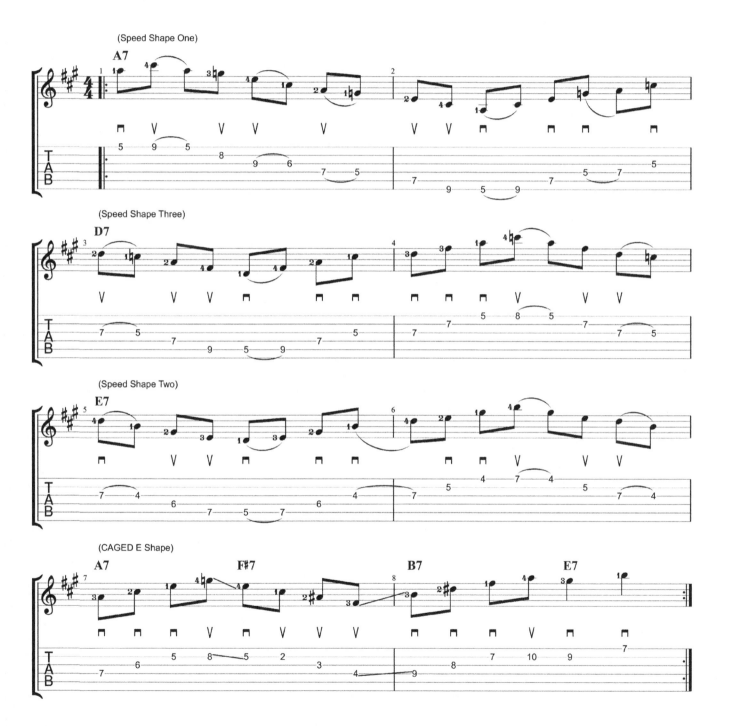

Example 10d uses the second speed shapes of Am7 and C7, the fourth speed shape of Fmaj7 and the third speed shape of Fm7. Despite the changing fingering forms, the etude uses the same melodic sequence for descending and ascending within each arpeggio, breaking early in the fourth bar to allow a brief respite before the repeat. Some common tones connect the arpeggios, with all four chords containing a C note, and three of the chords containing an E (which becomes Eb in bar four).

Example 10d:

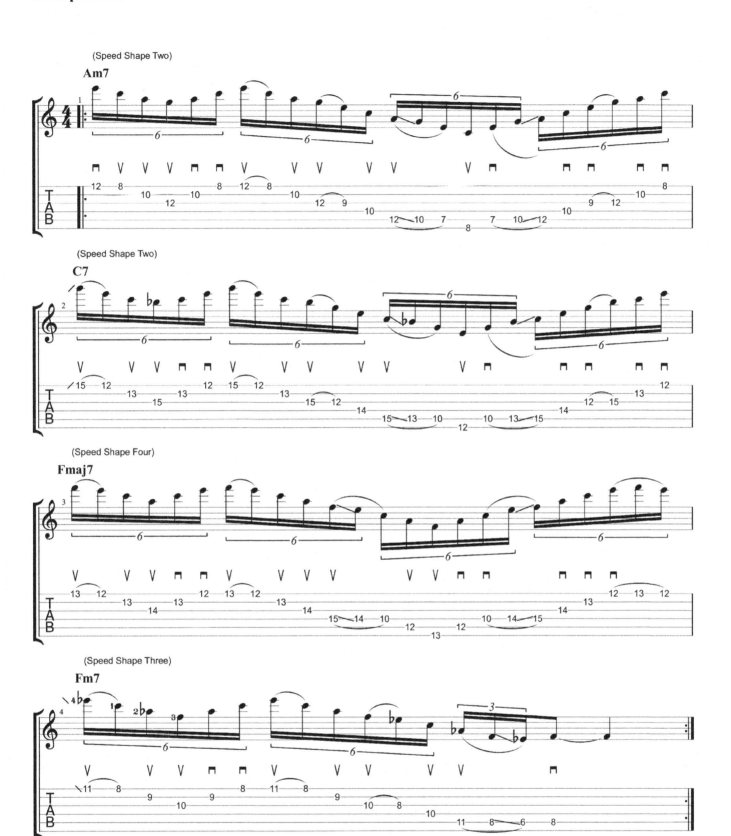

195

Introducing some syncopation to sweep picking lines allows us to break free of the notion that sweeping needs to be about a barrage of notes. Rests can augment a sense of clever phrasing within your lines. The next etude in B Minor has a funk-fusion vibe with even a little Latin influence, and rests in each bar.

Where rests occur, you should aim for silence in those spaces rather than letting the previous notes hang over. To punctuate the rests, try adding a little extra oomph to the preceding picked note in each instance.

Example 10e:

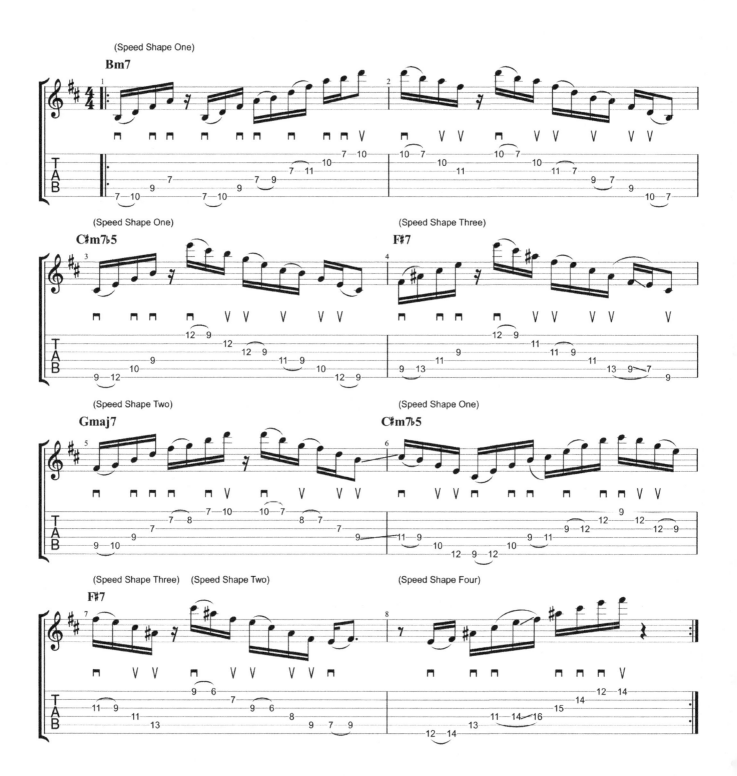

The final etude has a prog-rock feel in 5/4 time. Using the III and IV chords from the key of F Major, this example uses all four speed shapes for each arpeggio. In bar one, Speed Shape 4 of Am7 connects to the first pattern at the high E string mid-way through the 3rd beat. At the base of the latter pattern, a position shift up to Speed Shape 2 occurs at the low E string. This zig-zag approach happens one more time to the final Am7 speed shape on the 3rd beat of bar two before the entire sequence repeats within the inversions of the Bbmaj7 chord in bars three and four.

Take note of the altered fingering suggestions for the inversion transitions in bars one and three.

Example 10f:

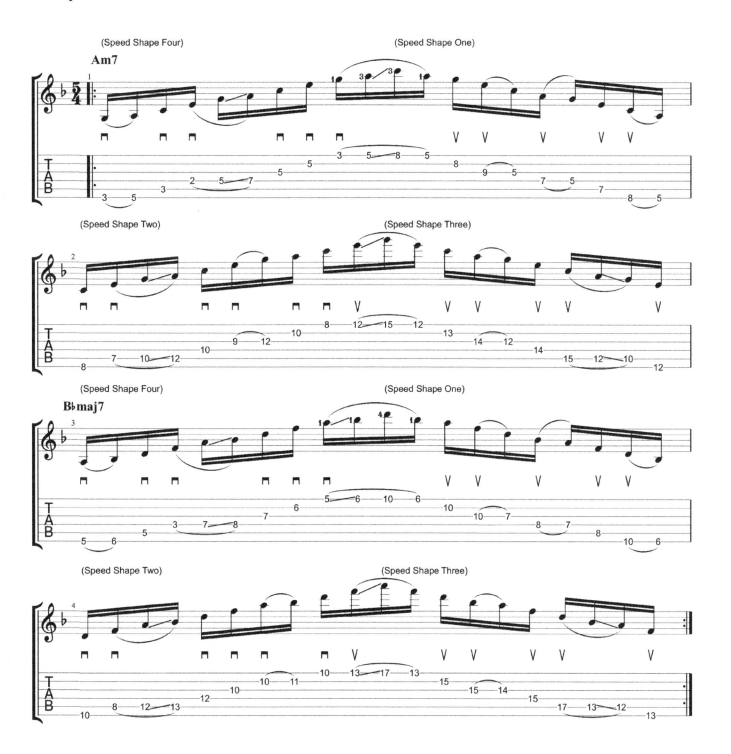

Long Term Practice Goals

Instead of rehashing the essentials of practice that have been cited in previous chapters, this *How to Practise* section contains a checklist of *essential attributes* for your performance of the examples provided within. You're making real music with sweep picking now, so it's important to aim high with your delivery, be highly self-aware, and honest with yourself about any areas of weakness.

When performing the etudes of this chapter, and indeed all drills and etudes in the book, can you:

• Ascend and descend with equal facility?

• Play in time when combining picked notes and slurs?

• Control the strings in use while silencing the others?

• Change positions without affecting the tempo?

• Apply dynamic effects like picking accents and muted notes at will?

• Play through examples at a constant tempo with a metronome or drum beat?

• Find and track your top clean tempo for future comparison?

If you answered, *"Totally, Chris dude. What else have you got for me?"* then you are becoming the sweep picker I know you can be! If not, keep working. You will get there. By focusing your practice on the end game, you have a gauge by which to judge your progress. Check the above list from time to time to remind yourself what you're working towards.

Conclusion of Book One

As you might have gathered through my books, I'm a big believer in strategy. Defined in the Oxford dictionary as *a plan of action designed to achieve a long-term or overall aim*, it almost doesn't matter what your approach is, so long as you have one and it serves you. Strategy is what turns aimless into purposeful. It's the plan that kicks into action when you need it.

Besides the biomechanical, musical, geometric and theoretical information presented in this book, my biggest hope for *Sweep Picking Speed Strategies for Guitar* is that it imbues you with the confidence to break down any aspect of guitar performance in a solutions-oriented manner.

What are my options?

Which one works best for me?

How can I take the optimal solution and use it to create a hundred new ideas?

These are the questions to ask yourself with any concept.

While it's important to me as an educator that the material in this book resonates with you and inspires your arpeggio execution systems, it's also okay to disagree with me! Do you like to pick notes that I hammered on? Do you wish to use outside picking where I opted for inside picking? Examine the reasoning and put it into practice. If it works best for you, then it's the right way for you.

However carefully you align with or diverge from the strategies in this book, the key is to know what you like, why you prefer it, and to be consistent in your application. That way, *your* system emerges, serving your aims and personalising a well-considered approach to your own playing.

It's been an absolute pleasure to present this material to you, and I hope you'll join me for the continuation of this subject in the next volume!

What to Expect from Book Two

The next book of speed strategies for arpeggios will venture into extended chord colours and how to use them to imply more intricate harmony. You will also be guided through seamlessly integrating scales and arpeggios, sequencing, additional techniques beyond sweep picking, and personalising your arpeggio vocabulary.

There will be an abundance of hands-on practical work to apply to real music, so I look forward to sharing that content with you!

Chris Brooks

LEGATO**GUITAR**
TECHNIQUE**MASTERY**

Legato Technique Speed Mechanics, Licks & Sequences For Guitar

CHRIS**BROOKS**

FUNDAMENTAL**CHANGES**

Introduction

Legato means different things to different people. According to the dictionary, legato means *bound* or *tied together*. To many musicians, it means playing *smooth* lines without a strong attack or space between notes.

To guitarists, legato is about playing those liquid lines with hammer-ons and pull-offs – the kind that recall the awe-inspiring playing of masters like Allan Holdsworth, Joe Satriani, Brett Garsed, Greg Howe and many more.

Licks are just one part of being a great legato player, however, so I wanted to create a method that delves deeply into the fretting hand mechanics, tonal control, fretboard approaches and developmental tools that can help any player create legato lines.

As you study the chapters of this book, you'll acquire a 360-degree view of playing in the legato style. The strategies contained within will most certainly have a flow-on effect in other areas of your playing, including melodic choices, musical devices, noise control and guitar tone.

Beginners can use this book to develop the essential skills required to execute legato passages. Intermediate players can advance their chops and troubleshoot existing issues they've encountered so far. Advanced players can add to their current arsenal with an array of lines from diatonic to chromatic and experiment with various fretboard strategies for new lick creation.

I hope that your study of the book will be as smooth as the licks you will create by the end of it!

Chris Brooks

Get the Audio and Video

The audio and video files for this book are available to download for free from **www.fundamental-changes. com.** The link is in the top right-hand corner. Simply select this book title from the drop-down menu and follow the instructions to get the audio.

We recommend that you download the files directly to your computer, not to your tablet, and extract them there before adding them to your media library. You can then put them on your tablet, iPod or burn them to CD. On the download page, there is a help PDF, and we also provide technical support via the contact form.

For over 350 Free Guitar Lessons with Videos Check out:

www.fundamental-changes.com

Twitter: **@guitar_joseph**

Over 10,000 fans on Facebook: **FundamentalChangesInGuitar**

Instagram: **FundamentalChanges**

Bonus videos are available at:

https://www.fundamental-changes.com/legato-guitar-technique-mastery-videos/

Or scan the QR code below with your smartphone:

Setting Up Your Tone

Before you play through the book, let's talk about pickups, pedals and amps to help you get the right tone for the right purpose.

Compression and sustain are important attributes for a legato-friendly tone on electric guitar, so it's essential to consider each component of your signal path to ensure that your sound is smooth and enables the techniques covered in the book.

Compression affects the dynamic range of a sound source, bringing dynamic peaks down in output and weaker sounds up to more regulated levels. Besides producing a more even signal saturation, compression can determine the average output of a signal. This is handy for legato playing to enable pick strokes, hammer-ons, pull-offs and slides to work in a single lick without seeming like there are stronger and weaker players on the field.

A typical signal chain for legato players includes humbucker pickups and a boost pedal running into a gain source like another pedal, or an overdriven amp. The outputs and gain settings for each component will differ depending on each player's requirements.

A bridge humbucker is very commonly used in legato for its output and tone, but a single-coil pickup with at least a moderate output and a sweet midrange EQ tone can sound great too. If you want the humbucker benefits in a single-coil space, there are lots of pickup replacement options like the Seymour Duncan *Hot Rails* and *JB Junior* as well as the DiMarzio *Fast Track* series.

From the guitar, it's important to compress the output before your signal hits the main gain stage. Running a boost pedal gives your amp a more regulated sound to amplify. Boost pedals can come in the form of *clean boosts*, which increase the output of the guitar across the board, *drive boosts* which add gain and affect tonal colour, and *compression pedals* which flatten the dynamics without changing the tone. An example of each includes the TC Electronic *Spark Boost* for a clean boost, Ibanez's famous *Tube Screamer* for drive boost and colour, and the BOSS *Compression/Sustainer* for clean compression.

When you've chosen a boost pedal, place it in between your guitar and amp but run it in bypass. Next, try setting up a drive tone on your amp. If you run a clean amp with a distortion pedal instead of a gain channel on your amp, engage it now. The amount of distortion you run at your main gain stage will depend on your genre and tastes, but the kind of tone you might use for a crunch rhythm is a good starting point.

Try some hammer-ons and pull-offs with your amp sound, then engage your front boost pedal for comparison. You should find a nice level of saturation present that enables legato without overly aggressive finger work. Tweak the drive, tone and output levels on your boost pedal until you find a tone that sounds and feels right.

If you feel that the tone is too saturated, or not saturated enough, spend a little more time getting the balance right between your boost pedal and primary gain source.

The audio for this book was recorded on a Kemper Profiling Amp using a Plexi amp sound (The 1987x profile from *The Amp Factory*) with a TS boost in front. I run the amp gain at about 60% and use the boost to add the rest of the gain and compression.

Chapter One: Biomechanics

This chapter covers the role of each hand in creating the notes for the best results in legato playing. You'll learn how to control unwanted sounds and maximise the variety of right-hand and left-hand articulation options. We'll cover,

• Fretting Arm Positioning

• Finger Orientation and Sound Control

• Picking Hand Function and Control

• String Changes and Articulation Options

By the end of the chapter, you'll understand the factors affecting your results, and be able to make some choices about how you'd like your legato approach to sound.

Fretting Arm Positioning

Optimal positioning of the fretting arm is a crucial first step in enabling your fingers to access and stretch across the fretboard. The ideal starting point involves the elbow, wrist, thumb and fingers all working together to create a good span without feeling like you need to be naturally gifted or born with big hands.

Figure 1a illustrates *ineffective* positioning. With tip of the index finger on the starting note, the rest of the index finger and the other fingers point away from higher notes along the string. The thumb is anchored gently but is resting a bit high up on the neck. Finally, the wrist is placed behind the index finger. Out of frame, the elbow usually sticks out in this position.

Figure 1a:

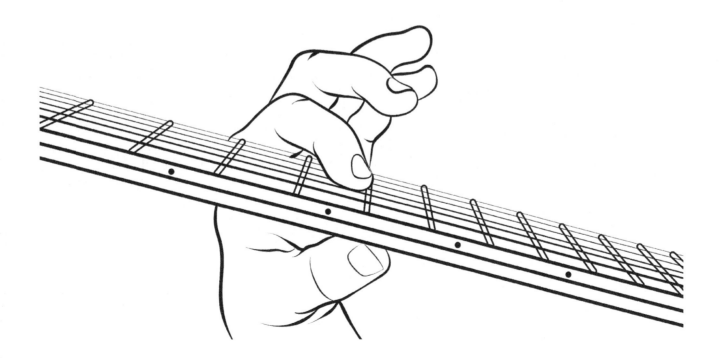

Figure 1b illustrates the result of some simple but necessary adjustments. To make these, keep using the tip of the index finger as a pivot point, but bring your elbow in towards your body. This will rotate the forearm and bring the wrist across to the other side of the planted finger. Next, place the thumb a little further up the length of the neck, and down a little on the width of it.

With the changes in effect, it should be possible to stretch from the 5th fret of the low E string to the 9th or 10th fret using the fourth finger. Even if the direction of the index finger in Figure 1a feels comfortable for the first note, you can use wrist and elbow positioning to compensate for different finger lengths as you ascend along a string.

Figure 1b:

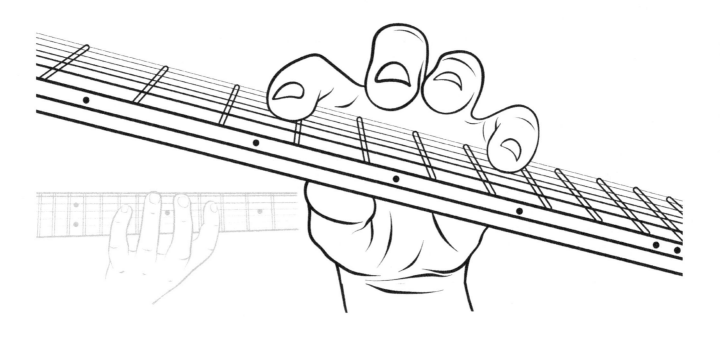

A *hammer-on* is articulated with pressure to the fretboard instead of a pick stroke. Rather than being in place before an articulation occurs, placing the fingers on the fretboard *is* the articulation. The way you set up each finger will be crucial to producing an even-sounding hammer-on each time.

Example 1a is a basic drill you can use to test your hand position. Create a pivot point with the thumb, then use the elbow and wrist to roll each finger onto the fretboard, one at a time. A standard error is to lock the wrist into a rigid position and expect finger strength to produce all the motion. On the 8th fret pull-off back to the 5th fret on both strings, avoid any drastic dragging motion that would cause you to play out of tune or with too much pressure.

Example 1a:

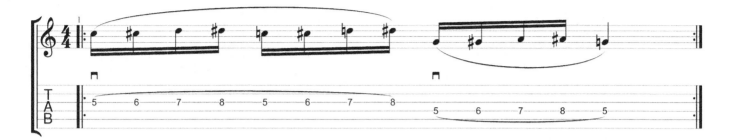

Finger Orientation and Sound Control

With the softer dynamics produced in legato playing, it's vital to preserve an acceptable signal-to-noise ratio i.e., maintaining the integrity of the notes compared to ringing strings or other noise issues.

We will explore the interplay between the left and right hands for noise control shortly, but for the fretting hand, let's look at how positioning and the combination of fingertips and pads help maintain the purity of legato notes.

Figure 1c illustrates two examples of finger orientation. On the left, a note on the D string is fretted using only the tip of the index finger. Fretting this way opens up the possibility of accidental noise from the pick, the other fingers, or even just the vibration of the instrument.

On the right-hand side of Figure 1c, the same note is fretted using a blend of the tip and pad of the index finger, controlling the strings beneath with a soft muted barre. No pressure need be applied to the other strings. A fingertip/pad blend can be incorporated into fretting with the other fingers too, but the index finger often does the lion's share of this noise control.

Figure 1c:

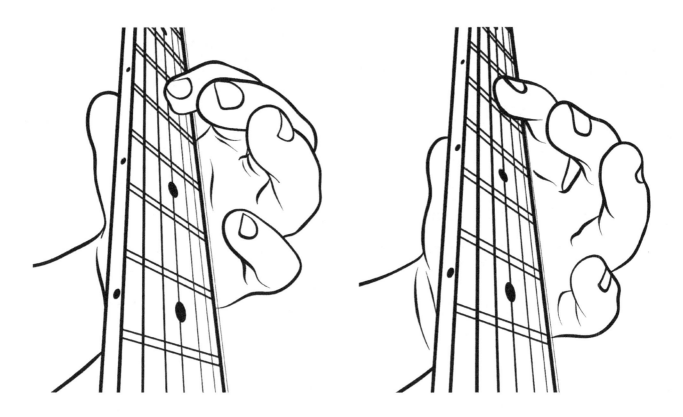

String-muting devices are commonly seen wrapped around guitar necks these days. Replacing the humble sock that many studio and home recording guitarists have used over the decades, elastic hair bands and commercially available Velcro wraps are often placed around the first fret of the fingerboard to deaden open strings or unwanted string noise.

Many people frown upon string-muting devices, they can be either a crutch or a useful tool depending on how much they are relied upon.

Picking Hand Function and Control

While the picking hand doesn't articulate each note in legato playing, it does play a big part in control, dynamic variation and trading off with the fretting hand to mute unused strings.

Picking hand functions used in this book can be divided into the following tasks:

- *Plectrum Initiation*: Many players use pick strokes at the beginning of strings to create the initial vibration that slurs will follow

- *Hybrid Picking:* Some players, especially in the Fusion genre, incorporate fingers of the picking hand into note articulation for a different attack

- *Palm Muting String Control:* When fretting higher strings, palm muting unused lower strings is a crucial noise deterrent. As licks descend to the lower strings, a balancing act occurs as the mute rolls off the strings to allow the fretting hand clean access to the lower register. The fretting hand then takes care of unused higher strings in noise control

- *Staccato Legato:* The term is an oxymoron, but in Chapter Eight we'll be using the picking hand for some muted legato to create a more extensive dynamic range within hammer-ons and pull-offs.

Example 1b will help you test the changing roles in sound control between the picking hand and the fretting hand. As you begin at the high E string, use your picking hand to mute everything from the B string to the low E string. When it's time to play the B string on the 3rd beat of bar one, roll the palm mute away from the B string and let the index finger of the fretting hand gently mute the high E string beneath.

As you descend to each new string, progressively roll away the palm mute so that by the time you play on the low E string, only the fretting hand controls the notes played, and the strings muted beneath. Avoid using barre-chord levels of pressure on the strings not being played. A light amount of contact on any otherwise noisy strings is all that is necessary.

Example 1b:

String Changes and Articulation Options

Before getting into the technique drills in Chapter Two, it's necessary to consider some options that not only require slight variations of technique but have flow-on effects on your personal tone, style and how you approach the chapters ahead.

To explore and discuss, here's a drill that will be repeated using various articulation techniques.

Example 1c:

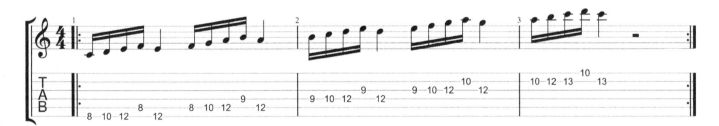

Articulation option 1 uses pick strokes to initiate the first note of each string, with hammer-ons used along each string where applicable.

Example 1d:

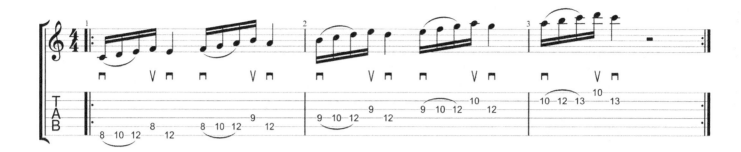

It's becoming more common in the fusion world to use picking hand fingers to replace upstrokes, so option 2 uses a finger to initiate the higher string of each pair, indicated with a *P* which you can think of as a *pluck*.

While the second finger is the closest available finger to the pick, I prefer the third finger for adjacent strings because of its similar length to the index finger. When you see the P indicator, use your preferred finger for picking.

Example 1e:

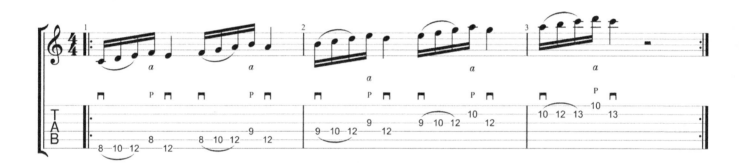

Because the fourth finger of the fretting hand has plenty of leverage, it is often unnecessary to initiate vibration on a lower string with a pick stroke. Option 3 in Example 1f uses a *hammer-on from nowhere* for each 1/4 note in the phrase. From now on, try to initiate lower strings this way unless otherwise indicated or impractical.

Example 1f:

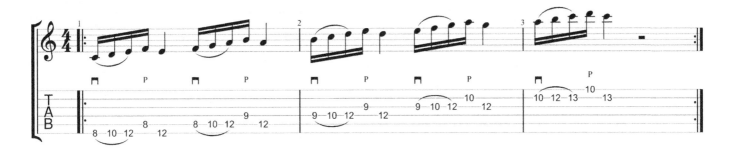

Option 4 is to use hammer-ons from nowhere for strings in either direction. A purely hammered approach requires each finger to apply enough pressure to produce notes, but not so much that each note sounds *slammed* down on the fretboard.

A legato effect should be maintained with string changes. Remember that legato means tied together, so the notes should meet up without space between them or any ugly-sounding overlap.

Example 1g:

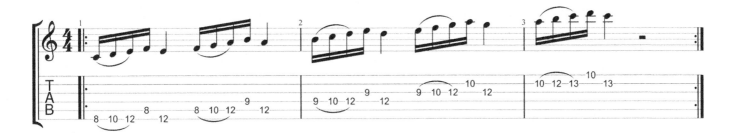

Using all hammers is excellent for strength building and also to become mindful of how little attack is required from the pick or fingers in the legato sound.

Descending Hammers

The hammer-ons from nowhere approach has applications in descending along strings too. *Re-hammering*, as it's sometimes called, is adopted by some legato players instead of overt pull-offs to replicate the evenness of Jazz horn playing and to create a consistent tone in any direction.

To apply descending hammer-ons, hammer each new note at the precise moment the finger on the previous note is lifted (not pulled). With a little development time, you might conclude that pull-offs don't need to be extreme in your playing to be effective.

Listen to the audio of Example 1h, which is performed with the same tone: firstly with pull-offs on the descents, and secondly with hammer-ons only.

Example 1h:

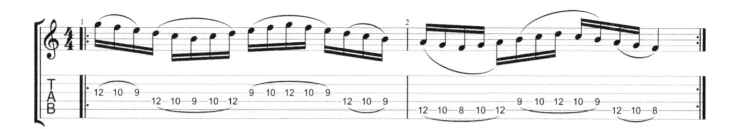

The late, great Allan Holdsworth, a pioneer of this approach, reportedly detested the sound of fingers pulled off the string to generate notes. By contrast, '80s high gain rock and shred guitar players often use pronounced pull-off sounds in descending lines. In the middle, some players who are credited as hammer-only exponents perhaps just use a light touch and less-obvious pull-offs.

My own view? It's important not to gate-keep a technique. It belongs to all of us. There are degrees of touch available, and it's essential to use what sounds and feels right to you. With so many great legato players out there, from jazz-inspired to extreme rock, it's part of your journey to either emulate or revolt against what those before you have done.

For future examples in the book, remember that you have the option to:

- Use pick strokes on each new string

- Use pick and finger strokes on each new string

- Begin lower strings with hammer-ons from nowhere

- Begin any string with hammer-ons from nowhere

- Use re-hammering to replace pull-offs

Experimentation is highly encouraged with each and all of the approaches!

Biomechanics Checklist

Before moving into the development drills that will fill your initial practice routines, check that you have accomplished the goals listed below as they will put you in good stead for the material in Chapter Two.

Goals:

- Establish functional and practical fretting using finger, wrist and elbow placement

- Master your fretting angles using the right balance of fingertips and pads to control adjacent strings

- Build a tag-team between fretting hand control and picking hand muting

- Begin strings using pick strokes, finger plucking and hammer-ons from nowhere

- Know the difference between pulling off and rehammering notes

Keep in mind:

- Once you know all the options, techniques become choices rather than laws

- Your preferences will help build your style and sound

Troubleshooting

- *Bad tone*: experiment with the interaction between your boost pedal and amplifier. Reconsider the gain, tone and volume settings in your setup and ensure that even a single note sounds pleasant.

- *Messy execution*: roll the gain back and spend more time on the Chapter One examples, taking care to fret each note cleanly, with the picking hand muting unused strings. Bring the gain back up and monitor the signal to noise ratio in your playing.

- *Legato timing*: try using the pick for each note, removing it on selected repeats until you can play the legato version exclusively with the same command of timing.

Chapter Two: Technique Builders

The exercises in this chapter focus on building technique for both hands using the principles covered in Chapter One. Through a variety of chromatic and diatonic drills, you will be able to construct your first legato practice routines that will develop hammer-ons, pull-offs, hammer-ons from nowhere, legato slides and hybrid picking.

To keep the examples clean for reading and open to personalisation, the tablature purposely avoids the clutter of excessive pick stroke indicators and other playing directions unless they are the specific target of development.

In cases where I've indicated my personal preferences, try the suggestions offered, then adopt any changes you wish to make as your chops develop and lead you in your own direction.

Chromatic Technique Drills

The first three examples draw from chromatic patterns in 7th position with a 1-2-3-4 finger allocation. Try each drill using a downstroke and a hammer-on, keeping pick strokes soft and moving from string to string smoothly with a sweep-like motion. For bonus practice, repeat the drills using both hybrid picking and hammer-ons from nowhere to begin each string.

As the drills move from the low E string to the high E string, mute each lower string with the picking hand when it's no longer in use.

Example 2a:

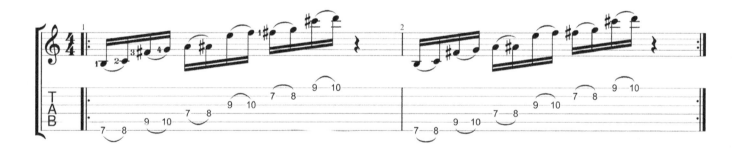

Example 2b is a variation which uses the third and fourth fingers on the lower string of each pair. If the discrepancy between the lengths of the third and fourth digits is a hindrance, remember to use your wrist to level the playing field.

Example 2b:

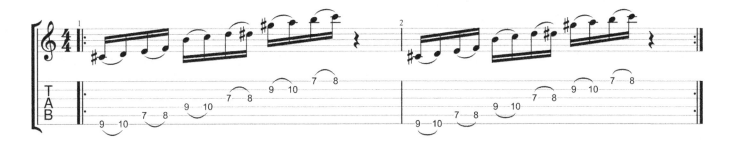

Dividing the fingers into different pairs, Example 2c begins with the first and fourth fingers, then the second and third fingers. Bar two switches the pairs.

Example 2c:

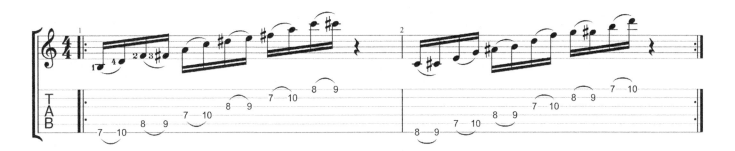

A *pull-off* requires a slightly different approach to a hammer-on because you will need to place the *catching note* (i.e., the note you will hear after the pull-off) right before you pull the higher finger away from the string.

In a descending chromatic exercise like Example 2d, you might be accustomed to stacking all four fingers on the fretboard and peeling them off one by one. Instead, use only the fingers required to play the pair of 1/8th notes in each beat. Doing so allows more flexibility in the wrist and less tension throughout several repeats.

Example 2d:

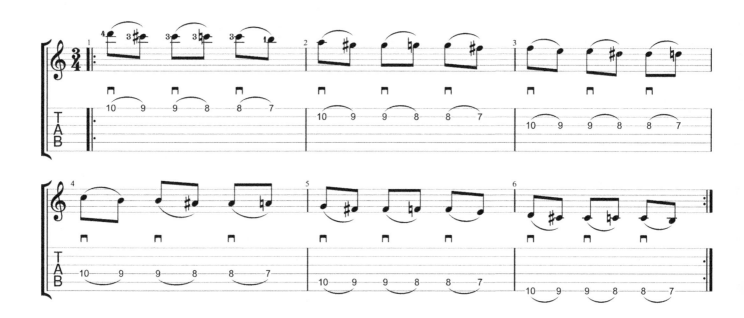

Example 2e combines the rolling hammer-on and pull-off approaches within chromatic stacks along each string. Long streams of slurred notes can be trickier to play in uninterrupted time, so try not to float around rhythmically.

Example 2e

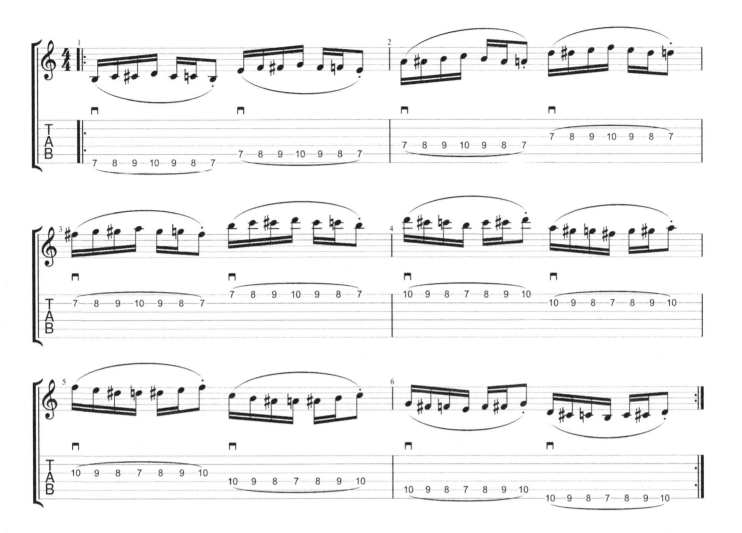

Example 2f is one of twenty-four chromatic fingering permutations and works well as a drill for pull-offs or exclusive hammer-ons. On the audio, you will hear a light pick stroke on the first note of the high E string, followed by soft pull-offs and hammer-ons with each new string initiated using a fourth-finger hammer-on from nowhere.

Example 2f:

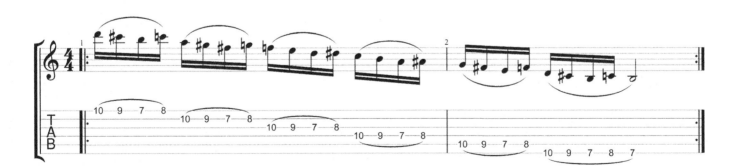

217

For extra chromatic homework, try replacing the previous example with some or all of the following twenty-four permutations. From 1-2-3-4 to 4-3-2-1 they are:

1-2-3-4	1-2-4-3	1-3-2-4	1-3-4-2	1-4-2-3	1-4-3-2
2-1-3-4	2-1-4-3	2-3-1-4	2-3-4-1	2-4-1-3	2-4-3-1
3-1-2-4	3-1-4-2	3-2-1-4	3-2-4-1	3-4-1-2	3-4-2-1
4-1-2-3	4-1-3-2	4-2-1-3	4-2-3-1	4-3-1-2	4-3-2-1

Before moving on to diatonic legato drills, let's use the fretboard simplicity of chromatic ideas to focus on some hybrid picking with Example 2g.

Bars one, two and three allow time to prepare the alternating pick and finger strokes that occur on each 1/4 beat. In bars four, five and six, the fingerpick stroke at the beginning of each two-beat phrase is immediately followed by a downstroke of the pick. This half of the drill may require more focus to achieve speed, so isolate the latter portion of the drill for further development if necessary.

Example 2g:

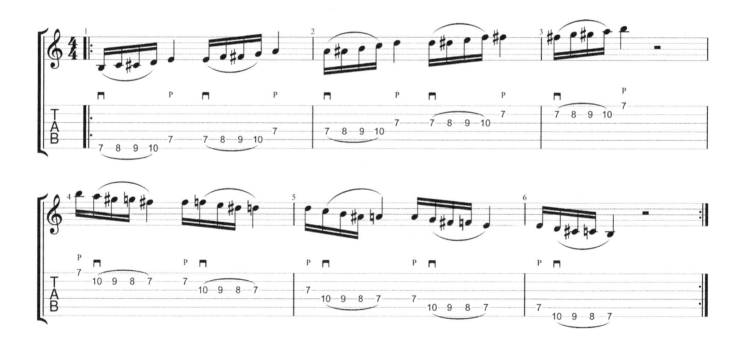

Diatonic Technique Drills

It's time to apply legato building to small licks that fit into everyday keys and expand them into complete scale lines. The exercises in this section will build stamina and improve string-changing.

These examples will draw on various three-note-per-string shapes within the key of C Major and its modes.

C Major Scale Across The Fretboard

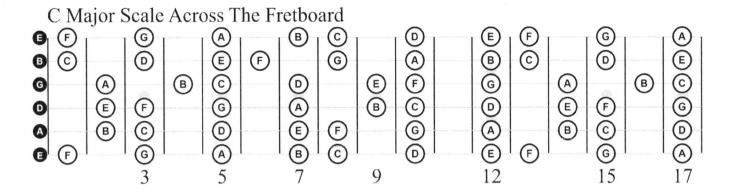

Example 2h will develop into a six-string sequence throughout the next few examples but begins as a two-string drill using two whole-tone stretches on both the D and G strings. These are fretted with the first, second and fourth fingers.

Example 2h:

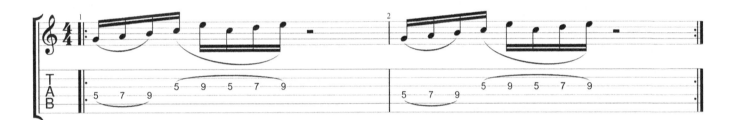

Expanding the lick to loop back to the starting note, both strings include two extra notes. Use a fourth finger hammer-on from nowhere to re-engage the D string on the third 1/16th note of beat 4 in both bars.

Example 2i:

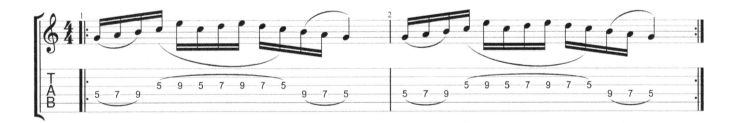

In Example 2j, returning to the 5th fret of the D string in bar one, beat 4 begins a repeat of the lick. The pattern crosses the bar line into the second measure, concluding on the 9th fret of the G string on beat 4.

Example 2j:

Moving through three octaves, Example 2k uses a similar motif to Example 2g, beginning on the G notes located on the 3rd fret of the low E string, the 5th fret of the D string and the 8th fret of the B string. The index finger will begin each octave of the lick.

Example 2k:

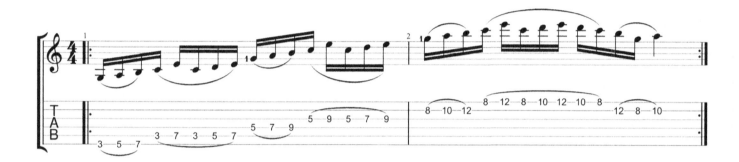

Diatonically transposing the previous lick upward by one pattern in the key gives us a shape consisting of a whole tone and semitone spacing on each string. Some players may prefer to use the first three fingers to fret this pattern but, in practise, use it as an opportunity to strengthen the changes between your third and fourth digits using the fingering suggested.

Example 2l:

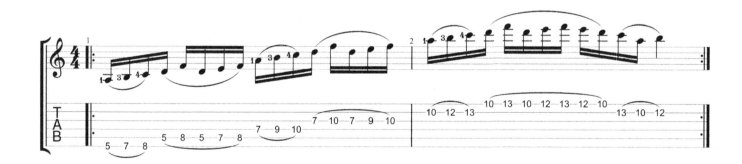

Let's use one string pair to try all the different combinations of two-fret and one-fret spacings that occur in diatonic three-note-per-string shapes.

Example 2m:

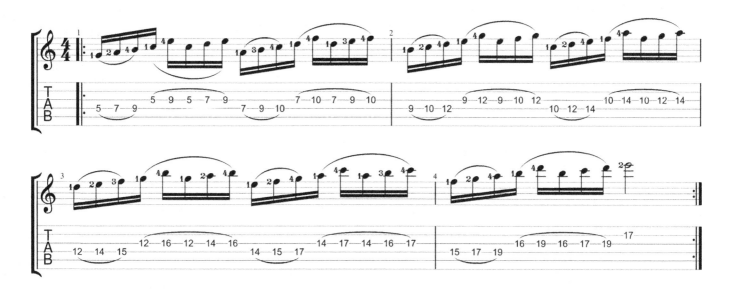

Legato Slides offer a way to connect patterns and avoid getting stuck using the same numbers of notes per string. Since you won't be picking your way through position shifts, it's essential to keep enough pressure on the fingerboard as you slide.

Example 2n includes a legato slide on the D string from the 10th fret to the 9th fret in both bars.

Example 2n:

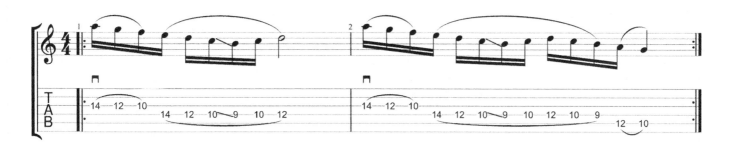

Taking legato slides through six strings, Example 2o uses an eleven-note pattern that repeats in a lower octaves and string pairs each time. Aside from the first note, each string change is initiated with hammer-ons from nowhere.

The notation in this example uses the odd time signature of 11/16 to help you isolate each octave for separate practice. In more practical usage, players like Richie Kotzen and Steve Vai might rush the phrase to force the eleven 1/16th notes into two beats of a 4/4 bar, as in Example 2p.

Example 2o:

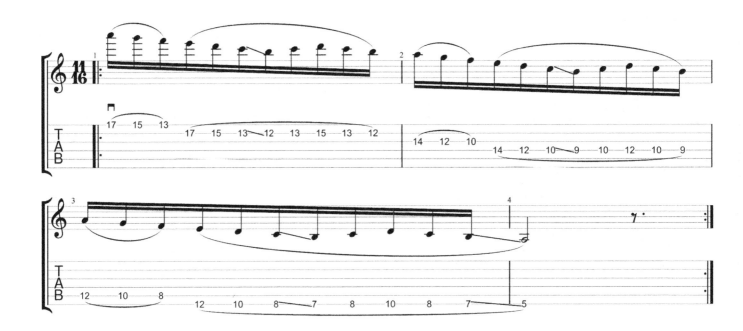

Example 2p:

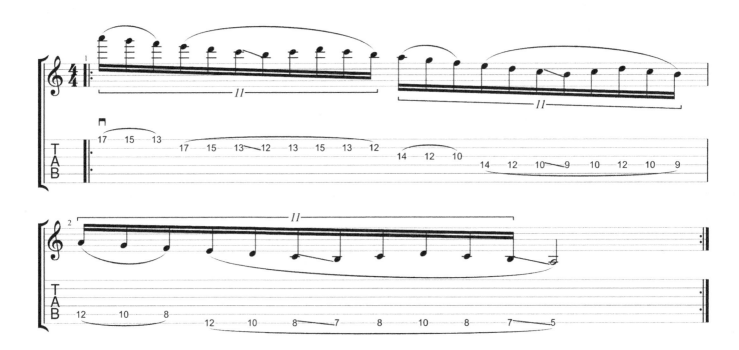

Let's try ascending slides in Example 2q. With four notes each on the low E and A strings, this C Major pattern moves from the 8th position to the 12th position. Often, but not always, the highest finger used along a string will slide up in an ascending position shift, and the lowest finger will slide down in a descending shift. For lone notes like the 12th fret of the G string in bar one, I generally use a finger pluck.

Example 2q:

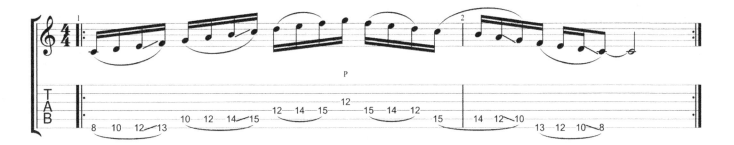

Using four notes on every string, the A Minor pattern in Example 2r starts in the 5th position but finishes up in the 17th position. Try sliding with the fourth finger as indicated but, as an alternative, compare it to sliding with the index finger between the first two notes of each string.

Example 2r:

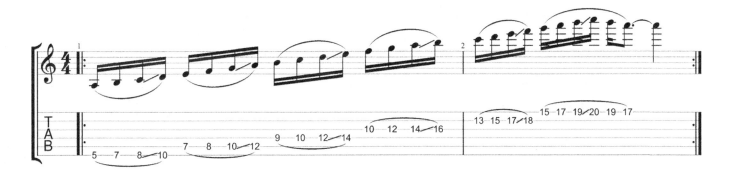

Sweep and Hybrid Compound Picking

A variant of hybrid picking switches between sweep picking and fingerpicking. The internet uses the term *Swybrid* picking to describe this compound of directional pick strokes and finger strokes. For legato playing, it can be useful to have a few moves like these to expand string-changing options.

Example 2s begins each eight-note unit with two downstrokes. Each note on the G string is played with a pluck of either the second or third fingers of the picking hand while the return to the D string starts with a hammer-on from nowhere.

For the sweeps, keep in mind that directional pick strokes should see the pick land on each new string as soon as it leaves the previous string. Avoid separated pick strokes.

Example 2s:

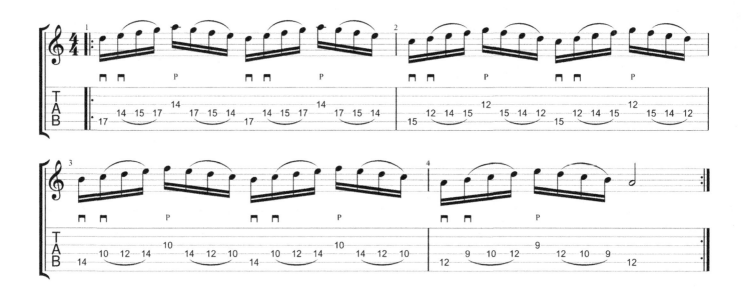

Example 2t ascends using a downstroke through the low E string and A string, a second-finger stroke (*m* or *medio*) on the D string and a third-finger (*a* or *annular*) stroke on the G string. This 50/50 split between pick and fingers creates tonal contrast and makes it simple to put the pick in position for each repeat.

All downward string changes are handled with hammer-ons. The notation here is in 7/8 time to make it clear where the pattern repeats. The fourteen-note phrase can be played in 4/4 time too, which will see it crossing the bar line at a different point with each repeat.

Example 2t:

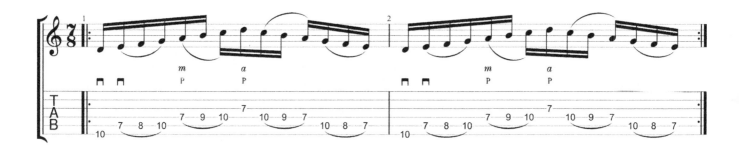

Upward sweeps can be incorporated into Swybrid string changes too. In Example 2u, the ascent from the A string to the D string uses the pick, second finger and third finger with an upward sweep from the D string to the A string, then to the low E string after two pull-offs.

Example 2u:

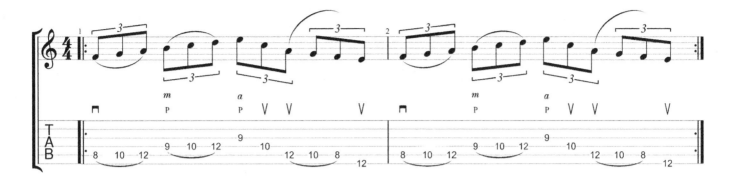

Building A Practice Routine

Practice sessions are often compared to training sessions at the gym. I use this analogy as well, not because guitar requires strength training, but because a good practice session requires structure to enable progress.

As you acquire more material to practise on guitar, life often dictates that your available time does not increase at the same rate. It's important to cycle exercises through your allotted practice time, replacing redundant material with new challenges.

I believe a good practice routine consists of something familiar, something unfinished, and something brand new. Not every session needs to stick to a formula, but a ratio approach might help you decide what should be tackled and what should be left behind. Applying these three attributes in a practical way might look something like this:

- Familiar: Use exercises you know well to warm up for the day's work

- Unfinished: Improve material you've begun already in previous sessions by developing it further, playing it faster, moving it to other keys etc.

- New: Prepare yourself for the next challenge by starting something brand new as a preview of future practice sessions

At the beginning of your legato development, all of the material in this chapter might be brand new, but even after a few days of practice, drills that used to fall into the *new* category can now be used as warm-ups. When an exercise becomes easy, it's time to replace it with another.

There are seven chromatic drills in this chapter. If each was assigned one minute of practice time, that's a seven-minute warmup. From there, you might spend ten minutes looking at the first five diatonic technique drills. Finally, a three-minute peek at the next few diatonic drills caps off a twenty-minute legato practice session.

Next week, you might be finished with the chromatic drills and, instead, promote the diatonic exercises to warmup-material status, using the bulk of practice time to work on the scales in Chapter Three. Cycling material helps your progress without the need for more time.

Be your own personal trainer when it comes to practice. Decide when a portion of the program has served its purpose and move ahead with new challenges. Remember that growth occurs outside the comfort zone.

Exercises in this book should be learned in free time to get the mechanics right before bringing out the metronome. If you find *click, click, click* uninspiring to practice to, check out the unaccompanied drum tracks in the audio of this book.

In the next chapter, you will learn to unlock the fretboard in major and minor keys using (and then losing) common and unorthodox scale patterns.

Chapter Three: Making (and Breaking) Scale Patterns

This chapter will help you put in place systems to navigate the fretboard in a thorough way to avoid limiting yourself to specific patterns or positions.

Good command of fretboard mapping allows you to make choices about where you play the notes you wish to use. Using Example 3a to illustrate this point, here are six pathways for a two-octave C Major scale. Each pattern has a slightly different timbre, layout, application of pick strokes and string changes.

Example 3a:

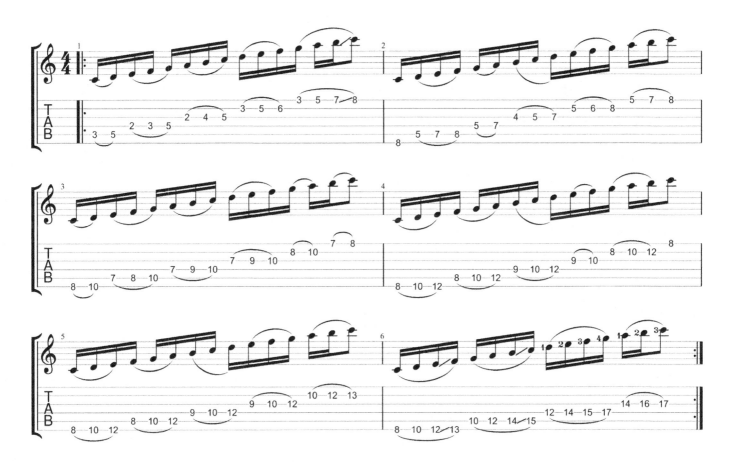

By the end of this chapter, you should be able to make choices about scale playing from various fretboard options. You can achieve this by mapping out the key of C Major in the common three-note-per-string (3NPS) patterns, then exploring the impact of using two- and four-note-per-string patterns.

Covering the key of C Major from the root note position, the seven 3NPS patterns look like this:

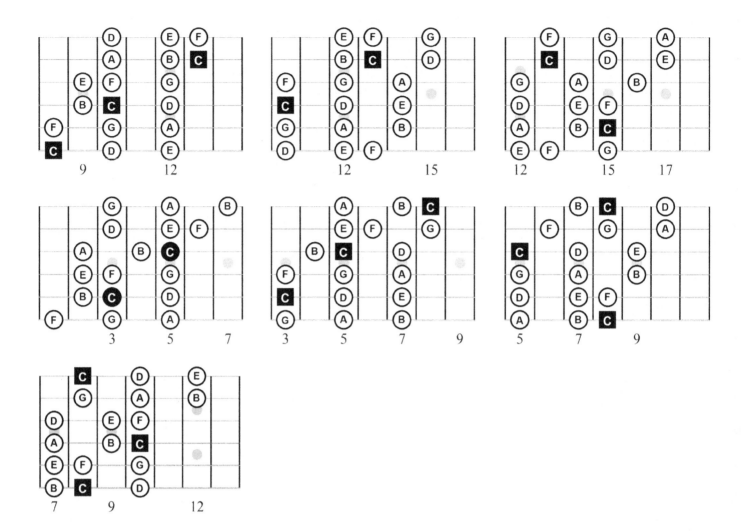

The numbering consistency and possibilities for applying sequences make the 3NPS system a favourite among rock players. Musically, each pattern contains two full octaves plus an extra four notes. To make sure you can connect each pattern to the next, take a look at Example 3b which begins on the fourth pattern.

This drill ascends and descends in alternating fashion by connecting each pattern with a legato slide. Ascending string changes use the pick while descending string changes begin with a fourth finger hammer from nowhere. Notated with 3/4 time signature to confine each pattern to a bar, you can play these patterns in any time signature as long as you maintain an even rhythm between each hammer-on, pull-off and slide.

Example 3b:

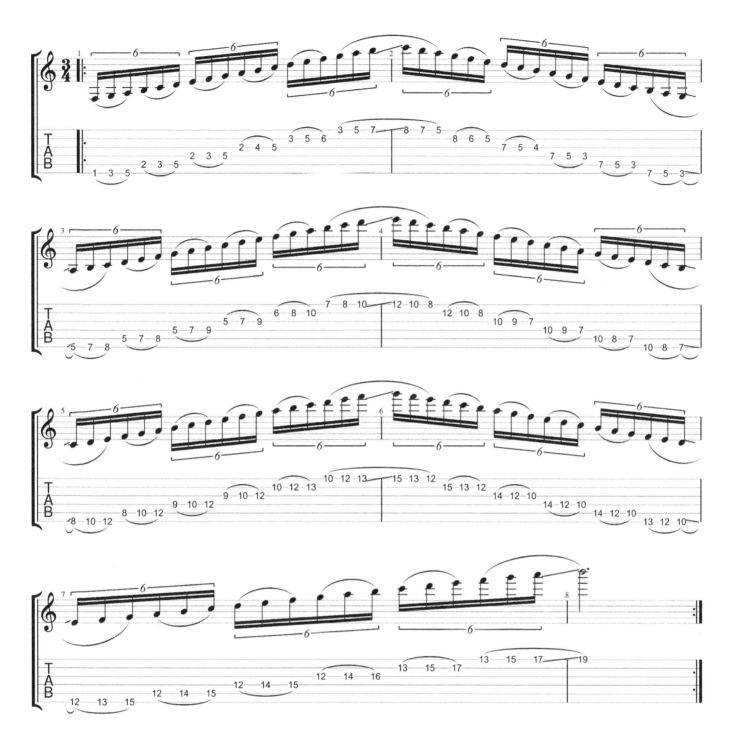

In the previous example, it was the fourth note on the high E string of each ascending pattern that created a position shift. We can use this trick to jump patterns at any point within a line.

Example 3c includes four notes on the A string, G string and high E string to enable us to move between four of the previous 3NPS patterns.

Example 3c:

Example 3d applies the same concept in both directions, using index finger slides on the B string, D string and low E string and fourth-finger slides on the A string, G string and high E string.

Example 3d:

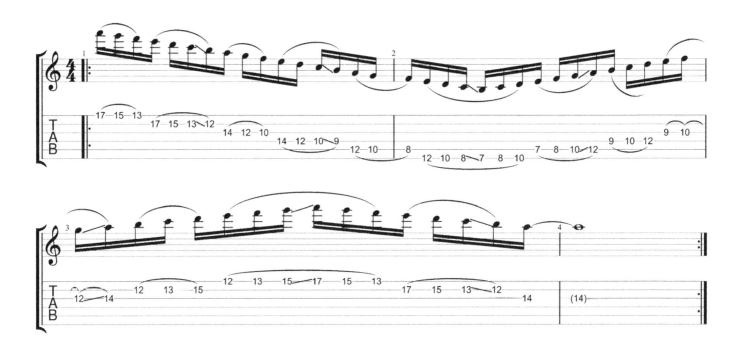

Changing positions and directions at various points, Example 3e is a great lick for creating a rollercoaster feel as you ascend and descend within an overarching upward direction. As you piece together longer and faster lines like this, you should begin to feel more fretboard freedom and flow between patterns.

Example 3e:

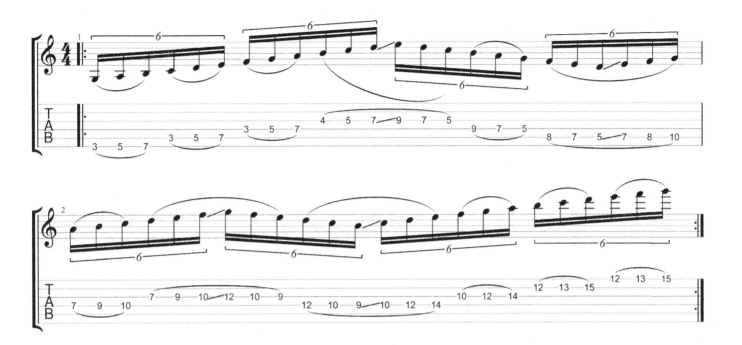

Playing four notes on a string needn't always include slides. While some patterns require quite a stretch to place four fingers along one string, a less strenuous example can be found from the 2nd and 6th degrees of a major scale (the notes D and A in the key of C Major). From both degrees, notes can be fretted a whole tone up, a semi-tone above that, and another whole tone higher, allowing the notes to roll on and off with the fretting hand.

In Example 3f, use your fretting hand wrist to roll each new note onto the fretboard, releasing the previous note so that you don't have to stretch across five frets on the low E string, D string and B string. Using the wrist will also make it easier to swiftly position your index finger onto the other strings, which require a smaller span.

Example 3f:

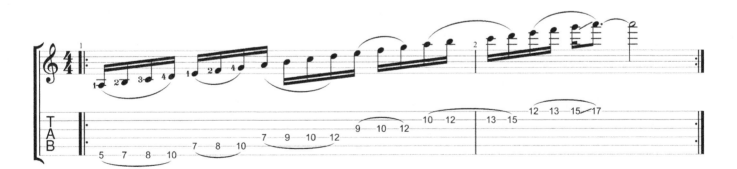

Let's try rolling back and forth within the larger stretch in Example 3g. Beginning with the D note on the 10th fret of the low E string, be sure to keep the fretting hand relaxed by lifting off each finger that is no longer needed. When fretting the three notes on the higher string of each pair, use fingers one, two and three for continuity with the other strings.

Example 3g:

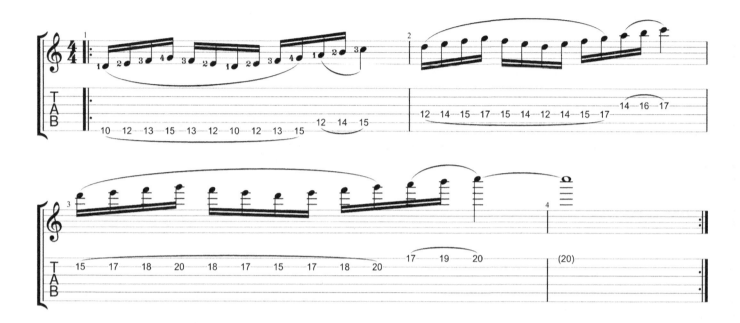

While scales played with 3NPS stay relatively in position and scales played with 4NPS shift upward or downward in the same direction as the last note on the string, two notes per string (2NPS) have yet another effect on fretboard positioning.

Ascending 2NPS diatonic scales will begin each new string in a lower position than the previous string in almost all cases. Descending scales have the reverse effect. Playing exclusively in 2NPS is not a common approach for major and minor scales but is worth exploring as an escape route from other pattern forms.

Example 3h is a routine ascent and descent using 3NPS, beginning on the F note on the 13th fret of the low E string, peaking at the C note on the 17th fret of the G string. We can compare this to a 2NPS approach in the next example.

Example 3h:

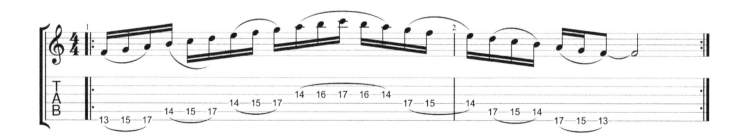

Containing the same notes, Example 3i is by no means a fast alternative but creates a different timbre as the scale cuts across all six strings in the ascent, two notes at a time. Upon leaving the high E string, we can connect to the descending 3NPS pattern that begins in bar one, beat 4 on the second 16th note.

Example 3i:

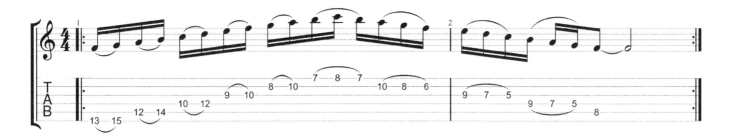

Combining the 2NPS approach with alternating three- and four-string groups, Example 3k again begins on the 13th fret of the low E string, concluding on the 1st fret an octave lower. Rather than view this example as an exercise in speed, use it to expand your scope of how notes connect on the fretboard.

Example 3j:

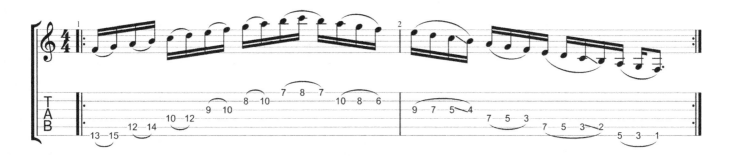

In Example 3k, an ascending 3NPS pattern beginning in 3rd position is escaped in bar two using descending two-note units on the high E string, B string and G string. The D note on the 7th fret of the G string is also the first note of a four-finger pattern up to the 12th fret, enabling another position shift for the remaining strings.

Example 3k:

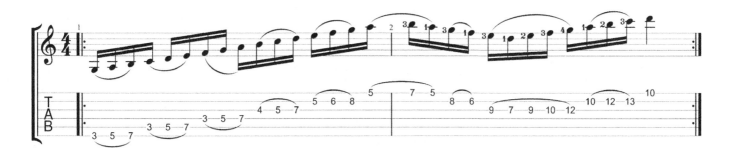

Two notes on a string occur systematically in the CAGED system as the 5th and 6th degrees of the scale occupy their own string in each pattern. If you've memorised the seven 3NPS patterns, it's easy to see how CAGED patterns that share the same starting notes will shift down into different 3NPS patterns any time a two-note string occurs.

In C Major, the five CAGED patterns are:

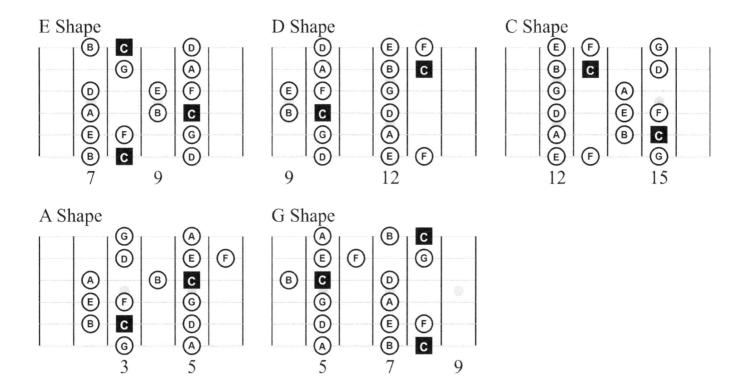

To summarise the theme of making and breaking patterns, Example 31 includes various numbers of notes per string and positions, executed with hammer-ons, pull-offs, slides and four-finger fretting.

On the strings containing four melody notes, pay attention to the presence or absence of position slides as the latter will be your cue to use a 1-2-3-4 fingering over the whole tone/semi-tone/whole tone stretches using the wrist-rolling approach.

Example 3l:

Exploiting the Options

The critical takeaway in this chapter is that versatility and flexibility will help you transcend the limitations of *systems* and keep you mindful of the endgame: complete fretboard mastery. You can achieve this in manageable steps by learning patterns, then learning not to be limited by them.

Using the shapes in this chapter and also the fretboard map at the beginning of Chapter Two, aim to complete the following list, slowly at first, moving to a moderate tempo.

- Play the seven 3NPS patterns in the key of C Major, ascending and descending

- Play the five CAGED patterns, ascending and descending

- Use four notes per string to any time escape other patterns

- Use two notes per string momentarily to shift downward on the fretboard when ascending, or upward on the fretboard when descending

When you've completed the above list, move on to Chapter Four to build a library of sequences and develop some serious speed!

Chapter Four: Liquid Lines and Scorching Sequences

With your technique developed and fretboard knowledge expanded, it's time to arm your lead playing with a selection of slick legato licks and sequences applicable to soloing.

Sequencing is a way of breaking up streams of consecutive scale tones by running different intervals or motifs through steps within the scale. By restating a theme or melodic passage in rising or falling steps, we can combine unity of concept with variety of pitch.

It's crucial to experiment with and document your own legato sequences to build a library of ideas, but I'm going to start you off with many of my own in this chapter. You'll also learn my legato approach to common sequences that are generally approached with picking.

Each sequence example is applied to a scale pattern within the key of C Major, but you are encouraged to apply each concept to every scale and mode in your repertoire. A suggested chord is included for practice, but you should try each example over various chords in the key and develop your own preferences.

My four-step approach to coming up with new sequences is:

1. Create a *unit*: a motif that will be moved up or down within the scale

2. Apply the unit to positional scale patterns

3. Extend the range of the sequence by cutting across scale patterns with the unit

4. Try the complete sequence in different subdivisions, e.g., 1/16th notes, 1/8th note triplets, 1/16th note triplets etc.

In Example 4a, the ascending C Major Pattern 1 is broken up with a twelve-note unit in string pairs. Taking place over 2 beats, each repetition of the unit goes up to the fourth note in each string pair, down to the first note, then back up to the sixth note. In the tab and audio, single notes on higher strings are finger-picked.

Example 4a:

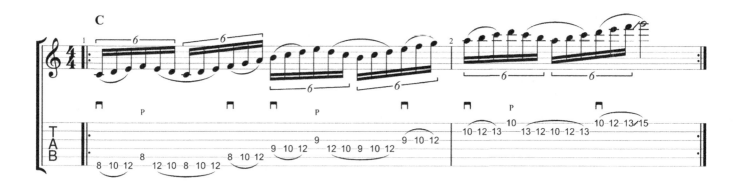

To cover more fretboard territory with the same sequence, Example 4b cuts across patterns to create a three-octave hexatonic pattern (using six diatonic notes out of seven in each octave), ending on the 20th fret of the high E string rather than the 15th.

Example 4b:

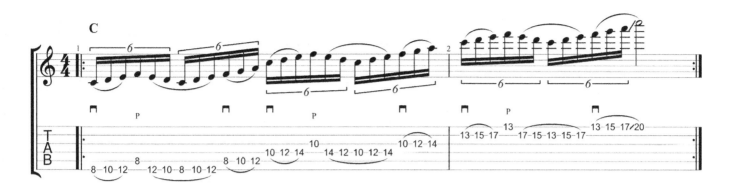

It's a good idea to have sequences that run in the opposite direction to your favourites. Reversing the note order of the core unit of the sequence is an excellent place to start.

Example 4c is a descending run designed to connect to Example 4a. When played after the previous example, a slide into the first note of this lick will get things moving. If adhering to the suggested sweep picking strokes, use a soft pick attack.

Example 4c:

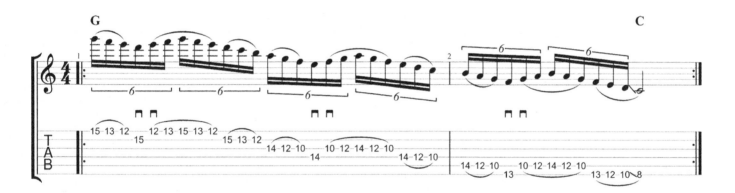

Using the sixth 3NPS pattern of C Major, Example 4d is played in 1/16th note triplets like the last three examples but uses a nine-note unit that is applied to five-string pairs. The result is a sequence that sounds displaced because each unit takes place over one and a half beats – a less predictable way to sequence.

Example 4d:

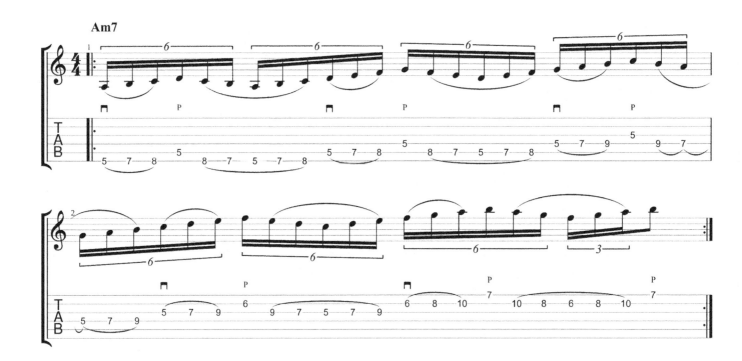

As a descending counterpart to the previous sequence, Example 4e reverses the nine-note unit and applies it to the fifth 3NPS pattern. Because single notes appear on lower strings in this direction, a two-string sweep is used to keep the momentum of the sequence. Keep picking attack discreet to maintain smoothness.

Example 4e:

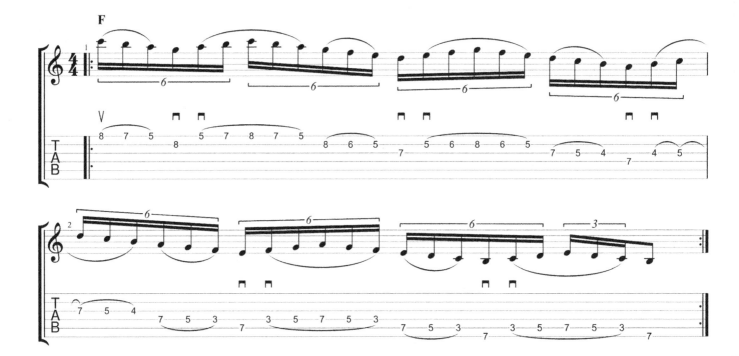

As the string layout in Example 4f indicates, the next sequence uses a melodic unit of six in another hexatonic pattern. While it works well as a sextuplet-based lick, the goal here is to maintain rhythmic control independent of the melodic unit. To avoid slipping into six notes per beat, tap one foot in 1/4 note beats, developing a feel for which notes fall on the beat.

Example 4f:

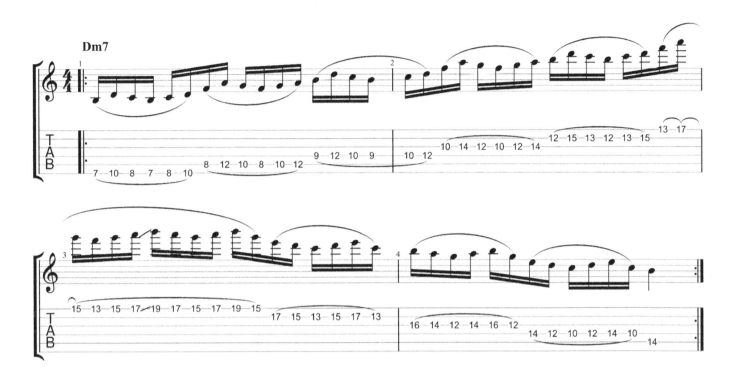

Instead of using the displacement sound of the previous examples all the way through, a *reset* can be used to begin sequences on downbeats again. In bar one of Example 4g, the nine-note motif is cut short on beat 4, with only six notes used. A position shift to the 7th fret of the D string in bar two begins a new iteration of the phrase, an octave higher than bar one.

Mechanically, each nine-note unit uses one downstroke, one finger stroke, and one hammer-on from nowhere.

Example 4g:

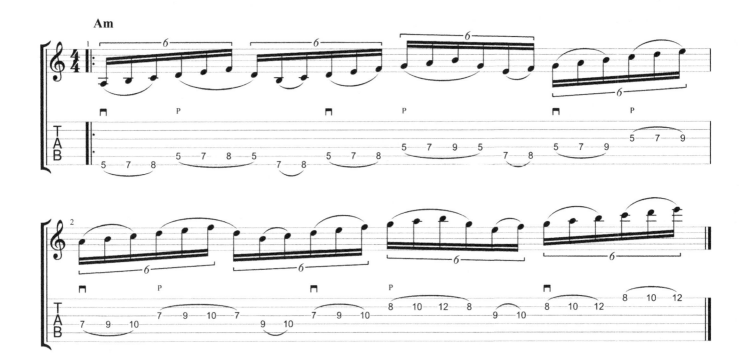

As a companion sequence to connect with Example 4g, Example 4h also uses two nine-note units followed by a group of six notes before a pattern switch in bar two.

As a descending line, there's lots of leverage to hammer on from nowhere when engaging lower strings. The notation and the audio for this example outline my own approach, which applies to both bars.

Look out for the fingerpicking on the first note of beat 1, the third note of beat 2 and the sixth note of beat 4. The pick strokes used in beats 2 and 4 could just as easily be replaced with hammer-ons from nowhere, but a downstroke right after a finger-picked note has a nice contrast.

Try a few mechanical approaches (including all hammers) and see what resonates with you.

Example 4h:

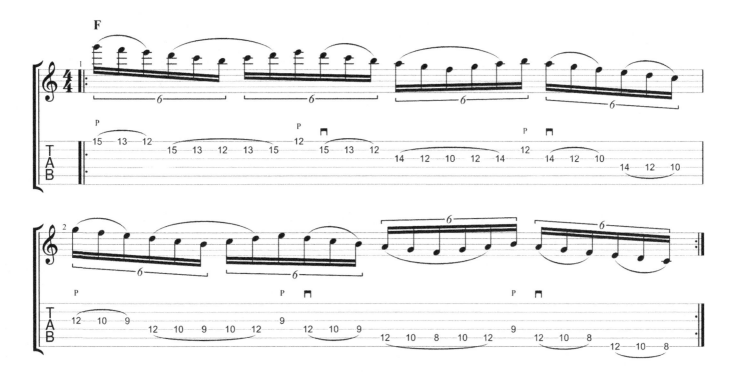

If you've been shying away from the hybrid picking suggestions so far, Example 4i might sell you on the approach. Using the third finger of the picking hand to pluck the single notes that pop up on the higher string in each bar uses less movement than pick strokes only, allowing faster and efficient string changes. Experiment with dynamics and see if you can reduce the volume of the hybrid picking to that of the slurred notes.

Each unit in this sequence begins a 5th higher than the previous step. In several cases, you will be rolling the fourth fretting hand finger across adjacent strings, so be careful not to overlap the notes. In bar four, a B note on the 7th fret of the high E string helps avoid an awkward reach to the 12th fret of the B string.

Example 4i:

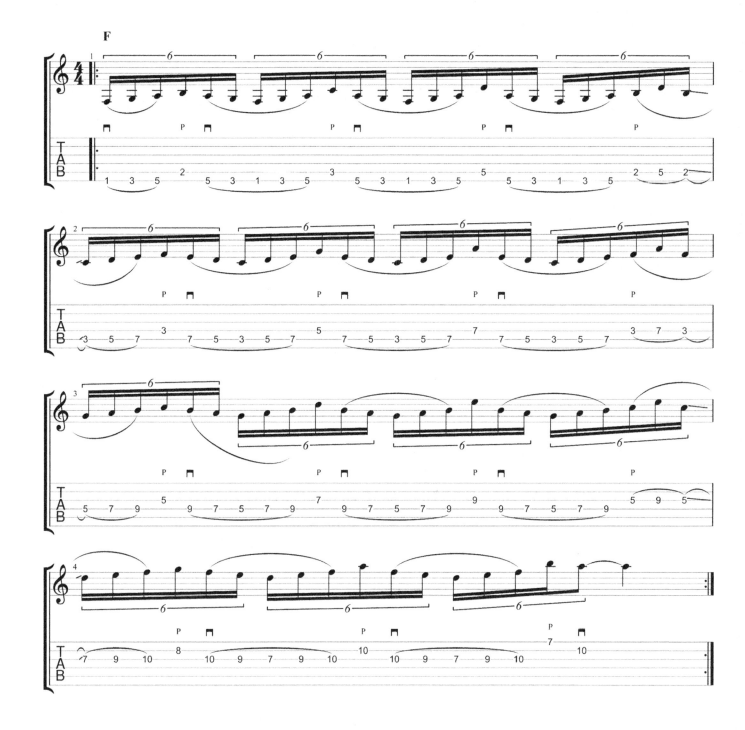

Getting back to 1/16th note subdivisions, Example 4j features an eight-note, two-string unit that *could* be used in a positional scale pattern. Instead, this lick takes the unit a diatonic 6th higher each time until the end of bar two, then shifts down the B string and high E string in diatonic thirds through bars three and four.

Example 4j:

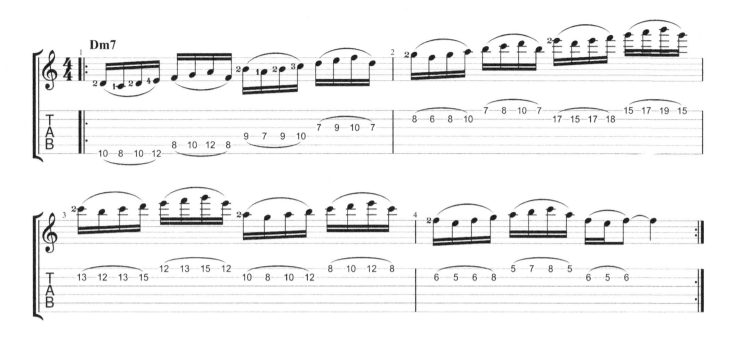

Using a 4NPS pattern with an eight-note sequential unit, Example 4k is a good test of fretting hand stamina as you work from the 19th fret of the high E string to the 3rd fret of the low E string. By now, you should find this possible without pick strokes, except for the first note in bar one.

Example 4k:

243

1/16th note sequences that change with the beat can sound a little too much like exercises after a while. A simple way to freshen things up is to displace the notes before or after a downbeat. Example 4l does this with the previous sequence, starting on the *-and* of the 1st beat in bar one.

Example 4l:

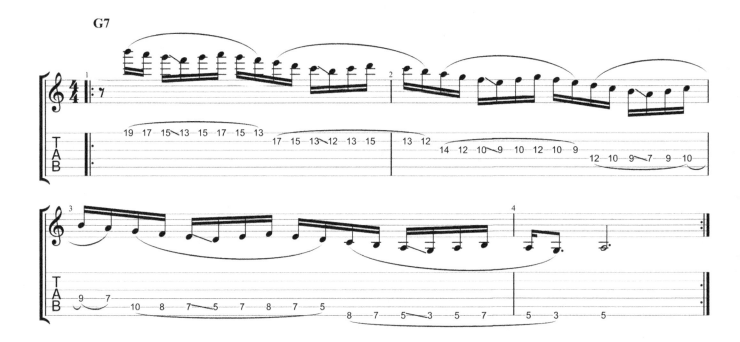

Fun with Odd Tuplets

For sequences based on melodic units of numbers like five, seven and nine, a rhythmic approach popular among legato players is to play the odd groups of notes within beats using tuplets or *artificial divisions.* Rather than have the melodic units *spill over* the beats, artificial divisions will see numbers like five, seven, nine or eleven notes take place within the space that four or eight notes might otherwise occupy.

Example 4m shows what a five-note melodic unit looks like when played as 1/16th notes.

Example 4m:

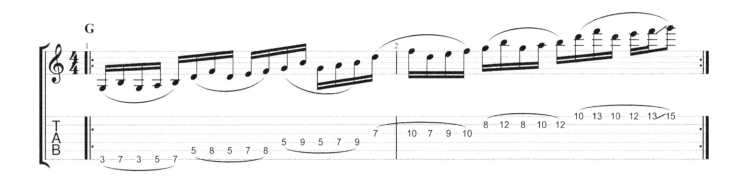

Fitting each five-note group into single beats (Example 4n) creates a rhythmic ratio of 5:4 called *quintuplets*, giving the previous sequence an accelerated feel that ends more than one beat sooner. The result is a more exhilarating sound.

Example 4n

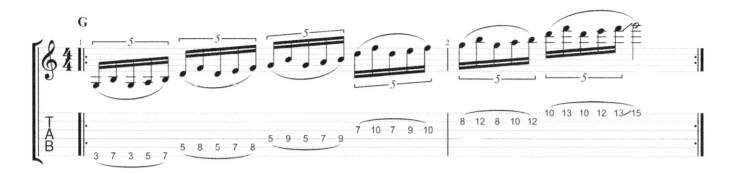

Your logical mind might attempt to break quintuplets into a pair of 1/16th notes and a set of 1/16th note triplets, but such an approach sounds quite different to five evenly placed notes. To help develop a more even distribution of quintuplets, play Example 4n again slowly, tapping your foot on each string change, which coincides with each beat. You can also try speaking any five-syllable phrase repeatedly and evenly. A made-up phrase of mine goes *Si Ki Ta Ka Ta*.

Try descending in quintuplets using the two-string unit in Example 4o. This time, string changes and beats are not mutually exclusive.

Example 4o:

Septuplets are another artificial division, comprised of seven 1/16th notes over a 1/4 beat. Example 4q runs a septuplet motif through the sixth major scale pattern and incorporates Swybrid technique into the execution.

To prepare for the full sequence, Example 4p isolates a portion for development. Take note of the three articulation points using the pick and one finger. The pick stroke on the last note of beats 1 and 3 sweeps through to begin beats 2 and 4. In the longer version (Example 4q), each sweep will initiate another septuplet.

Example 4p:

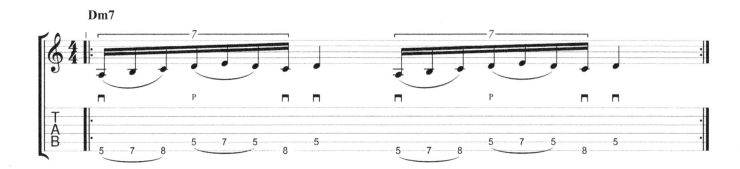

Example 4q:

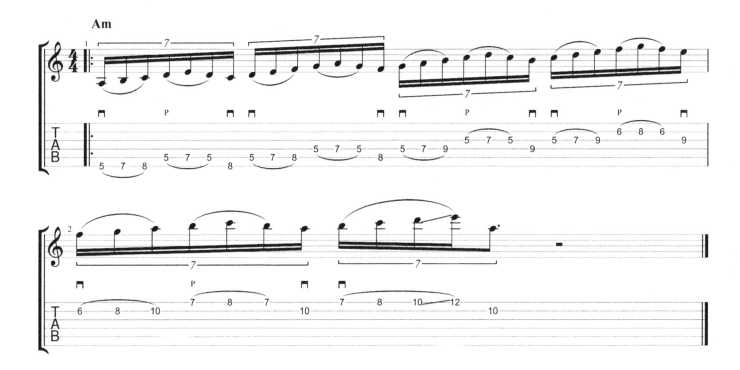

Flipping the motif to create a descending counterpart, Example 4r can mostly be played without pick strokes, but I prefer to outline the groups of seven in the manner indicated.

Example 4r:

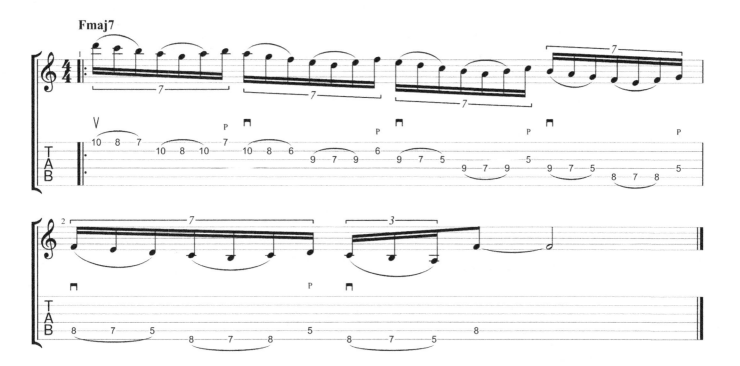

Nonuplets or nine-note tuplets are interesting because unlike quintuplets and septuplets, they are divisible by the common rhythmic number three. Depending on the subdivisions, nonuplets can be thought of as three lots of three or a *triplet of triplets* spread over two beats or one beat.

1/16th note nonuplets take place over two 1/4 note beats. The first, fourth and seventh notes in each nine also coincide with 1/4 note triplets. Consider the following:

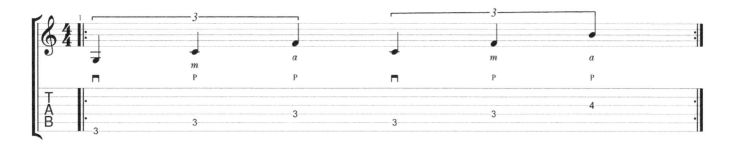

Using the 1/4 note triplets as marker points, try Example 4s. You can reinforce the *three x three* approach by using the pick, 2nd finger and 3rd finger to pick each of the marker points, followed by two hammer-ons for each string. The beams in the notation also serve as a visual reference for this approach.

Example 4s:

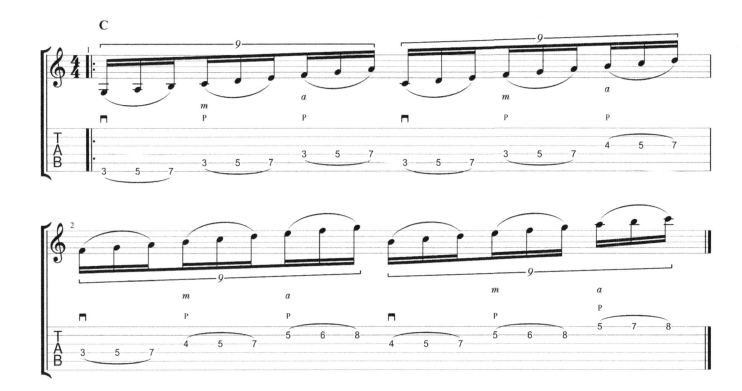

Although tempo will place limits on the use of 1/32nd note nonuplets, the *triplet of triplets* approach works using 1/8th note triplets as the basis for the nine 1/32nd notes that will occur in each beat. Each of the notes in the following bar becomes a marker point for the nonuplets in Example 4t.

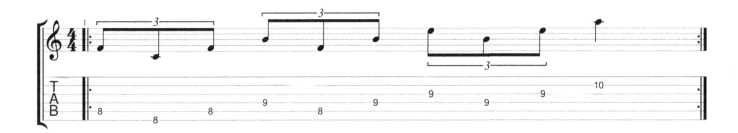

Example 4t:

Traditional Sequences Played with Legato

Sequences that are often used as picking exercises or phrases can also be adapted to a legato approach with the tools you've developed in this book.

Ascending and Descending Fours

Using each note in the scale to launch four ascending notes in each step is commonly executed with alternate picking. In Example 4u, a sweep/hybrid picking approach is taken, with each mechanical template taking place over three beats. The example is written in 3/4 time to make the mechanical repeats obvious.

Example 4u:

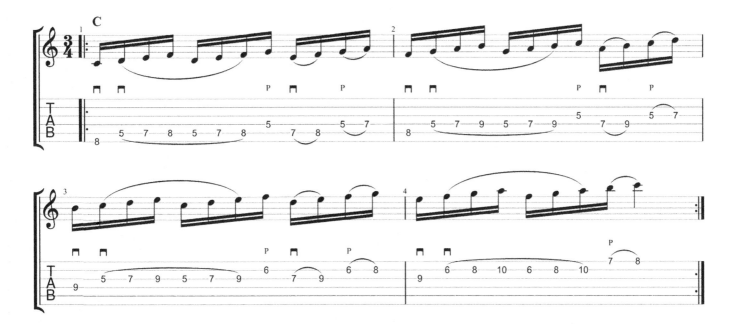

The descending fours pattern in Example 4v also uses Swybrid execution and fits perfectly with Example 4u for combined practice.

Example 4v:

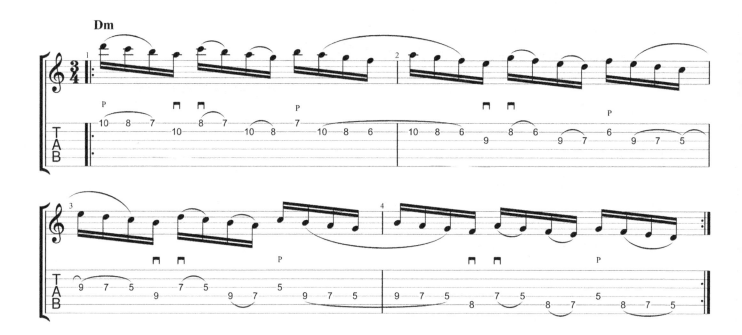

Ascending and Descending Threes

For moving up and down the scale in threes, sweeping also comes in handy for string changes.

In both the ascending (Example 4w) and descending (Example 4x) versions, the G string is used as a position-changing point between the fifth and sixth patterns of the C Major scale. Instead of slides, the position shifts are handled with the fingering changes indicated.

Example 4w:

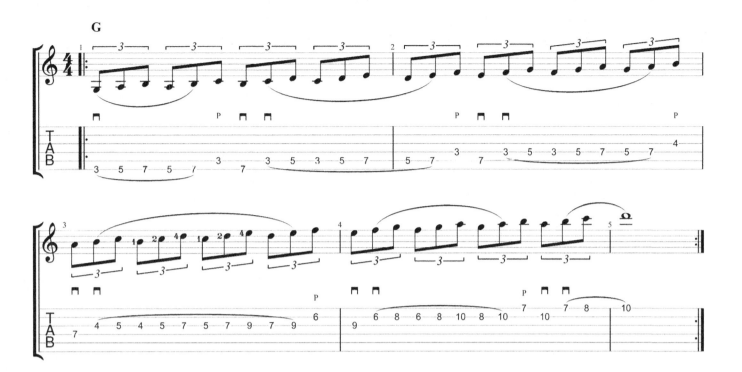

Example 4x:

Ascending and Descending Seconds

Based on an intervallic approach, the last example of this chapter moves descending diatonic 2nds up the scale in bars one and two, then ascending seconds going down the scale in bars three and four. Swybrid picking is used in the ascent, but only sweep picking strokes are required in the descent.

Example 4y:

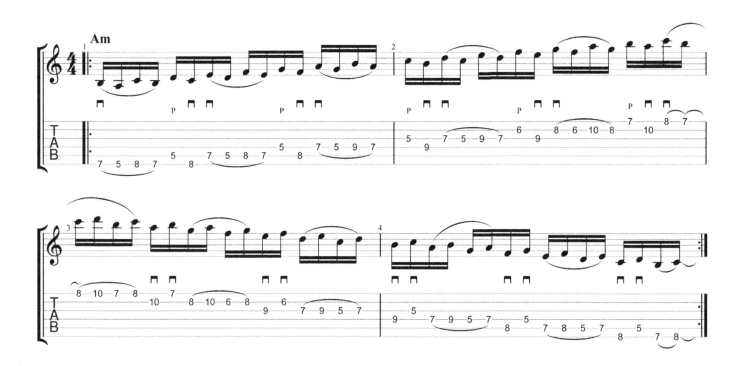

To make the most of the sequences in this chapter, apply your favourites to each scale you regularly use. Draw on whole and partial sequences in improvisation and aim to connect them fluently with the other concepts used in your solos.

Next, create and catalogue your own sequences, incorporating different intervals, tuplets and scale shapes to build a vocabulary that is uniquely your own.

Chapter Five: Number Systems and Omissions

In the previous section, you learned to break out of up and down scales by applying motifs, sequences, melodic displacement and odd tuplets. This chapter looks at another way to avoid playing consecutive scale notes by systemising mixed numbers of notes per string.

Using numbers to decide what notes you play sounds decidedly unmusical and very much a *guitar player thing* to do. What number systems *can* do, however, is force us to look beyond our established playing habits and explore options which might then form musical choices. By omitting notes with these systems, something as simple as playing up and down sounds more appealing. When sequencing, even more melodic interest is created.

In each system, the numbers are listed from the low E string to the high E string. In the examples, expect to see some overlap between different scale patterns to produce practical and musical results. When you can play the examples, experiment with substitute note choices if you find other preferences within the number systems presented.

System One: 1-3-1-3-1-3

Alternating between one and three notes per string is a handy way to move within a position in fewer steps than an entire scale but preserve a linear sound more scalar than an arpeggio lick.

Starting from a D note on the 10th fret of the low E string, Example 5a ascends using a sweeping downstroke for string changes and can use an upward sweep or hammer-ons from nowhere for descending string changes. This lick sounds excellent over a IIm chord because the notes used belong to a *minor eleventh* arpeggio. The pattern in this example draws from the first and seventh C Major scale shapes.

Example 5a:

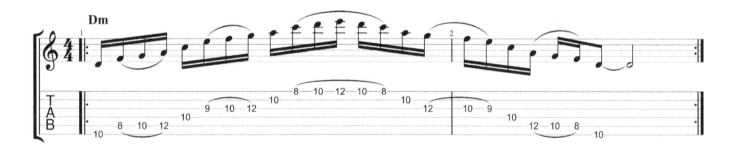

Let's apply a five-note motif to each of the three-note strings in the ascent. Example 5b takes a little longer to get to the highest note in the lick but creates musical interest and variation from the normal descent.

Example 5b:

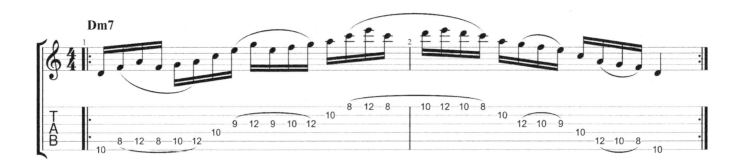

Next, let's sequence in both directions. In Example 5c, an ascending motif weaves through the first fourteen notes of bar one, beginning a new iteration on the third 1/16th note of beat 4. In bars three and four, the descending fourteen-note unit travels from the high E string to the D string, then from the G string to the low E string.

Example 5c:

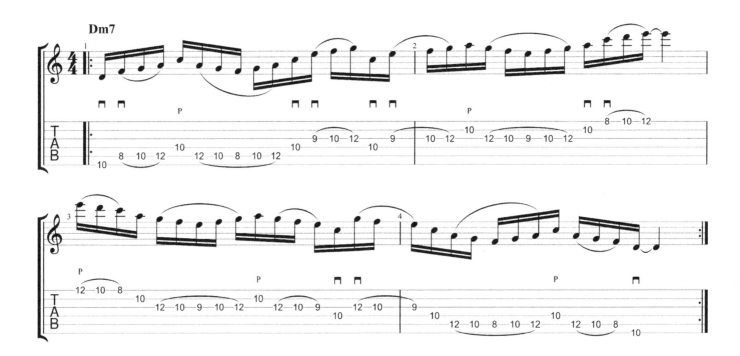

System Two: 3-1-3-1-3-1

Flipping the order of where the numbers occur, System Two outlines slightly different notes in each string pair. Using the II chord again for comparison, Example 5d starts with three notes on the low E string, one note on the A string and follows in alternating fashion across the other strings.

Example 5d:

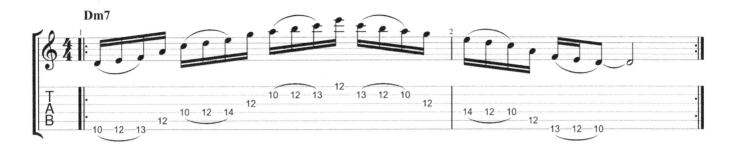

Sequencing your way through a mix of consecutive scale notes and diatonic 3rds with the 3-1-3-1-3-1 format creates licks that can sound more complicated than they actually are. With a combination of one, three and five notes per string at various points, Example 5e demonstrates the benefits of using a number system layout while still sounding creative.

Example 5e:

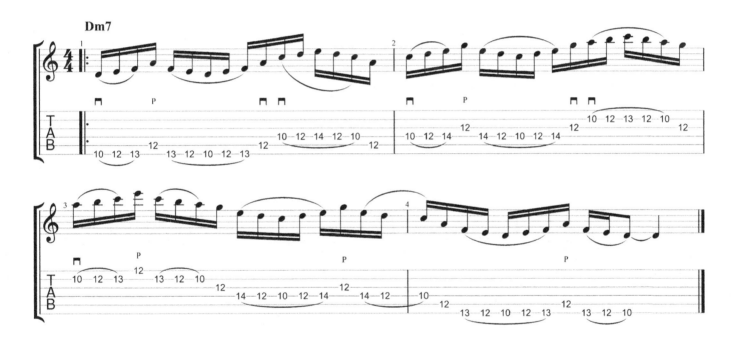

Transposing the format to suit a dominant chord, Example 5f works nicely over a G7 chord while drawing on notes from the fourth and fifth 3NPS patterns of the C Major scale.

Example 5f:

Thinking in combinations of *three* and *one* can work in horizontal position shifts and still sound perfect over a single chord. Using three melody notes each on the A string and G string and one note each on the D string and B string, Example 5g traverses three positions that begin on triad tones of the F chord underneath (F, A and C).

Example 5g:

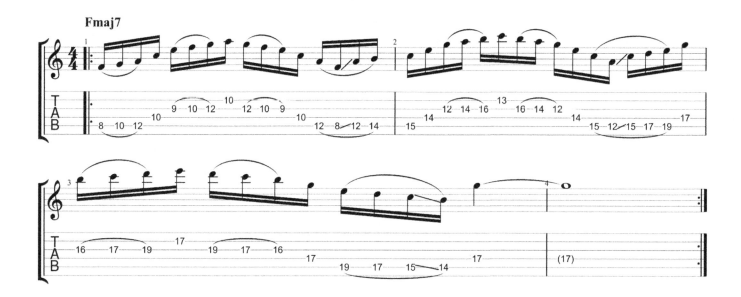

256

System Three: 3-1-3-3-1-3

The third system draws from both of the previous formats by having 3-1-3 on the bass strings and 3-1-3 on the treble strings. Selecting notes from the 8th position using this form, Example 5h ascends and descends while Example 5i applies a more creative approach.

Example 5h:

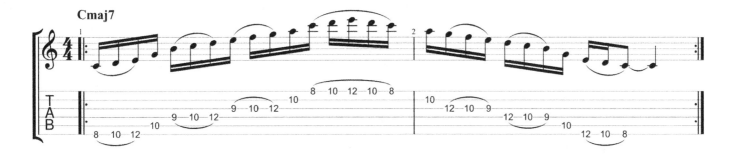

Example 5i:

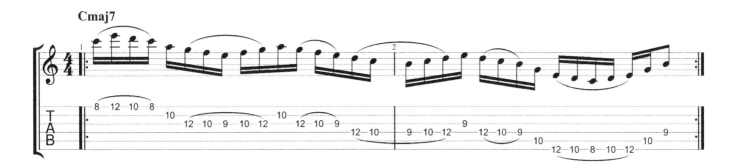

Example 5j breaks positions by using the 3-1-3 format from the low E string, then the A string, the D string and finally the G string. Each time, the seven-note melodic unit is diagonally transposed a 5th higher. The lick concludes on the 19th fret of the high E string, giving the lick a twelve-fret span.

Example 5j:

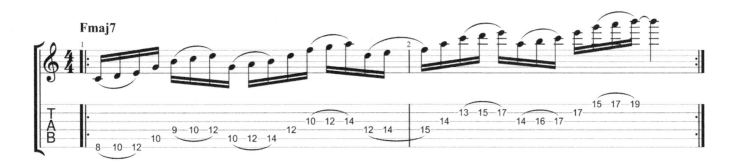

Example 5k applies descending 3-1-3 forms to the sixth, seventh and first 3NPS patterns of C Major.

Example 5k:

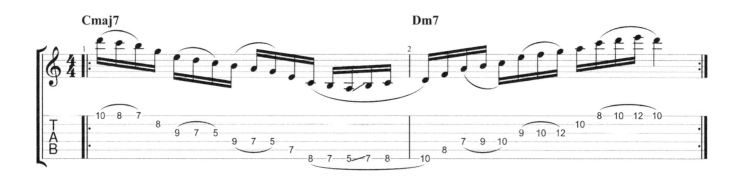

System Four: 4-1-4-1-4-1

I use this system to move five notes through three-octave patterns. In the four-note groups, slides can be placed at the beginning or end of each string.

Example 5l:

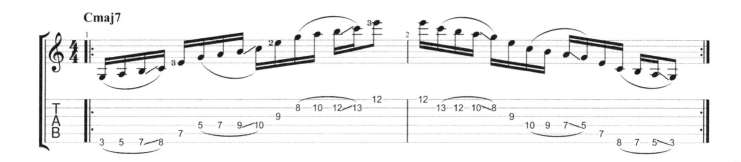

A longer ascending path can be created with a few detours on the way up, with Example 5m taking two bars to reach the highest note in the pattern.

Example 5m:

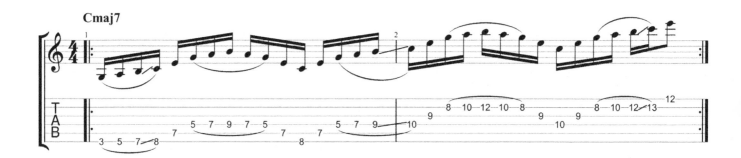

Example 5n transposes the 4-1-4-1-4-1 concept a diatonic 3rd higher than the ascending pattern in Example 5l, placing the slides at the semitone intervals this time. Example 5o represents a more lick-oriented descending version.

Example 5n:

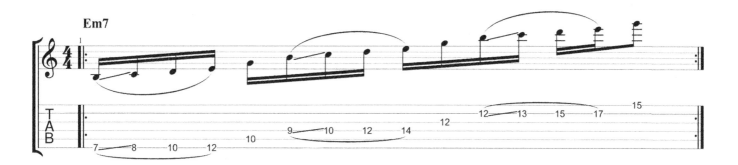

Example 5o:

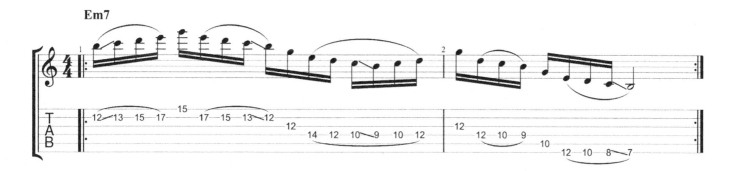

Sequencing along each four-note string, Example 5p re-introduces 1/16th note nonuplets rhythms, each taking place over two beats.

Example 5p:

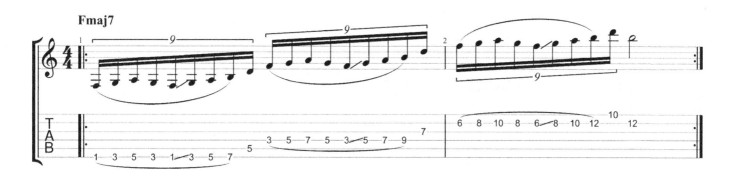

Pentatonic Number Systems

Number systems make the Pentatonic scale a powerful tool for legato playing. Because pentatonic scales only contain five notes, number systems can be used to play the full scale across all strings without any omissions.

Example 5q demonstrates how the 3-1-3-1-3-1 format can cover the same notes as the standard A Minor pentatonic box. The key of C Major contains the notes of two other pentatonic scales (D Minor and E Minor pentatonic), so if the stretch in this example is too wide for now, transpose it a perfect 4th or perfect 5th higher.

Example 5q:

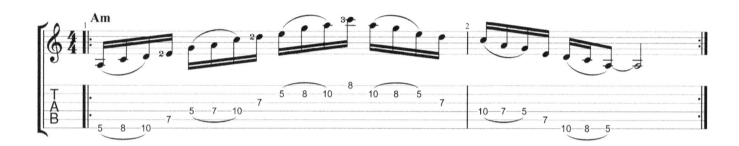

Using the E Minor pentatonic scale in the 12th position, Example 5r shows a very different side to the pentatonic than the blues-based runs commonly played within the *box shapes*.

Example 5r:

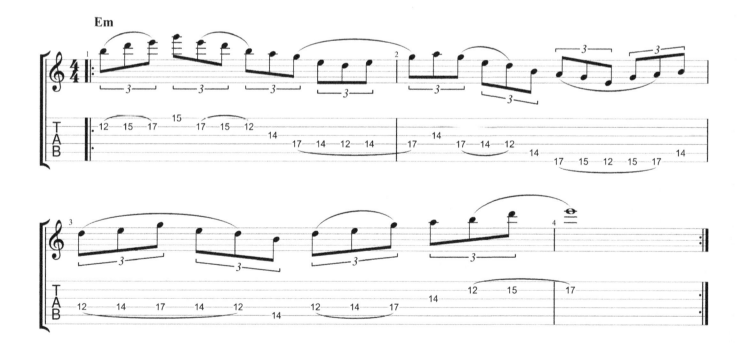

Beginning with the D Minor pentatonic in 10th position, Example 5s brings Swybrid chops to the pentatonic realm with a repeating motif in bar one. The next bar shifts to E Minor pentatonic to copy the previous phrase before ascending to the high E string by beat 3.

Example 5s:

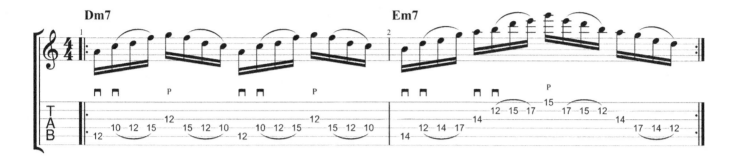

Where 3-1-3-1-3-1 pentatonic forms kept the pattern within one position, 3-1-3-3-1-3 pentatonic patterns break out by connecting to a higher pattern on the treble strings to reach two extra scale notes.

Compare Example 5t with the shape used in Example 5q. When you've memorised the differences, proceed with the sequence in Example 5u.

Example 5t:

Example 5u:

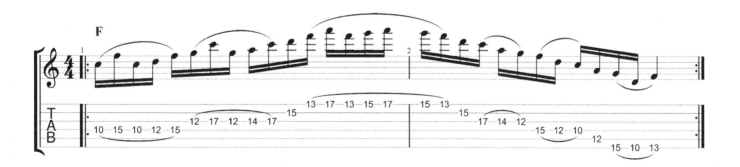

To play Example 5v as written, keep to the sextuplet subdivisions indicated, even when the melodic units switch between fives and sixes on the three-note strings.

Example 5v:

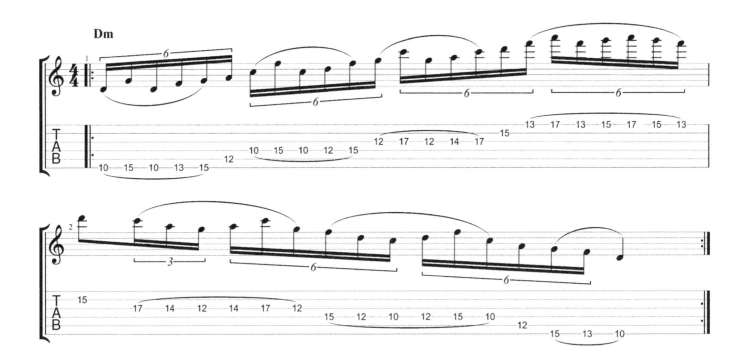

Finally, in pentatonic land, the three-note-per-string format can create some vast fretboard-spanning licks in the style of masters like Brett Garsed.

Example 5w maps out the format using the A Minor pentatonic and Examples 5x to 5z provide sequencing ideas in the Garsed style.

Example 5w:

Example 5x:

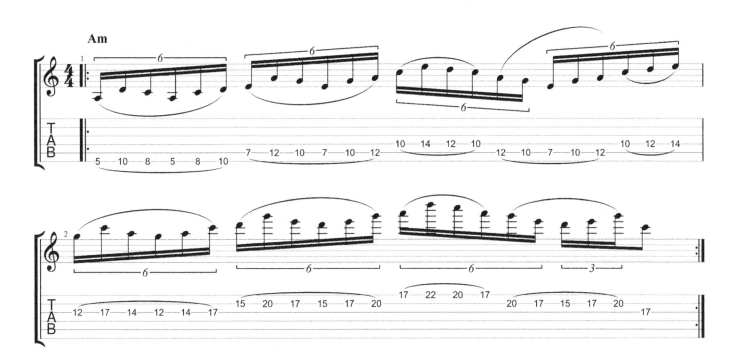

263

Example 5y:

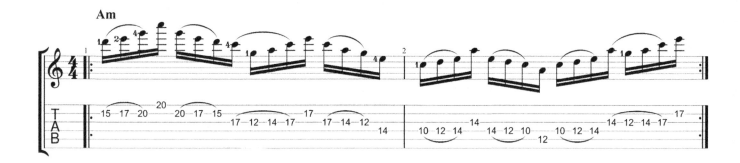

Example 5z:

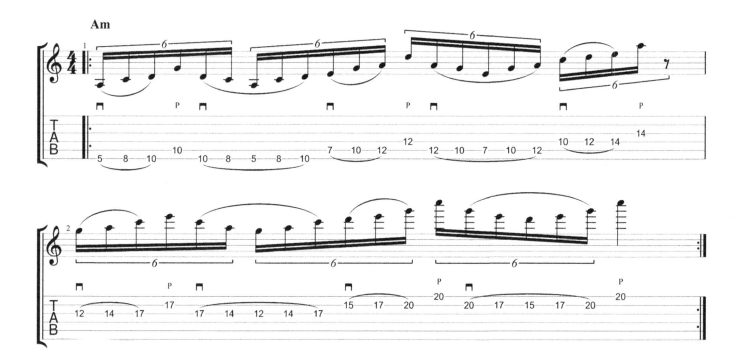

In Chapter Nine, fragments of these pentatonic forms will be combined with diatonic scale patterns.

Chapter Six: Chromatic Passing Tones

Chromatic passing tones are notes that don't belong to the key but are used above and below the diatonic notes. Passing tones from outside the key can create colour, build interest and maximise the number of notes accessible to the fretting hand for legato passages.

This chapter uses chromatic passing tones without forsaking the desired tonality of licks. Scale shapes will be used as a framework for passing tones, with an emphasis on *filling in the blanks* using available fingers not already in use on each string.

By the end of the chapter, you'll be able to engage and disengage passing tones to create an array of new rolling legato lines for your lick bag and have a process to follow to create your own licks and patterns.

The three scale boxes below illustrate:

1. The first pattern of the major scale (used here in the context of a D Dorian tonality).

2. The scale with chromatic passing tones between every whole-note space. Where five notes exist on a string, legato slides will be necessary.

3. A scale shape with only one passing tone per string to maintain a four-note-per-string system.

Box three is an excellent device for getting the passing tone flavour without impacting the fingering of the diatonic notes from box one.

D Dorian in 8th position

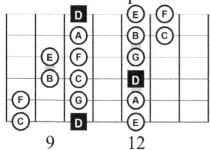 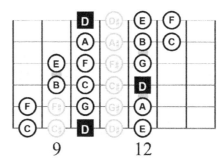 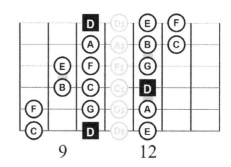

Example 6a is a D Dorian mode played from the 10th fret of the low E string to the 10th fret of the high E string. Take note of the fingers used on each string since the unused fingers will be covering the passing tones in the next example.

Example 6a:

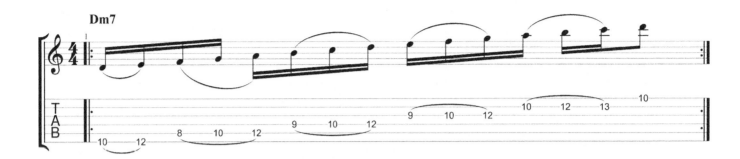

In Example 6b, passing tones are added to the A, D, G and B strings using the third finger of the fretting hand for all except the B string (handled by the second finger).

Example 6b:

Played over a G7 chord and passing through the seventh, sixth and fifth major scale patterns, Example 6c provides a more real-world look at switching between *inside* (diatonic) and *outside* (accidental) notes.

Both the D string and G string feature a small trick to avoiding consecutive semitone overkill. In bar one, beat 3, a row of four notes on the D string is broken up by a note on the G string before returning to the D string for the 10th fret. In bar two, beat one, a similar move occurs between the G string and B string.

In bars three and four, be careful with the timing of position-shifting slides to ensure that the 1/16th notes are played as written.

Example 6c:

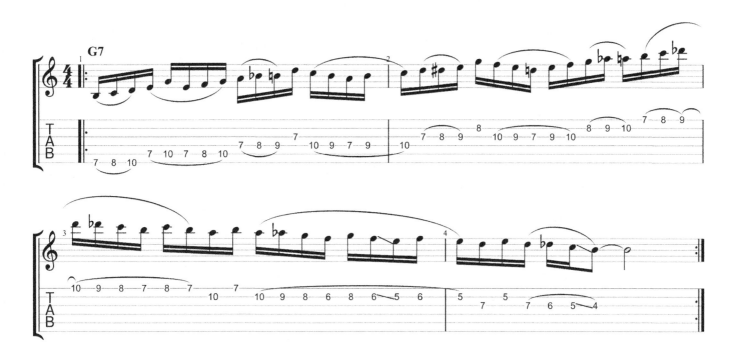

Ideal to be played over an Am triad or Am7 chord, Example 6d dials back the level of chromaticism for a subtle approach with only two passing tones.

Example 6d:

If you have experience playing major scales using the *CAGED System*, you might be familiar with the patterns used as the foundation of Example 6e. Combining the shapes *G* and *A* from CAGED in C Major with selected chromatics, this lick takes another step away from being predictable by mixing sequences and the numbers of notes per string. For best results, memorise and practise this example one bar at a time before getting up to speed.

Example 6e:

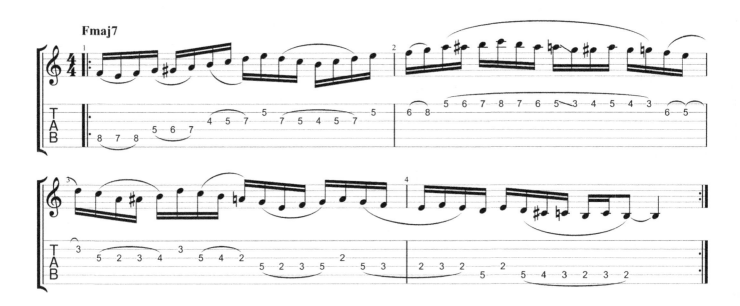

Using passing tones to turn 1-3-1-3-1-3 layouts into 1-4-1-4-1-4, Example 6f works as an Aeolian sounding lick over an Am triad. It can also be transposed a perfect 4th higher over a Dm triad or Dm7 chord.

Example 6f:

Thanks to one chromatic passing tone per unit, a 3-1-3 unit becomes 3-1-4, creating an eight-note motif. Example 6g features units of eight notes that alternate between beginning on D notes and A notes. To add interest, the lick is displaced by half a beat, thanks to the 1/8th note rest at the start of bar one.

Example 6g:

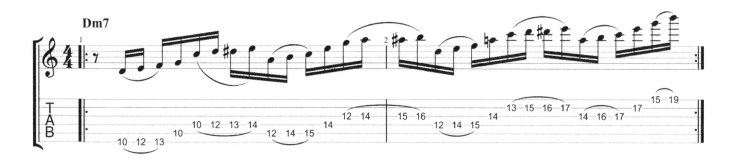

Pentatonic scales make great enclosures for passing tones, as utilised in the next four examples.

Example 6h is based on the classic minor pentatonic box shape in A Minor but can also be transposed to the other pentatonic scales within the key (D Minor and E Minor).

Example 6h:

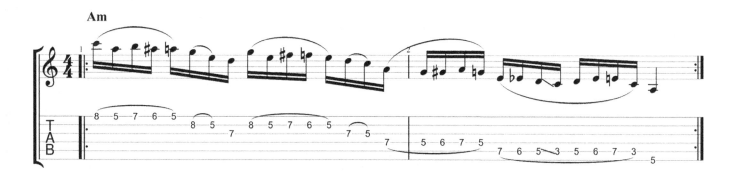

With a small chromatic twist at the end of each string pair, Example 6i uses the pentatonic layout of Example 5y. For additional lick mileage, each two-beat portion of this example can be looped multiple times before moving on to the next.

Example 6i:

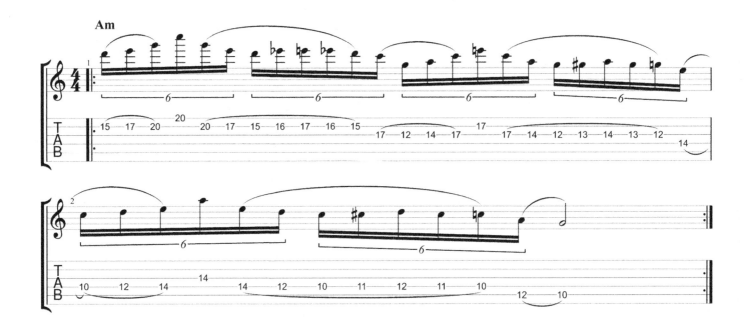

Example 6j begins as a combination of the D Minor pentatonic scale and passing tones, but the inclusion of a D Dorian scale run in bar two makes the combined lick specifically suited to ii chords.

Example 6j:

Played over a C chord, Example 6k displays a very overt use of chromatic passing tones using streams of hammer-ons, pull-offs and slides to get the most mileage out of the high E and G strings. Groupings of septuplets and sextuplets indicate suggested marker points for you to arrive at using the beats of each bar.

Example 6k:

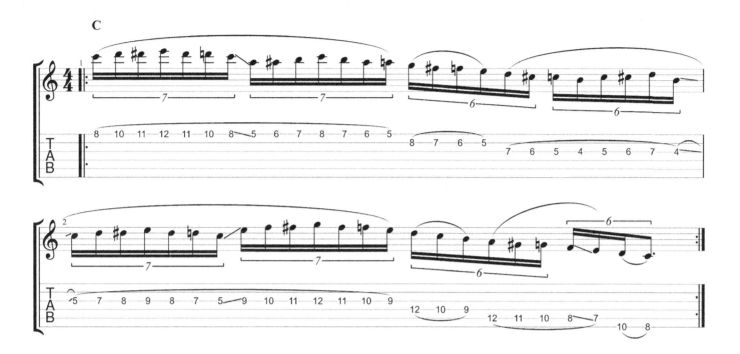

Bonus Tips for Chromatic Passing Tones

While the bulk of this book is about techniques and their many applications, some additional suggestions might help you get the most out of the flavour of chromaticism.

Tension is best accompanied by *release*

When it comes to tonality, the notes we play are either *inside* (belonging to the scale at hand) or *outside* (everything else). The power of passing tones is not just in the tension they create, but in the release when passing tones are resolved to something pleasant, like a chord tone. The longer you spend playing outside the key, the more pressure there is on delivering a resolution.

In the *filling in the blanks* approach used in this chapter, it should be easy to remember where the *in* notes are. Make sure that you don't get so carried away with passing tones that you lose sight of where the safe notes are.

Too much of a good thing

Passing tones are often taught from the perspective of *spicing up your playing*. Keeping with the culinary comparison, you wouldn't cook a steak with twice its weight in pepper. Likewise, chromaticism – at least in the development stage – shouldn't overpower a scale to the point where its tonality is lost in a sink full of semitones. Try to apply passing tones in a measured, tasteful manner.

Ratio Concepts

A methodical way to start applying your passing tone ideas is what I call *ratio concepts*. An inside/outside ratio allocates certain bars or beats to chromatic exploration, using the rest of the time to establish tonality by playing in the key.

For three bars of a four-bar cycle, you could commit to playing in key, and use the fourth bar to go completely experimental with passing tones, resolving in the next repeat of bar one. You might come up with other ratios, like two bars inside, two bars outside. For a beat-based approach, try assigning beats of bars to passing tones, like the fourth beat of every bar, or the last two beats of every second bar etc.

The concept might seem too formulaic, but is a practical way to keep the use of passing tones in check.

Chapter Seven: Legarpeggios

Triads and arpeggios are normally associated with alternate and sweep picking techniques. Besides outlining the notes of a chord, arpeggios employ wider intervals than scales and shorter distances between the high and low registers of the guitar.

This chapter covers some layouts and sequences to include arpeggios in your legato approach. Since many arpeggios partially or exclusively utilise one-note-per-string layouts, hammer-ons from nowhere will be an important device for execution. Noise control will be a crucial part of playing the licks in this chapter cleanly and accurately.

To begin, Example 7a features an A Minor triad on the first three strings. Hammer-ons from nowhere begin each string. As with other hammer-only licks in this book, a careful balancing act between picking hand muting and fretting hand string control is crucial. Before speeding this drill up, ensure that each note is accurately and evenly fretted with consistent attack.

Example 7a:

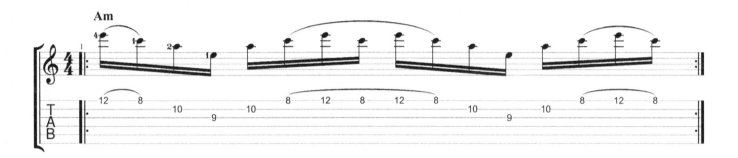

Example 7b applies the sequence from the previous drill to the triads of D Minor, C Major, A Minor and G Major. Your goal in this example is to shift positions without affecting tone or timing, particularly from the C Major triad to the A Minor triad, which both occupy the 12th fret of the high E string in the transition.

Example 7b:

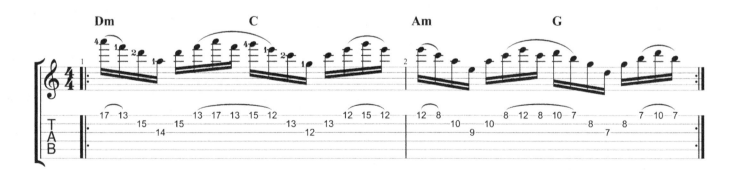

One way to approach larger shapes is to combine the flow of ascending sweep picking with the fretting hand leverage of descending hammers from nowhere. This combo is especially useful when tapping is required.

In Example 7c, a six-string A Minor triad is approached with ascending sweep picking and descending legato.

Example 7c:

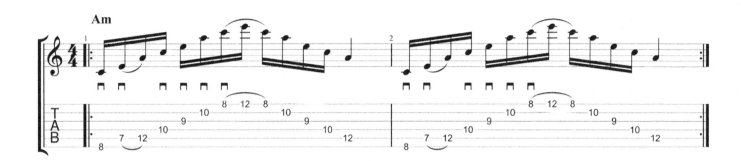

If you've seen Joe Satriani perform the track *The Mystical Potato Head Groove Thing*, you may have noticed a section in which he places his right hand across the strings behind the fretting hand for an arpeggio lick (2:19 on the recorded version). A combination of function and stagecraft, this overhand muting technique allows the picking hand to completely silence the strings while the fretting hand executes an all-hammer arpeggio in both directions.

Example 7d is performed on the audio using the overhand technique. The advantage of this approach is that it is easy to apply and remove and requires no rolling on and off. With the picking hand in the overhand muting position, it's easy to sequence the A Minor triad in this example and focus on hammering the right notes with a consistent dynamic.

Example 7d:

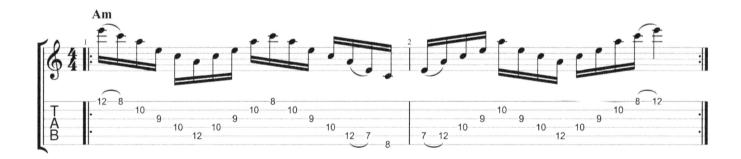

Branching out into extended arpeggios, Example 7e uses the overhand mute while the fretting hand spells out Major Ninth arpeggios over matching chords.

Example 7e:

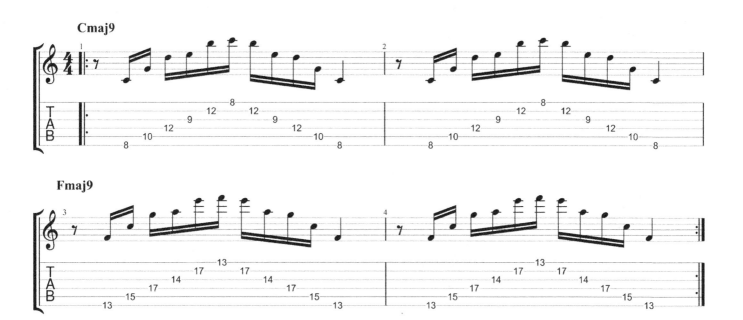

For Example 7f, the picking hand can resume its normal position as the fretting hand uses hammer-ons and sliding position shifts to execute the four triads. Aim to keep your hammer-ons, slides and pull-offs consistent in volume and timing.

Example 7f:

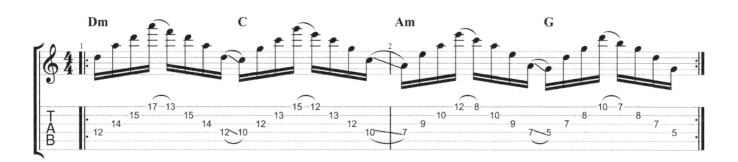

A good exercise for warming up and improving your all-hammer arpeggio chops involves running through every diatonic arpeggio using one zone of the fretboard. With various shapes for seventh arpeggios in the key of C Major, Example 7g maps the root, 3rd, 5th and 7th of each scale degree within a five-fret range.

Example 7g:

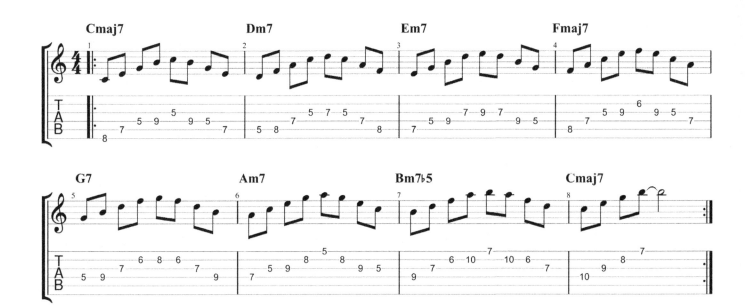

Another helpful approach for seventh arpeggios covers the four notes of the arpeggio in string pairs across three octaves. Played from the lowest fretted position, Example 7h maps out C Major Seventh arpeggios, beginning with the second inversion before moving to the third inversion, root position and first inversion. Example 7i repeats the process for the A Minor Seventh arpeggio, beginning with the third inversion.

Example 7h:

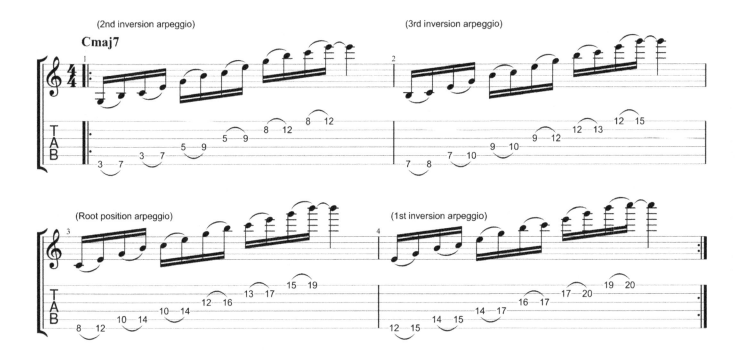

Example 7i:

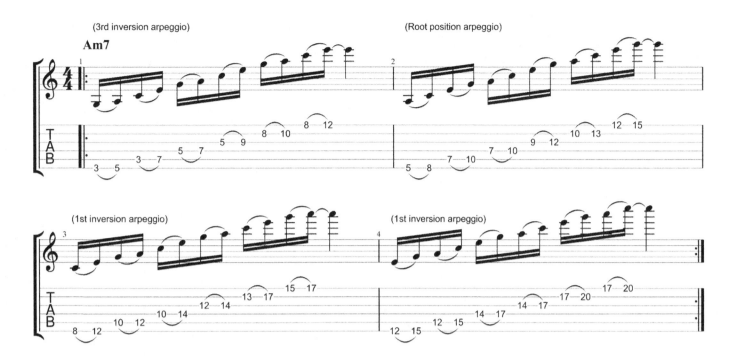

Applying sequences to 2NPS seventh arpeggios, Examples 7j and 7k take a six-note melodic unit and phrase it in 1/16th notes. Bars one and two of both examples are answered with descending versions in bars three and four. The ascents are articulated with hybrid picking. A finger pluck is used to begin the descents and to articulate each of the single-note strings the rest of the way down.

Example 7j:

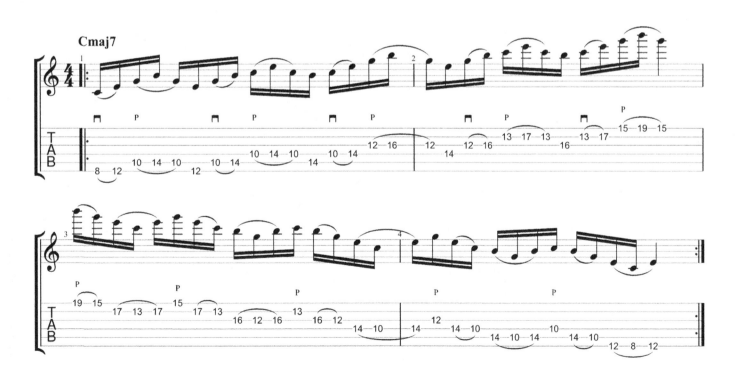

Example 7k:

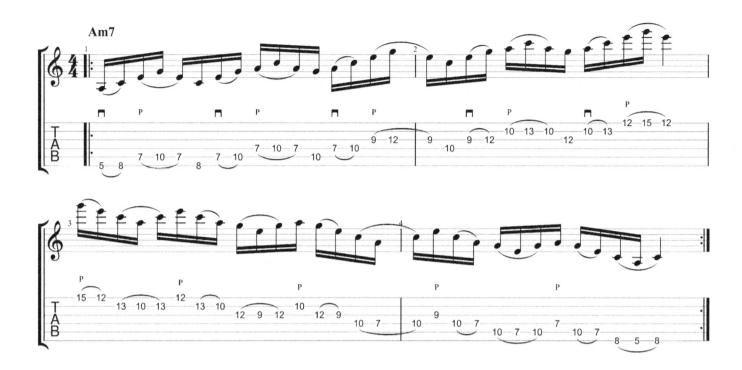

Example 7l applies ascending and descending fours to a G Dominant Seventh arpeggio (1, 3, 5, b7). A swybrid picking approach works well for the ascending sequence in bars one and two. In the descent, only hammer-ons from nowhere and pull-offs should be required, with one exception. On the 4th beat of bar four, the G note on the 5th fret of the D string requires the picking hand since the index finger is busy rolling out of the previous note.

Example 7l:

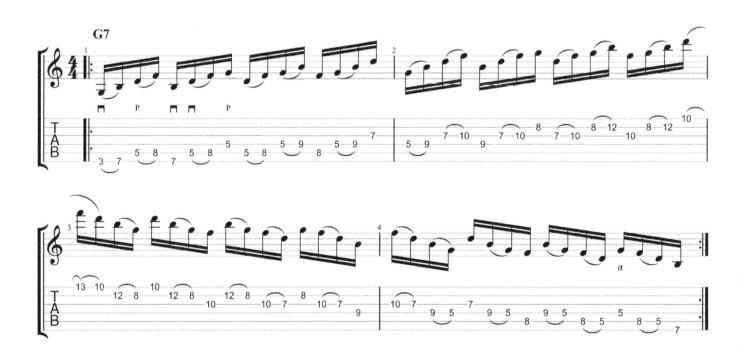

Using a mixed number approach, Example 7m alternates between one and three-chord tones per string using major seventh, minor seventh, dominant seventh and minor seventh (flat 5) arpeggios from the key of C Major. In these shapes, sliding position shifts are handled by the index finger in both directions.

Example 7m:

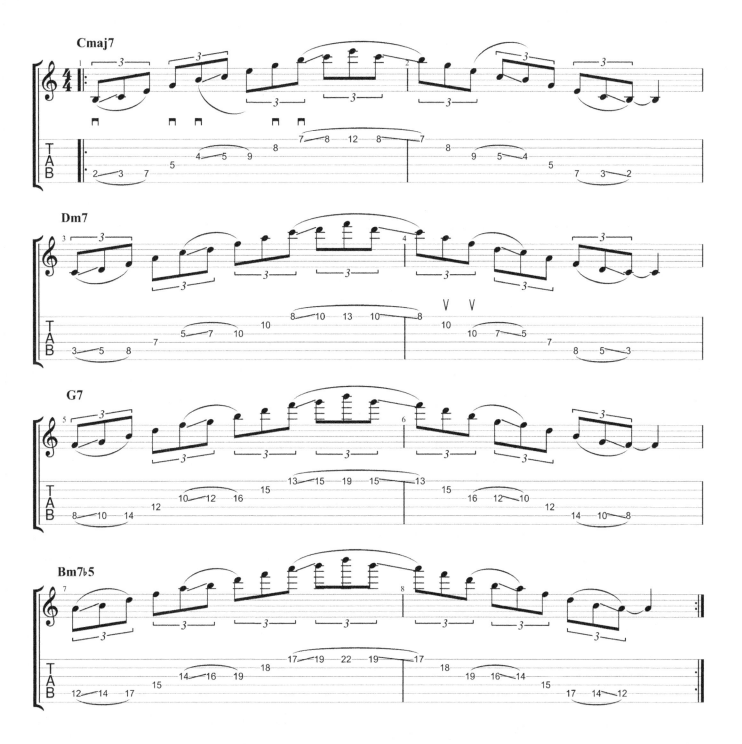

Now that you have a few different arpeggio strategies for legato, it's vital to integrate them with scale-based lines within licks. The last three examples do so with the arpeggio forms of Example 7m.

Example 7n offers a seamless transition between the notes of the C Major scale (F Lydian) and a 3-1-3-1-3 F Major Seventh arpeggio.

Example 7n:

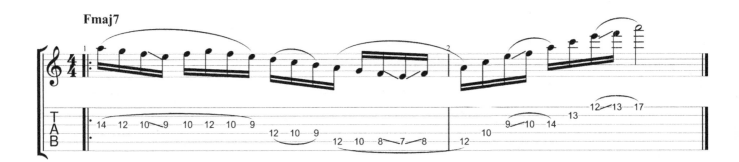

Example 7o uses the framework of a G Dominant Seventh arpeggio to add one extra note (A) to the A string, G string and high E string in bar one while sticking to the arpeggio in bar two.

Example 7o:

To complete this chapter, Example 7p represents another fully-formed, solo-ready lick suited to an A Aeolian tonality. At the end of the book, lines like this will be combined with many of the other concepts to create *Monster Licks*.

Example 7p:

Chapter Eight: Styling and Ornamentation

Throughout the previous chapters, you've accumulated a wealth of concepts for your legato vocabulary and technique. Taking it a step further, this chapter delves into additional musical and technical devices to inspire your improvisation and allow expressive personalisation to develop within your legato playing.

By the end of this chapter, you will have incorporated the following:

- *Whammy bar technique*: dips and pre-dips, vibrato and horn emulation

- *Rubato:* borrowing and returning time within phrases

- *Burst phrasing*: a staggered time feel made famous by Joe Satriani and Steve Vai.

- *Staccato Legato*: an oxymoron in name, but a useful dynamic device!

If your guitar is fitted with a vintage-style tremolo, make sure it is well set up to enable strings to return to pitch. If your guitar is not equipped with a moving bridge at all, jump ahead to Example 8e.

Whammy Bar Technique

A whammy bar *dip* is a simple but effective way of rearticulating a note that is already ringing. While the note is sustained, a small tap and release of the bar creates a subtle scoop sound in which the note is lowered by an interval like a quarter-tone or semitone before quickly returning to pitch.

In Example 8a, whammy bar dips are used in beats 1-3 of bar one and beats 1 and 2 of bar two. The dips imply a 1/8th note rhythm within the applicable beats.

Example 8a:

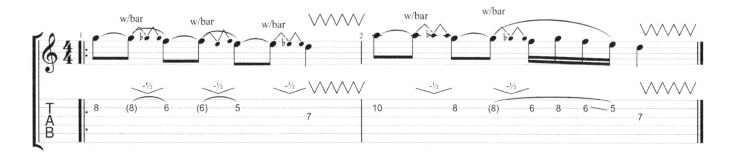

A *pre-dip* is a scoop of the whammy bar that occurs coming into the articulation of a note rather than after it. In the tablature, the marking indicates that pre-dipped notes will start flat and be brought up to pitch.

In bar one of Example 8b, a slide on the B string from the 8th fret to the 10th fret is embellished with a pre-dip on the 10th fret. The same move occurs in bar two from the 7th fret to the 9th fret of the G string. If done correctly, you'll hear the correct pitch of each note in the position shift, with the semitone in between implied with the whammy bar.

Vibrato is also applied using the bar. Whammy vibrato is different from finger vibrato since the bar can move above and below the fretted pitch.

Example 8b:

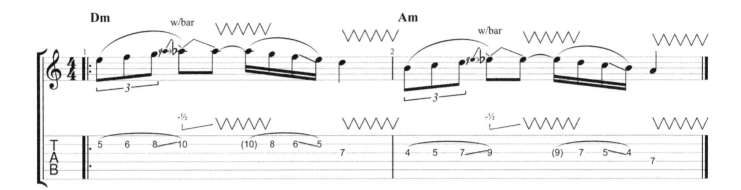

In Example 8c, a pre-dip is placed at the beginning of each beat in bar one. For longer notes like the last note in bar two, experiment with a slower reversal of the pre-dip to emulate a vocal or horn-like approach.

Example 8c:

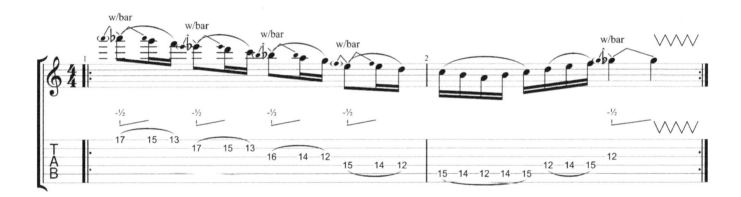

Example 8d is another faux-horn lick that includes the three whammy bar techniques covered so far and introduces a fourth: the *flutter*. In contrast to the small push of a whammy dip, a flutter is an upward pull of the bar that snaps back after release, causing a dramatic *gargle* sound. The flutter in this example occurs on the last note of bar one as it ties over into bar two.

Example 8d:

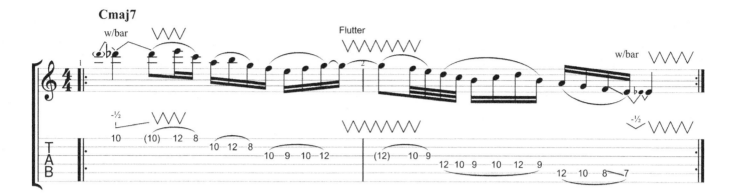

Rubato (Robbed or Borrowed Time)

In Italian *rubato* literally means *robbed*. In phrases that use rubato, expression is achieved by quickening or slackening the time feel without altering the overall tempo. I prefer to use the description *borrowed time* when talking about rubato because what is taken should also be returned. Where some notes are lengthened, others will be shortened.

Demonstrating rubato, the next few phrases compare straightforward notation to the result of borrowing and returning note duration. The audio for these examples will display a true *before and after*.

Example 8e is our first straightforward phrase, played on the audio with strict adherence to the notated rhythm.

Example 8e:

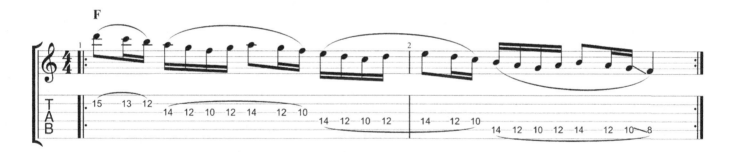

Holding selected notes longer and speeding up others to complete the phrase within the same two bars, Example 8e2 is trickier to sight-read but sounds way more expressive. This is just one way to apply a lot of rubato to a phrase, so after listening to the audio and studying the notation, experiment with your own *push and pull* time feel of the previous example.

Example 8e2:

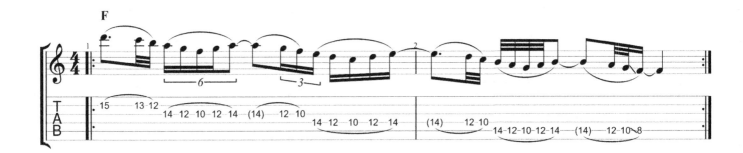

To take a step back and develop a knack for rubato, start with a simple scale shape, then explore your options. In Examples 8f and 8f2, a C Major scale pattern is played firstly as straight 1/16th notes (8f), then deviated with different note groupings (8f), including a nonuplet grouping in bar one, beats 3 and 4.

Example 8f:

Example 8f2:

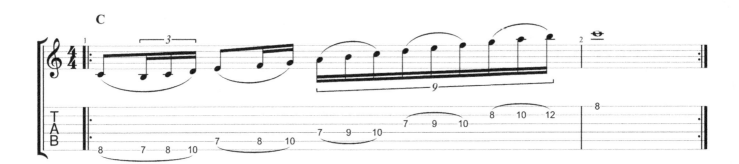

As you develop your command of rubato, maintain your awareness of where beats are, targeting specific marker points to lock back into the beat.

Burst Phrasing (Ornamentation)

Legato works well as a vehicle for *ornamentation*, a way of embellishing a melody. Ornaments are notes that are not crucial to the main melodic line but provide interest, variety and another option for expression, often played as fast notes that circle the important notes of a melody.

Guitarists Joe Satriani and Steve Vai are renowned for ornamented phrasing, aided by small bursts of legato before, after, or around melody notes.

Example 8g begins with three 1/4 note triplets followed by a descending legato phrase.

Example 8g:

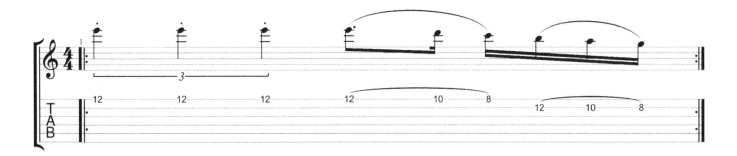

In Example 8h, the four E notes on the 12th fret of the high E string are preceded by C and D notes in quick hammer-on bursts. For extra drama, a rubato effect is created by lengthening the E note on beat 3 and rushing the remaining notes as a sextuplet.

Example 8h:

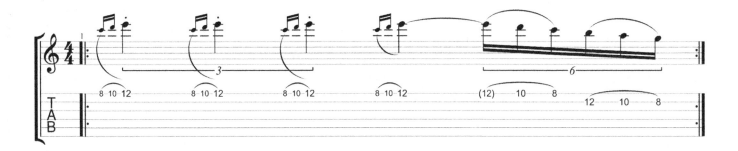

Example 8i, played as a sliding 1/4 note scale fragment would make for a boring lick. Using bursts of 1/32nd notes after each melody note, Example 8j highlights the ascending and descending notes of the previous example but provides a far more exciting alternative.

Example 8i:

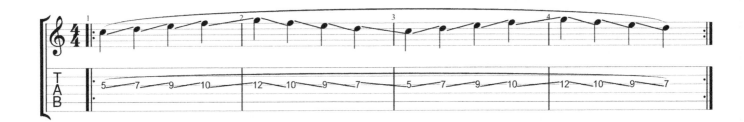

Example 8j:

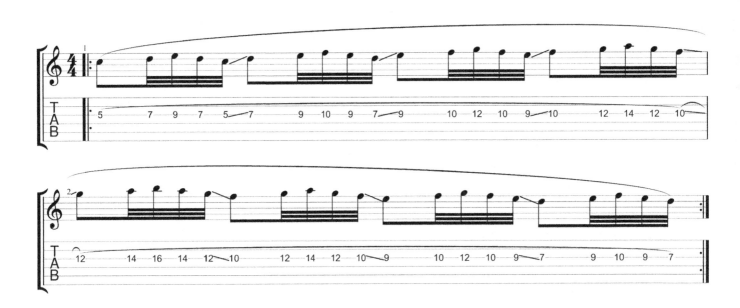

Example 8k contrasts the simple melody of bars one and two with the 1/32nd note ornamentations of bars three and four, executed with legato, hybrid picking and slides. In both halves of the lick, the main melody notes land in the same spots. Bars three and four can also be played as straight 1/16th notes for an extra descending sequence for your lick bag.

Example 8k:

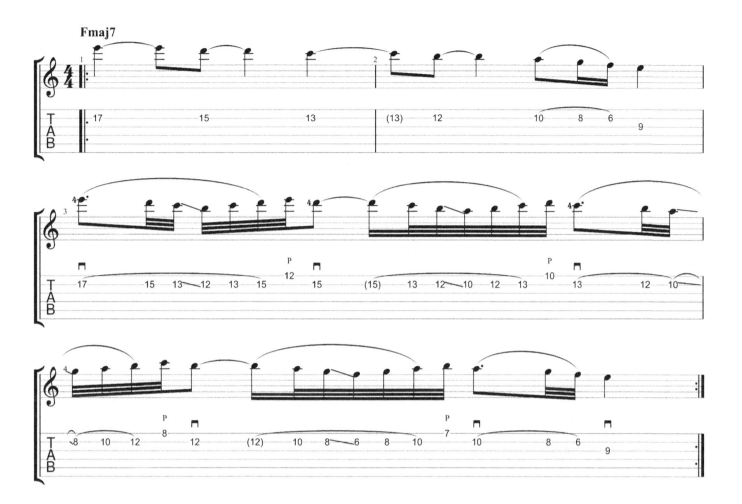

Staccato Legato

Staccato Legato is a phrase I coined in the early 2010s for some YouTube content that explored the technique of muting legato lines to create new options for attack and dynamics. Staccato (meaning *detached* or *separated*) and legato (*tied together*) are musical opposites according to the dictionary, but the combination of fretting hand slurs and picking hand muting creates a sound that is unlike either true legato or picking.

Any legato line can become a muted one, but hammer-ons from nowhere work particularly well in this approach.

Example 8l is a two-string drill played without any pick strokes. With your picking hand in a palm-muting stance, repeat the lick with various amounts of muting pressure to experiment with the *dynamic range*.

Dynamic range is the difference between the softest and loudest notes in a phrase. Very light muting will allow the pitch of the notes to come through and heavy muting will create a very percussive tone with indeterminate pitch.

Example 8l:

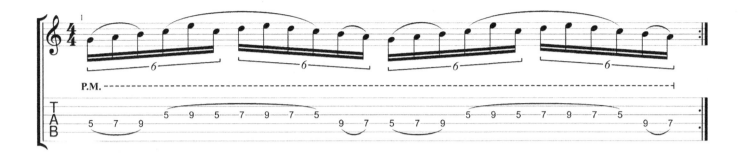

Using the notes from the previous drill, Example 8m alternates between the fluid sound of bar one and the restricted sound of bar two. The amount of pressure applied in the mute will decide how much dynamic range exists between the two bars.

Example 8m:

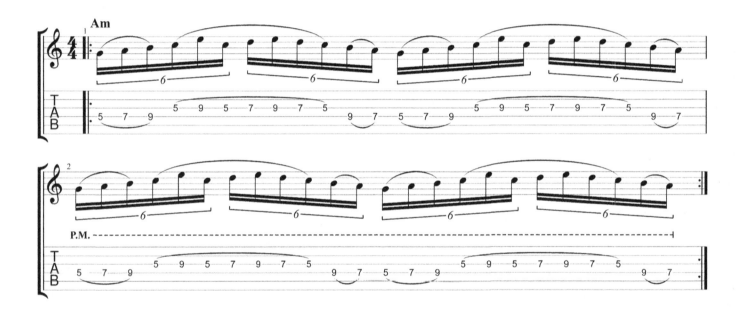

For the muting aspect of this technique, any scale can become a practice drill. In Example 8n, a muted C Major scale ascends from the low E string to the G string, becoming unmuted at the halfway mark and descending back to the low E string. This can be practised in free-time but is notated in two sets of 1/16th note *undecuplets* – a feel similar to sextuplets but with a slight lag since there are twenty-two notes instead of twenty-four.

Example 8n:

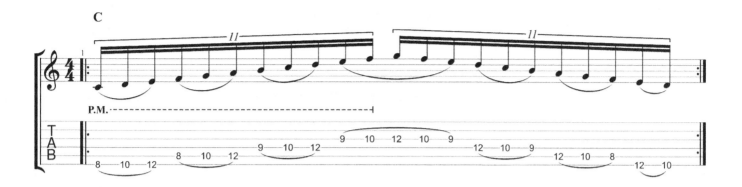

Bringing the pick back into play, Example 8o is a string skipping lick with muted and unmuted portions. The higher string in each two-beat pair should ring nice and clear and be contrasted by heavy muting on each lower string.

Example 8o:

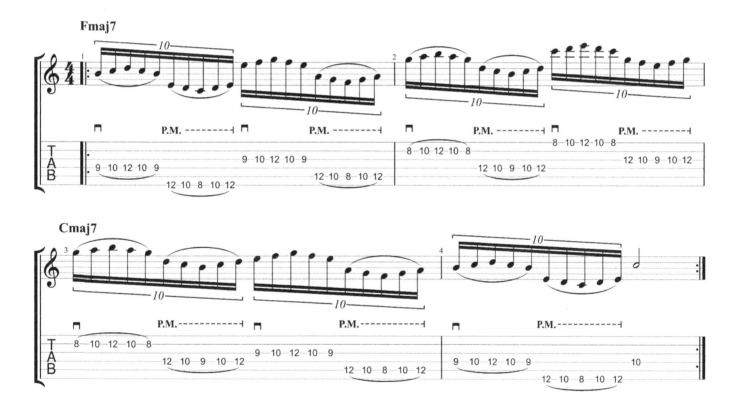

On my debut album *The Master Plan* (2002), the opening track, called *Kryptica*, featured a lick that I'm still often asked about. Using a sound that I describe as *cascading overtones*, the fretting-hand figure in Example 8p repeats while the palm mute (beginning on bar one, beat 3) slides inward from the bridge to the neck pickup.

The sliding mute passes through different harmonics to create an attention-grabbing sound that almost sounds like an effects pedal. To get the right overtones, be sure not to mute too heavily.

Example 8p:

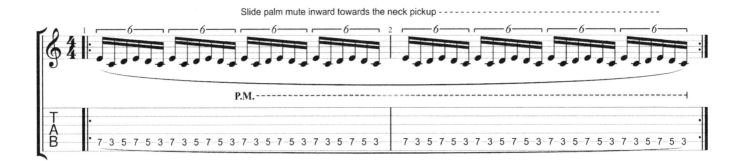

Chapter Nine: Monster Licks

This is where it all comes together! Using all of the techniques and musical devices covered in previous chapters, this collection of licks will put your dexterity, timing and finger tone to the test.

The audio for this chapter includes backing tracks at full speed and half speed. To practise in other increments, computer programs like *Audacity*, *Transcribe* and *Riffstation* will allow you to find the tempo best-suited to your ability as you progress.

Straight out of the gate, Example 9a fuses the D Dorian mode with chromatic passing tones, pentatonics, string skipping and muted legato! A *push and pull* rhythmic feel is created by regularly switching between 1/16th notes and 1/16th note triplets and sextuplets.

Example 9a:

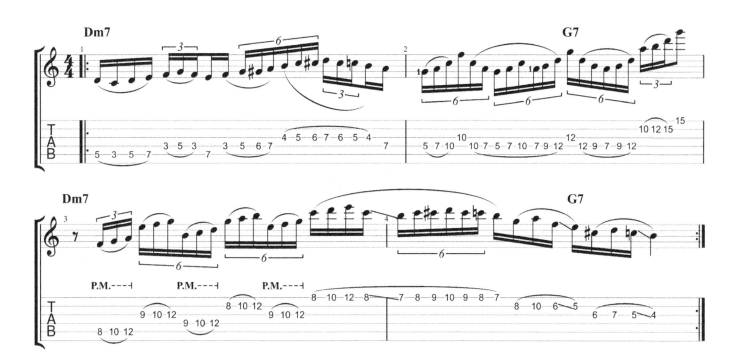

In Example 9b, the 1/16th note phrasing of bars one, two and four are contrasted with rhythmic bursts on the G string. The ascending lick in bar four is created from a two-note-per-string F Major Seventh arpeggio.

Example 9b:

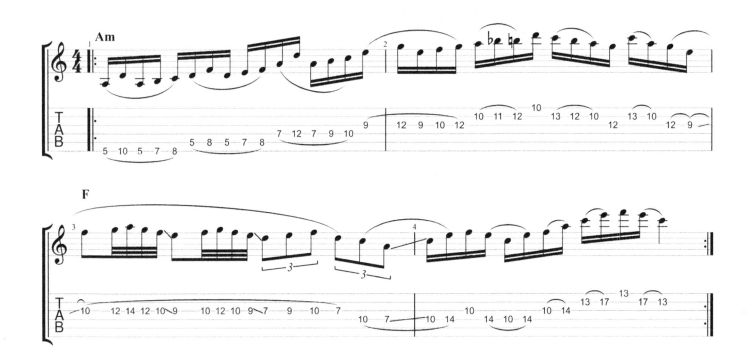

Played over alternating C Major Seventh and F Major Seventh chords, Example 9c includes 1-3-1-3-1-3 scale layouts (bars one and two), scales sequences with additional passing tones (bars three and four), a three-octave shifting pattern (bars five and six), and C Major Seventh arpeggios (bar seven) before concluding with the descending run of bar eight.

Over an F Major Seventh chord, the notes of the C Major Seventh arpeggio represent the perfect 5th, major 7th, major 9th and augmented 4th (11th) of the F Lydian mode.

Example 9c:

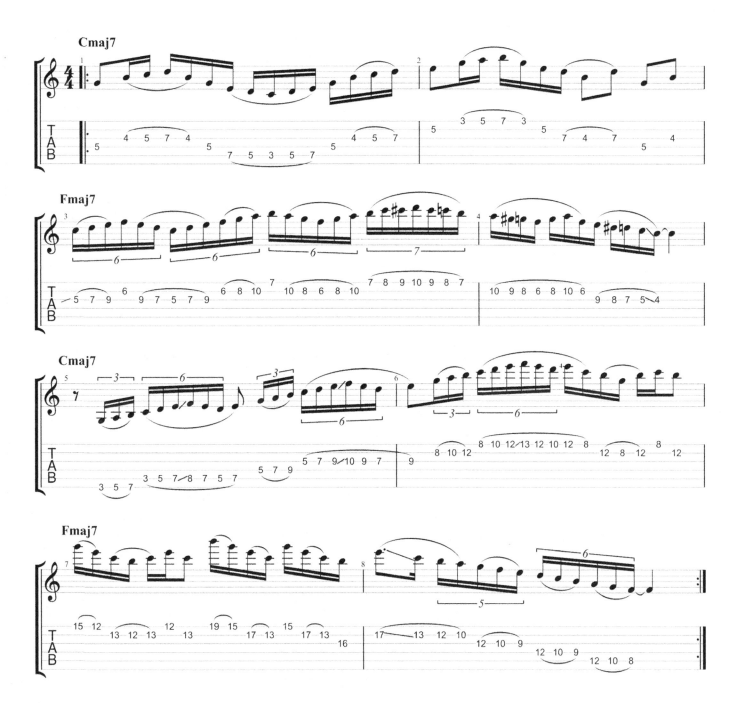

Example 9d is played exclusively over a G Dominant Seventh chord to produce the Mixolydian tonality throughout. Of particular melodic interest are the arpeggios in bar two (crossing over into bar three) which use B Minor Seventh (flat 5, flat 9), G Dominant Ninth and F Major Ninth arpeggios as a way of cutting through the scale in wider intervals.

The string-skipping in bars seven and eight gets wider with each instance, so be sure to maintain the timing notated. The low E string is muted every time while each higher string is unmuted and accelerated to 1/32nd note bursts.

Example 9d:

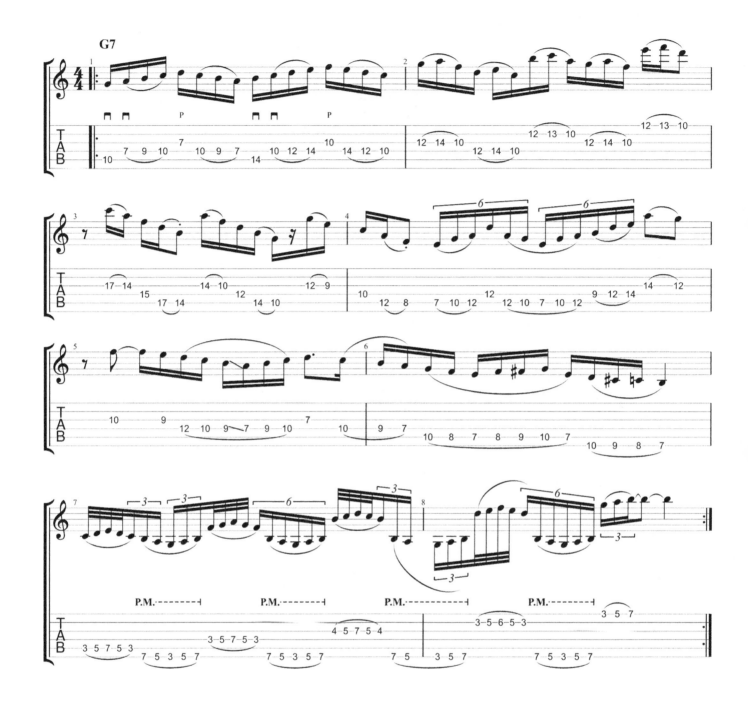

Applying some of the whammy bar techniques covered, the next study begins slow and allows time for dips, pre-dips, a flutter and a small dive bomb. Other notable attributes include E Minor Seventh arpeggios in bar three, single-string burst phrasing in bar four, and a 4-1-4-1-4 scale layout in bar six.

Example 9e:

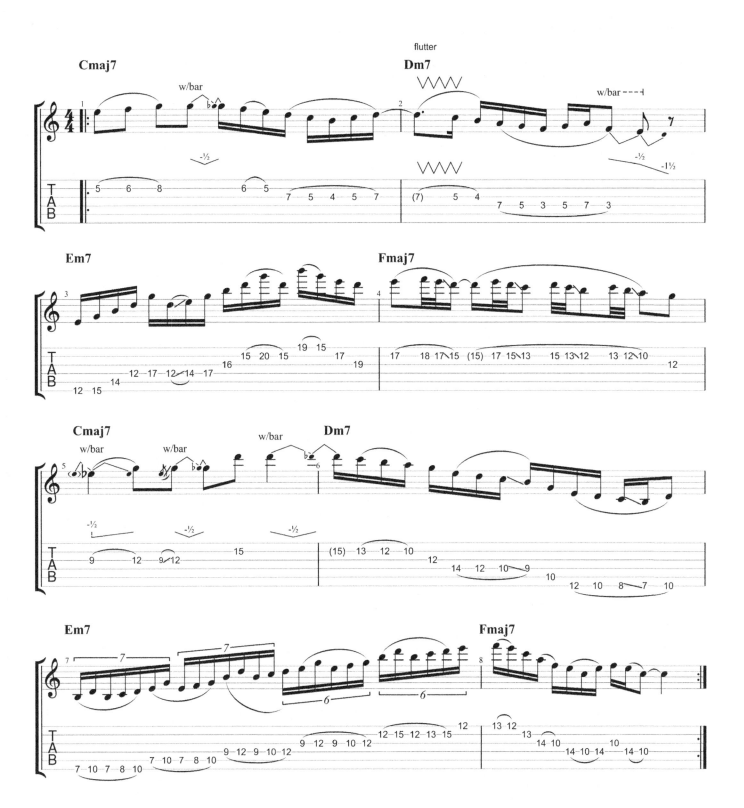

To finish the chapter (and the book!), Example 9f is played over a I – IV – V progression in A Minor. The V chord in bars seven and eight is a dominant seventh chord formed from the 5th degree of A Harmonic Minor.

Melodically, bars one and two combine a 1-3 Aeolian pattern, a six-string A Minor arpeggio and a 2NPS C Major Seventh arpeggio. Continuing over the same A Minor Seventh chord, bar three sequences a 3NPS scale pattern while bar four descends along the G string using whammy bar dips.

In bars five and six, look out for the alternating four-note and three-note-per-string patterns, the former of which is fretted using all four fingers rather than slides.

Borrowing from A Harmonic Minor, bars seven and eight play host to a G# Diminished Seventh arpeggio played in descending fours. The relationship between diminished arpeggios and the harmonic minor scale is covered in my book, *Neoclassical Speed Strategies for Guitar*.

Example 9f:

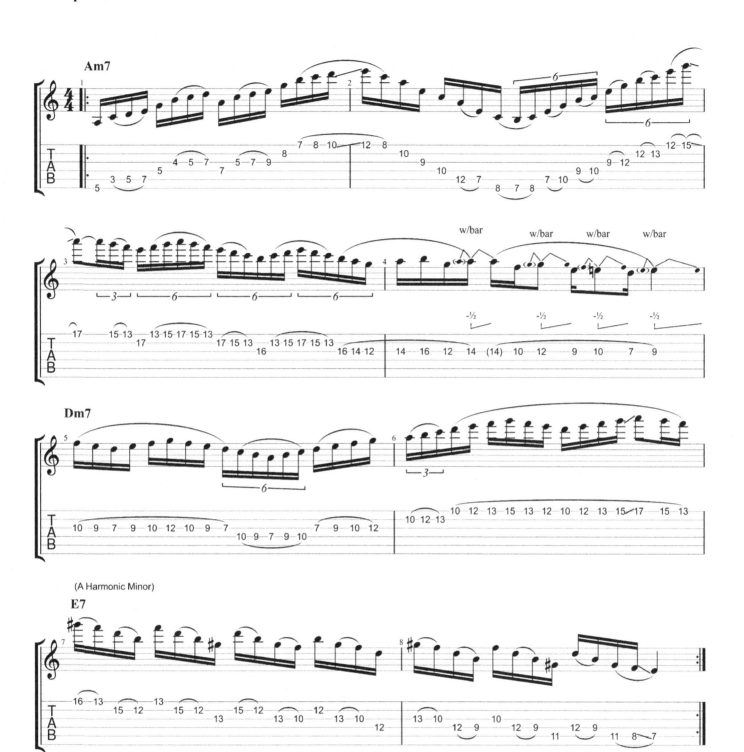

297

Conclusion

The cool thing about legato as both a musical device and a *guitar-centric* skill set is that it can be used as often or as seldom as your creativity calls upon it. Whether you build an entire style out of it or use it to contrast the aggression of your picked lines, the material in this book should be applied to real-life playing situations as soon as possible.

Learn the material as-is, but don't just stop there. Adapt the licks, transpose them, reverse them, combine them and see where the journey takes your playing. Similarly, with the mechanical approaches, try all of the options presented and systemise the strongest ideas into a personal blend that represents *your* choices.

I hope this book has been a source of enlightenment for developing a technical command of legato, and that it continues to be a source of inspiration with repeated reading.

Thanks for letting me be your guide to *Legato Guitar Technique Mastery*.

Chris Brooks

More From Chris Brooks

Neo-Classical Speed Strategies for Guitar

Sweep Picking Speed Strategies for Guitar

Advanced Arpeggio Soloing for Guitar

Sweep Picking Speed Strategies for 7-String Guitar

Find out more by scanning the QR code below:

Made in the USA
Monee, IL
14 February 2021